SCOTS LAW TALES

SCOTS LAW TALES

Edited by

JOHN P GRANT

*Professor of Law at Lewis & Clark Law School, Portland, Oregon, and
Professor Emeritus of International Law at the University of Glasgow,
Scotland*

and

ELAINE E SUTHERLAND

*Professor of Child and Family Law at the Law School,
Stirling University, Scotland, and
Professor of Law at Lewis & Clark Law School, Portland, Oregon*

DUNDEE UNIVERSITY PRESS
2010

First published in Great Britain in 2010 by
Dundee University Press
University of Dundee
Dundee DD1 4HN

www.dup.dundee.ac.uk

ISBN 978 1 84586 067 7

No natural forests were destroyed to make this product;
only farmed timber was used and replanted.

British Library Cataloguing-in-Publication Data
A catalogue record for this book is available on request from the British Library

Typeset by Waverley Typesetters, Warham, Norfolk
Printed and bound by Bell & Bain Ltd, Glasgow

CONTENTS

AUTHORS

Alistair Bonnington was Solicitor to BBC Scotland from 1992 to 2008. Prior to 1992, he was in private practice in Scotland, specialising in media law, including the law of defamation. He is a member of various European and North American legal groups dedicated to the promotion of freedom of speech. He has contributed to academic and professional journals on the subject of media law. He has also written newspaper articles on the subject and been used as a commentator by TV and radio. He has taught at Glasgow and Strathclyde Universities.

David L Carey Miller is Emeritus Professor of Property Law at the University of Aberdeen and a Senior Associate Research Fellow at the Institute of Advanced Legal Studies, London. A corporeal moveable property specialist, he has a special interest in title to cultural property and has lectured on the St Ninian's Isle treasure case at home and abroad. Appointed to Aberdeen in 1971 after work under T B Smith in Edinburgh in the 1960s, David Carey Miller's more recent work includes "Three of a Kind? Positive Prescription in Sri Lanka, South Africa and Scotland" (2008) 19 *Stellenbosch Law Review* 209 and "National Report on the Transfer of Moveables in Scotland" (with M M Combe, A J Steven and S Wortley) in W Faber and B Lurger (eds), *National Reports on the Transfer of Moveables in Europe* (2009).

Clare Connelly is a Senior Lecturer in Law at the University of Glasgow and a solicitor. She teaches and researches in the fields of criminal law, criminal justice and domestic abuse. Her recent publications include "Domestic Abuse: The Violence of Privacy" in *Scottish Life and Society: A Compendium of Scottish Ethnology* (2010); "Institutional

Failure, Social Entrapment and Post-Separation Abuse", 2010 *Juridical Review* 43; *Criminal Law* (2008); "Lockerbie Trial" in P Cane and J Conaghan, *The New Oxford Companion to Law* (2008); "Domestic abuse, civil protection orders and the 'new criminologies': is there any value in engaging with the law?", 2007 15 *Feminist Legal Studies* 259 (with K Cavanagh). She has conducted a number of empirical studies on mentally disordered offenders, domestic abuse and drug use and crime. She is a regular commentator on Scottish criminal law to the national and international media and regularly attended the Lockerbie trial and appeals in Camp Zeist and Edinburgh.

John P Grant is Emeritus Professor of International Law at the University of Glasgow and Professor of Law at Lewis & Clark Law School, Portland, Oregon. He attended parts of the Lockerbie trial and appeal and authored *The Lockerbie Trial: A Documentary History* (2004) and "The Lockerbie Trial" entry in the *Max Planck Encyclopedia of Public International Law* (2007, 2010). Among his other recent publications is *The Harvard Research in International Law: Contemporary Analysis and Appraisal* (with J C Barker, 2007), *The Harvard Research in International Law: Original Materials* (3 vols, with J C Barker, 2008) and *The Encyclopædic Dictionary of International Law* (3rd edn, with J C Barker, 2009).

Gavin Little is a Professor at the School of Law, Stirling University, of which he was the founding head. He writes on Scots public and environmental law and has recently contributed chapters on the regulation of nuclear energy and genetically modified organisms to the Scottish Universities Law Institute title *Environmental Law in Scotland*. He is a co-editor of, and a contributor to, *Law Making and the Scottish Parliament: The Early Years* (Edinburgh University Press, forthcoming 2011).

Sheila A M McLean is the International Bar Association Professor of Law and Ethics in Medicine at the University of Glasgow, where she established the Institute of Law and Ethics in Medicine and the Centre for Applied Ethics and Legal Philosophy. Her recent publications include *Assisted Dying: Reflections on the Need for Law Reform* (2007), which won the Minty Prize of the Society of Authors and the Royal Society of Medicine Book Award in 2008, and *Autonomy, Consent and the Law* (2009).

Kathleen Marshall was Scotland's first Commissioner for Children and Young People, holding office for a 5-year term from April 2004 with a remit to promote and safeguard the rights of children and young people in Scotland. She is a qualified solicitor and child law consultant, and was Director of the Scottish Child Law Centre from 1989 to 1994. She chaired the Edinburgh Inquiry into Abuse and Protection of Children in Care, which reported in February 1999. Her consultancy work has addressed a wide range of children's rights issues, for example, in relation to support for children and families, child protection, health, education and the court system; and she has long been a supporter of the campaign to ban all physical punishment of children.

Kenneth McK Norrie is Professor of Law at the University of Strathclyde. His primary research interests include family law, sex law, private international law, and delict, with particular reference to professional negligence. He has acted as adviser to committees of the Scottish Parliament in relation to family law, adoption and children's hearings, and served on a Scottish Government Working Group on No-Fault Liability for Medical Injuries. His major publications include *Parent and Child* (2nd edn, 1999), *Defamation and Related Actions in Scots Law* (1995), and *100 Cases that Every Scots Law Student Needs to Know* (2nd edn, 2010).

Elspeth Reid is a qualified solicitor and Senior Lecturer in Law at the University of Edinburgh where her teaching responsibilities are in the area of private and comparative law. She has published extensively in Scotland and abroad on topics in the law of delict. She is currently Series Editor of the *Edinburgh Studies in Law* monograph series published by Edinburgh University Press, and a member of the Editorial Boards of the *Edinburgh Law Review* and of the *Electronic Journal of Comparative Law*. Among her recent publications are *Personal Bar* (with J Blackie, 2006) and *Confidentiality, Personality and Privacy in Scots Law* (2010).

Robert Rennie has held the Chair of Conveyancing in the University of Glasgow for17 years and is the author of many books and articles on property law and conveyancing. He was a member of the advisory group set up by the Scottish Law Commission to consider the abolition of the feudal system and real burdens and has given many opinions on the interpretation of wills and titles. His recent publications include

Land Tenure in Scotland (2004), *Conveyancing in the Electronic Age* (with S Brymer, 2008) and *Land Tenure and Tenements Legislation* (3rd edn, 2009).

Elaine E Sutherland is Professor of Child and Family Law at the Law School, University of Stirling, Scotland, and Professor of Law at Lewis & Clark Law School, Portland, Oregon, spending 6 months of the year researching, writing and teaching at each. She is a former "safeguarder" in the children's hearings system, participates in the law reform process through regular responses to consultation papers from government and other bodies, and has served on the Family Law Committee of the Law Society of Scotland for many years. She has lectured and written extensively on child and family law in Scotland and abroad and her most recent publications include *Child and Family Law* (2nd edn, 2008) and *Children's Rights in Scotland* (with A Cleland, 3rd edn, 2009). She is a co-editor of, and a contributor to, *Law Making and the Scottish Parliament: The Early Years* (Edinburgh University Press, forthcoming 2011) and editor of, and a contributor to, *The Future of Child and Family Law: International Predictions* (Cambridge University Press, forthcoming 2012).

PREFACE

Scots Law Tales follows in what is a long tradition in Scotland of publications telling the story of major cases. The doyen of this literary phenomenon was William Roughead who, in the 82 years of his life (and right up to his death in 1952), published some 38 books and countless articles, many in the *Juridical Review*, each telling the tale of some important criminal case. He was a solicitor in Edinburgh, a Writer to the Signet, but, as his interest in, and fame for, accounts of criminal trials grew, he practised less and published more. According to the *Dictionary of National Biography*, Roughead "excelled in that peculiarly Scottish province of the kingdom of letters, the recounting of criminal trials, not as a criminologist, still less as a psychologist but, like Robert Louis Stevenson, as a 'tusitala', a teller of tales."[1] He "wrote in a style that combined intelligence, witty skepticism, and a flair for old-fashioned storytelling and moralizing; his accounts of murder cases and trials have the advantage of being concise and pointed, like folk tales".[2]

Roughead was immensely popular in his day on both sides of the Atlantic, counting among his American fans Henry James, Raymond Chandler and President Franklin D Roosevelt; in the UK, Dorothy L Sayers and Arthur Conan Doyle enthused about his work. Many of his tales were collected into anthologies.[3] However, in the second half of the twentieth century, the genre split between the literary, exemplified

---

[1] *47 Oxford DNB 136.* Tusitala is the term the Samoans used to describe Stevenson, a story-teller.

[2] J C Oates, The Mystery of JonBenét Ramsey, *New York Review of Books,* 24 June 1999.

[3] See, in particular, *Classic Crimes. A Selection of the Works of William Roughead* (1951) and *Tales of the Criminous: A Selection from the Works of William Roughead* (1956).

in "nonfiction novels" like Truman Capote's *In Cold Blood* and Norman Mailer's *The Executioner's Song*, and a straighter, more factual account of criminal cases, which increasingly became the province of television. Interest in the Roughead approach seemed to have waned until an American law publisher, Foundation Press, revived it in a slightly different format with a series of slim volumes, offering something more than the pared down and technical account of leading cases that appear in the law reports. Foundation's *Stories* series aimed at – and sometimes attained – the full story of leading cases, making them three-dimensional and setting them in their social, historical and cultural context. Foundation's *Stories* presently has 32 volumes, ranging in topic from the conventional *Contracts Stories* and *Family Law Stories* to the more esoteric *Death Penalty Stories* and *Presidential Power Stories*.

While Scots law does not have the number and range of cases to justify similar collections of tales on its sub-divisions, the corpus of Scots decided cases readily supports a volume like this. We decided that there were readers – law students and potential law students, lawyers in practice, at leisure and in retirement, and those non-lawyers who are fascinated by the law and its workings – who would enjoy an in-depth, interesting and rounded account of cases that might be familiar in name though not in detail. Fortunately, Dundee University Press agreed that there was indeed a readership for this book.

We consulted colleagues and friends and came up with 11 cases that qualified as important in themselves and, crucially, involved fascinating facts, events or personalities. We then identified expert authors for these cases and gave them a simple mandate: pen a readable chapter on the case, drawing out the personalities involved, the events leading up to (and, where appropriate after) the case, what the court decided and why, and the role that the case played in the development of its area of law – and do all this in whatever length is appropriate, but no more than 8,000 words. One author interpreted "appropriate" as 4,000 words; four other authors interpreted the cap of 8,000 words as including a plus or minus (in all cases, a plus) of 10 per cent. We suggested minimal footnoting, which one author took to mean none and another to mean 116. We then applied some light-touch editing to the manuscripts submitted; and the result is this volume of *Scots Law Tales*.

The cases chosen range from the miscarriage of justice perpetrated against Oscar Slater to the Lockerbie trial; from the decomposing snail in a bottle of ginger beer to allegations of high jinks by a prominent politician; from unplanned pregnancy to children being beaten at school to switching off life support; from McCaig's Folly at Oban to the lettering "EIIR" on pillar boxes; and from St Ninian's treasure in Shetland to allegations of ritual child abuse in Orkney.

The authors not only fulfilled their mandate, but went further in arguing that the case was rightly or wrongly (invariably wrongly) decided or that there are serious lessons to be learned from what happened in the case. So, Clare Connelly (in Chapter 3), pointing out that the wrongful prosecution and conviction of Oscar Slater for a crime he manifestly did not commit reflects poorly on all involved, argues that those in the criminal justice system at all levels have a responsibility to act honestly and ethically. John Grant (in Chapter 11), noting the deficiencies in the conviction of the Lockerbie bomber, condemns the current obsession with the return of Abdelbaset Ali Mohmed Al Megrahi to Libya and questions why there is not the same interest in finding out what actually happened in December 1988 and at the trial.

In discussing what many would regard as Scotland's leading case, *Donoghue v Stevenson*, Elspeth Reid (in Chapter 5) points out that, while the snail may have been English, the case cannot be described as the leading *English* authority on the law of negligence; and she emphasises the extent to which the principles enunciated in this *Scottish* case have been applied abroad. Alistair Bonnington (in Chapter 6) analyses the unreported defamation action of *Sheridan v News International*, his particular barbs being directed against tabloid journalism in general, the Faculty of Advocates and the subsequent prosecution of Tommy and Gail Sheridan for perjury at the trial.

In his chapter on the *McFarlane* case (Chapter 4), Kenneth Norrie discusses the confused and confusing state of the law on unplanned pregnancies, condemning the rules as nothing but distributive justice, something more appropriate for Parliament rather than the courts. Sheila McLean (in Chapter 9) analyses the law relating to the non-treatment of people in a permanent vegetative state arising out of the *Law Hospital* case and calls for consolidation of all the law relating to end-of-life decisions. In analysing the European Court of Human Rights' decision in the *Campbell and Cosans* case, Kathleen Marshall (in Chapter 10) traces the long road to the abolition of corporal punishment in schools and calls for the end of all physical punishment of children.

In discussing the rationales of the cases involving "follies" instructed to be built in a will or trust document, Robert Rennie (in Chapter 9) laments the variety of factors used to accept or reject the legitimacy of the deceased's clear intention and the lack of consistency in the case law. Gavin Little puts the "EIIR" case, *MacCormick v Lord Advocate*, under the microscope (in Chapter 2), in the course of which he argues that the case has had a profound effect on the constitution and politics of Scotland and the UK. David Carey Miller analyses the litigation on the ultimate destination of the St Ninian's Isle treasure (in Chapter 7), and argues that this ingenious action was made possible through the efforts of two remarkable lawyers, Principal Thomas Taylor of Aberdeen University and the redoubtable Professor T B Smith. In telling the story of the Orkney child abuse debacle, Elaine Sutherland (in Chapter 1) not only brings out little-known facts about the affair, but also sets Orkney in the context of the on-going debate about whether or not, and when, to remove children from potentially dangerous homes.

If this slim volume finds favour with readers, the editors might suggest, and DUP might accept, another volume of *Scots Law Tales*, this time dealing exclusively with cases decided prior to 1900 – the "golden oldies" of Scots law.

JOHN P GRANT
ELAINE E SUTHERLAND
Edinburgh
February 2010

Chapter 1

A KNOCK AT THE DOOR
Sloan v *B*: The Orkney Case

Elaine E Sutherland

"Nine children from four families in Orkney have been seized from
their beds and taken into care after allegations of ritualistic abuse.
Social workers helped by police flown in from the mainland carried
out the dawn raids."

The Times, 1 March 1991

A society can be measured by how well it protects its weakest members.
Children are undoubtedly among any society's weakest members,
since they are least able to lobby on their own behalf, least aware of
what their rights are and least able to enforce such rights as they have.
Thus, if the individual and collective rights of children are to have
any real meaning, it falls to adults to ensure that they are respected
and enforced. Of course, that does not preclude children and young
people from playing an active role. It is simply to acknowledge that
they cannot do it alone.

There is ample evidence that some children are abused and
neglected by their parents or other family members. Like many
countries, Scotland has long had sophisticated laws and procedures
aimed at protecting children from such conduct. Enforcing these laws
and procedures is a matter for the police, the various local authorities
across the country, the children's hearings system and the courts. In
individual cases, the task falls to a range of professionals: that is, to
individuals who, just like the rest of us, are fallible human beings. In
carrying out their tasks, they often face a "damned if you do, damned
if you don't" dilemma.

On the one hand, if they suspect a child is being abused, they can
remove the child from the home. If it turns out later that their suspicion

was unfounded, their action will be criticised as high-handed state intervention that caused needless harm and suffering to the child and the family. On the other hand, if they do not remove the child when faced with suspicion of abuse and that child is later harmed, or dies, at the hands of a family member, they have failed the child and will, quite rightly, be condemned for that failure. What are they to do? A further question arises – one that may throw light on continuing failures of the child protection system. If officials are criticised for over-zealous intervention, are those operating the system likely to respond with increased caution in the future, running the risk that children will be left unprotected? If they are criticised for failure to act, will they become more willing to remove children? In short, is there a pendulum effect at work in child protection practice?

That dilemma – and how it was resolved – lay behind what came to be known as the "events in Orkney" in 1991. The removal of nine children, ranging from 8 to 15 years old, from their homes on South Ronaldsay, one of the Orkney Islands, located some 10 miles to the north-east of the Scottish mainland, brought hitherto unprecedented publicity to their families, their community and the child protection system in Scotland. The case led to radical reform of child protection law and practice and the debate continues about whether these reforms struck the right balance. In all of this it is important to remember the nine children who, as we shall see, were failed, so abysmally, by the system.

The irony is that, at that time, the Scottish system of child protection seemed to be working reasonably well. There had been no Scottish equivalent of over-zealous intervention that occurred in the English towns of Cleveland[1] and Rochdale,[2] when large numbers of children were removed from their homes on the suspicion that they had been sexually abused, only to be returned home later without abuse having been proven. Nor had Scotland had its equivalent of the catalogue of English cases, from Maria Colwell,[3] in 1973, to Kimberly Carlile,[4] in

[1] See *Report of the Inquiry into Child Abuse in Cleveland 1987* (Cm 412, 1988). A journalist's account of the events can be found in S Bell, *When Salem Came to the Boro'* (1988).

[2] See Social Services Inspectorate, *Inspection of Child Protection Services in Rochdale* (DOH, 1990).

[3] *Report of the Committee of Inquiry into the Care and Supervision Provided in Relation to Maria Colwell* (DHSS, 1974).

[4] *A Child in Mind: Protection of Children in a Responsible Society* (London Borough of Greenwich, 1987).

1987, where failure to respond appropriately to clear warning signs of abuse resulted in the child's death.[5] A distinctive feature of child protection in Scotland, the children's hearings system, was hailed at home and abroad as a model for how to proceed. Certainly, it was accepted that child protection could be improved, since a thorough-going review had just been completed.[6] But had an element of complacency – "Here's tae us, wha's like us?" – crept in?

A knock at the door

The morning of Wednesday, 27 February 1991 began like any other for the four families, known only as Families B, H, T and M. All the families were "incomers" to Orkney, having migrated there from England. That is not to suggest that they were a homogenous group and, indeed, the little that is known about them suggests considerable diversity. Mr and Mrs B had lived on South Ronaldsay for some 15 years, whereas the H family had arrived only a couple of years before these events. Two of the fathers, Mr B and Mr H (until his brain tumour prevented him), worked away from home, in England. Mr and Mrs M farmed, with Mr M supplementing the family income by part-time teaching. Mr and Mrs T had lived in various parts of the world, prior to their move to South Ronaldsay in 1988, and Mr T designed and made jewellery. The M family belonged to the Society of Friends (Quakers), the T family was Jewish and the religious affiliation, if any, of the others is not known.

Only the three B children – two girls (WB and EB), aged 13 and 11, and their brother (SB), aged 7 – were born after their parents move to the island. The other six children, arranged neatly in two children per family – brother, PH, aged 9, and his sister, TH, aged 8; the two M brothers, SM, aged 15, and JM, aged 11; and the T siblings, BT, a boy, aged 12, and his sister, MT, aged 8 – had all arrived on the islands with their parents.

Most of the parents and children were asleep when two cars, containing social workers, RSSPCC officers and police officers, pulled up outside each of their homes just after 7 am. The parents were roused by the officials knocking on the front doors and informed that place

[5] These are just two of the many names that feature in inquiry reports for the period. See *Child Abuse: A Study of Inquiry Reports 1973–1981* (DOH, 1982) and *Child Abuse: A Study of Inquiry Reports 1980–1989* (DOH, 1991).
[6] *Review of Child Care Law in Scotland* (HMSO, 1990).

of safety orders (the procedural step in place at the time) had been granted by the local sheriff, authorising the officials to take the children away. Many of the children were awakened by a parent shouting, screaming or, at least, protesting. Each child and parent responded in his or her own way, with some of the children locking themselves in the bathroom in a futile attempt to avoid removal. The general picture is of distraught children and distressed and angry parents, albeit that most of the parents began to focus on helping their children prepare for their hasty and inevitable departure.

The B children were not allowed to take any personal possessions with them, save the inhaler and medication EB needed for her asthma. The H children fared rather better, being permitted to take cuddly toys with them since the police officer present was not aware of the prohibition on personal items. PH was allowed to say goodbye to his budgie and TH to her pet rabbit. No toys or books were permitted the M children, although the cream JM needed to treat his dermatitis was taken by one of the officers. Mr T gave each of his children one of the small pendants he made, BT's being a dolphin and MT's a seal, but the request to take books and teddy bears was turned down. Only the H parents were allowed to give their children breakfast. The children were then driven away and would not see or hear from their parents again for 35 days.

It is clear that at least some of the parents were not wholly surprised by the removal of their children. Mrs M, one of the parents to maintain her calm throughout, said simply "Oh, so you have come". What would make an ordinary mother accept that the authorities might just turn up one morning and take her children away? The answer lies in earlier events on the island and a case involving the W family whom,[7] thanks to subsequent litigation by one of the now-adult children, we now know to be the Willsher family. The Willshers were a large, boisterous group, comprising the parents and 15 children. In 1987, Mr Willsher was convicted of physical and sexual abuse of a number of his children and sentenced to two periods of imprisonment, the longer being for 7 years. Social work concern about the family continued after his incarceration and, ultimately, a number of the Willsher children were taken into care.[8] Medical

[7] See n 44 below, and accompanying text.
[8] Some of the Willsher children were to remain in care for years and two were adopted subsequently.

examinations revealed that some had been subject to penetrative sexual activity that post-dated their father's departure. It was during the interviewing of one of the Willsher girls that allegations of more widespread sexual abuse of children on South Ronaldsay emerged. In particular, 8-year-old MW drew pictures which she explained in a way suggesting group sexual activity involving a number of adults and children whom she identified as including the Orkney children, their parents and the Reverend McKenzie, the local Church of Scotland minister.[9]

Understandably, Mrs Willsher was distressed at the removal of her children and a number of her neighbours, including Mr and Mrs M, Mrs T and the Reverend McKenzie and his wife, sought to offer her support and assistance in seeking their return. When the other nine Orkney children were removed from their homes later, the question asked by their parents and the media was whether the removal resulted from legitimate concern over the children's welfare or was a punishment meted out to their parents for daring to challenge officialdom over its conduct in respect of the Willsher family.

After the nine children were taken away on 27 February, their parents' homes were searched by police officers, as was the McKenzies' manse and the nearby church. A curious array of items were removed, including a broken cross, some animal masks and a black cloak which the minister explained he used for funerals. A number of the parents were taken to the local police station and interviewed. On returning home from the police station, Mr H telephoned his solicitor, his Member of Parliament, a local councillor, the local doctor and a reporter at *The Orcadian* newspaper and a number of the parents visited each other and received visits from other members of the community. The parents were beginning to mobilise.

A community meeting was organised for 1 March, with some 300 people, attending. While this was designed to show support for the parents whose children had just been removed, there was real anxiety over the prospect that other children might be taken away. The "Orkney parents" accepted invitations to attend and gave their accounts of what had happened. A later public meeting led to the creation of the Parents Action Committee, chaired by the local surgeon and having as its goal the return of the children and a public

[9] *Report of the Inquiry into the Removal of Children from Orkney in February 1991* (HMSO, 1992) (hereafter "Clyde Report"), para 2.69.

inquiry into their removal. Members of another group, Parents Against Injustice, arrived on the island and made various public statements. Of course, all of this created tension with the local social work department which, in breach of good practice, had failed to make any follow-up visits to the parents.

Five weeks on the mainland

After some detours and periods in safe houses on the island, all of the children were taken, by plane, to the mainland. Most of the children were to remain in Highland Region, with the B children and SM being located in Strathclyde. The girls, WB and EB, remained together while SB was taken to a separate home. WB and EB were placed with a couple who had very considerable experience as foster carers and the girls seemed to draw comfort from being together, causing the foster mother to oppose social work suggestions that the girls should be separated. WB sometimes became distressed and bewildered about why she had been taken away from home. EB was more chatty, generally, but reserved about expressing her feelings. Both girls declined offers to go swimming or ice-skating. SB was placed with a couple with four children of their own and one other foster child. He joined in family activities, going swimming and to the cinema, as well as to visit relatives. His foster mother did not realise that he should not be allowed contact with his sisters and let him telephone them early in his stay. When she discovered the prohibition, he was not permitted further calls and, quite understandably, he found this confusing and frustrating.

The H children went first to TH's foster home in the belief that it would comfort PH to see his sister settled. This may not have been the effect since TH became tearful, recovering sufficiently to give her brother a cuddly toy she had brought with her before he was taken away to a separate placement. TH was placed with a woman who had seven adult children and seven grandchildren of her own and considerable experience as a foster carer. Despite being upset on her arrival, TH had a cuddle with her foster mother and settled in well, eating dinner that evening and later attending school and making friends. She missed her brother and home. PH settled in reasonably well at his placement with a couple with two daughters, albeit that he kept his feelings to himself. Initially, he asked to telephone his sister but, having been given excuses, stopped asking. He made friends at school and experienced no problems there.

BT was upset at the prospect of being separated from his sister, MT, and they went together to MT's foster home first. MT's foster carers were vegetarians, as was she, and the mother looked after three young children during the day and a fourth after school, having four children of her own. MT appeared to settle in reasonably well and, while polite, kept her distance. She attended school but was not particularly happy there. BT was distressed on arrival at his foster care placement with a couple who ran a bed and breakfast business in their home on the edge of a village. He settled down with his foster carers who gave him tea and cake and introduced him to their cats, but he missed his sister and parents throughout his stay, not sleeping well and often crying at night. Despite that, he settled in well at school and enjoyed playing football. The T children were permitted visits from a rabbi, at Passover, at their parents' insistence.

Brothers JM and SM were separated upon arrival on the mainland, with JM going to a foster home where he was subsequently examined by a doctor. His placement was with a family on a farm where there were two other children and he was allowed to drive a tractor and do other farm chores for which he was paid. He attended the local school. After his return JM's mother wrote to thank the foster carers for the trouble they had taken with him and JM also wrote a thank-you note. Fifteen-year-old SM appears to have fared worst since he was housed in a residential establishment, along with troubled children, many of whom had committed offences. As he was to observe later: "I was stuck in a school with people I did not know and who thought differently from me. I was the only one not in there for crime. I was taught to steal cars and that sort of thing." He found the strict regime at the school difficult and it did not provide educational courses at Higher level, although he had access to books and the headmaster lent him one of his own. The headmaster also broached the subject of SM being transferred to a Quaker school but SM did not appear particularly concerned about that. He was the only one of the children whose Mother's Day card actually reached his mother. On learning that he was going home, SM's good manners prevailed and he thanked the staff and the other boys and said that he had enjoyed his stay.

Not only was separation of siblings a feature of their care while on the mainland but they were denied contact with each other. Similarly, there was no communication between the parents and their children. Letters and gifts were sent by the parents but never reached the

children due, in part, to confusion over whether the social workers or
RSSPCC officers were dealing with the matter. Perhaps most traumatic
of all was the fact that neither the parents nor the children knew of this
breakdown in communication and one can only imagine frightened
children wondering why their parents had not been in touch. Each
of the parents was sent a form seeking their consent to their children
being medically examined and, while all refused to sign, the children
were examined anyway.

A particularly disturbing aspect of this case, and one that attracted
considerable criticism from the subsequent inquiry, was the interviewing of the nine children during their time on the mainland. The
interviews were conducted by police and RSSPCC officers, with Liz
MacLean taking on "a substantial burden" in this respect.[10] The
children were interviewed on numerous occasions, with the duration
of interviews varying considerably, from a little over 10 minutes to
in excess of an hour. Some of the children were angry during the
interviews, some were unduly withdrawn and others were quite
communicative. The reaction of individual children sometimes varied
between interviews, with foster carers reporting that the children had
often been distressed or angry afterwards.

The court proceedings

Meanwhile – and unknown to most of the children – further legal
steps, aimed at ensuring their safety, were being taken. The place of
safety orders, authorising removal of the children, only permitted their
detention for up to 7 days, although the statute in force at the time
required that a children's hearing be convened on the next lawful day,
if practicable, to address the concerns.[11] All of the Orkney children
were referred to a children's hearing on two grounds: (i) that they had
been the victims of sexual abuse or lived in the same household as
such a victim; and (ii) that they were falling into bad associations or
were being exposed to moral danger.[12]

At the first *children's* hearing, held on 5 March, the most striking
feature was the absence of the children, since the hearing dispensed

[10] Clyde Report, para 14.64.
[11] Social Work (Scotland) Act 1968, s 37.
[12] *Ibid*, s 32. These grounds of referral are currently found in the Children (Scotland)
    Act 1995, s 52 and the Children's Hearings (Scotland) Bill (SP Bill 41 (2010)),
    currently making its way through the Scottish Parliament, will provide for new
    grounds, expressed in more modern terms.

with their presence. It continued the warrants to detain them in a place of safety for 21 days and, since their parents did not accept the grounds of referral, instructed the reporter to apply to the sheriff for a finding-in-fact as to whether the grounds of referral were established. The reporter petitioned the *nobile officium* of the Court of Session to have the proof before the sheriff moved from Kirkwall Sheriff Court, on Orkney, to Inverness Sheriff Court, on the mainland, since the children were located on the mainland by this time and they might be called to give evidence. The children's parents opposed the application and, in the event, it was refused by the court although authority was granted for any evidence from the children to be taken in the sheriff's chambers in Inverness.[13] A second children's hearing, on 25 March, renewed the warrants to detain the children for a further 21 days, again having dispensed with the children's presence. Their parents' appeal against this renewal was refused.

The case to establish the grounds of referral came before the redoubtable Sheriff Kelbie in Kirkwall Sheriff Court on 3 April 1991 and, without hearing the evidence, he dismissed the reporter's application on the basis that the proceedings were "so fatally flawed as to be incompetent".[14] He criticised the detention of the children, the questioning to which they had been subjected and the quality of the evidence on which the case was based. He was particularly concerned that the presence of all of the children, including a 15-year-old boy, was dispensed with throughout the children's hearings proceedings. The reporter appealed to the Inner House of the Court of Session against the sheriff's decision. On the advice of counsel, the reporter decided that, even if the appeals were allowed, the effect of the sheriff's attack on the proceedings and evidence, while incalculable, had so prejudiced the interests of justice that it would not be possible to proceed with the case.

Sheriff Kelbie's decision prompted an immediate reaction from the crowd gathered outside the court. It marched upon the social work department, entering the office of Mr Lee, the Director of Social Work, but not before the procession was stopped at one point by a television crew anxious to get better footage. There were angry exchanges in Mr Lee's office but, eventually, everyone except Mr Lee and the Orkney parents was prevailed upon to leave. It was agreed that the children would be returned home that evening.

[13] *Sloan, Petitioner* 1991 SLT 527.
[14] *Sloan v B* 1991 SLT 530 at 537.

It was not until 12 June that the Inner House heard the reporter's appeal against Sheriff Kelbie's decision. In the event, the court found in favour of the reporter.[15] The sheriff's interlocutor was recalled and the court directed that any further proceedings were to be heard before a different sheriff. In the course of its decision, the court took the opportunity to examine a number of aspects of the case and to provide valuable guidance for the future operation of the system. In particular, the then relevant mechanism for emergency protection, the place of safety order, came under scrutiny, as did the issue of the child's right to participate in proceedings relating to his or her protection. No matter that he prevailed before the Inner House, the reporter had decided that there would be no further proceedings. Thus, the evidence, if any, about abuse of the Orkney children was never tested in court.

The children return home

On the evening of 4 April, 35 days after the nine Orkney children had been taken away, a Hawker Siddeley 784 carrying them and accompanying social workers landed at Kirkwall Airport to a reception from 200 supporters, media representatives and a lone piper playing "Scotland the Brave". No-one from Orkney Social Work Department was present and a police officer boarded the plane to warn the accompanying social workers that their safety could not be guaranteed and to suggest that they should not disembark along with the children. It is to his great credit that one of these social workers, Mr Greene, insisted on escorting the children through the throng to the terminal building. The children were then reunited with their parents in the relative privacy of the airport's customs room.

The Orkney families engaged the services of solicitors and, despite opposition from Orkney Islands Council, obtained legal aid to pursue actions for damages. An initial writ was served on the council in February 1994. In the event, there was no need for litigation, nor for the services of an attorney from a Los Angles law firm who appeared on the island, apparently uninvited. The families accepted an apology and compensation from the council. It was widely reported that the payments were in the order of £10,000 to each child and £5,000 to each parent.

---

[15] *Sloan* v B 1991 SLT 530.

The Clyde Inquiry

We have become all too familiar with failures of the child protection system being followed by an inevitable, and often inconclusive, inquiry. In the early 1990s, such inquiries were a rarity in Scotland and the report of the inquiry set up to examine the events in Orkney was anything but the mealy-mouthed collection of predictable generalisations, holding no-one personally responsible, that so mars many of its modern counterparts.

On 20 June 1991, Lord Clyde was appointed to conduct an inquiry into how and why various decisions were taken in the child protection process and the conduct of the officials involved in implementing these decisions.[16] Therein lay a problem. It was not the inquiry's function "to investigate the truth or falsity" of the allegations surrounding removal of the children.[17] Undoubtedly, that was frustrating for the parents and Reverend McKenzie since, after all the publicity surrounding the case, they had hoped for public vindication.

That limitation aside, the resulting *Report of the Inquiry into the Removal of Children from Orkney in February 1991*, known as "the Clyde Report", was meticulous and comprehensive, with all involved being given every opportunity to recount his or her recollection of events and point of view. That evidence is recorded in considerable detail in the Report and is followed by incisive analysis of what went wrong, who was responsible and, most important of all, recommendations for reform designed to avoid any repetition of the debacle. The handling of the inquiry came as no surprise, given Lord Clyde's reputation for a keen intellect, attention to detail and unfailing courtesy – not qualities that always coincide. The inquiry cost some £6 million, took 16 months to complete and resulted in a report running to 363 pages and making 195 recommendations.

So what went wrong in Orkney? In the words of Lord Clyde, "It is not easy to find any individual at least among the principal actors out of the whole story of the events relating to the removal of the nine children who is not open to some criticism".[18] What emerged was a picture of a lack of communication between individuals within various agencies, a lack of trust between certain individuals and agencies, an absence of any clear procedure and a lack of clarity about the roles of

---

[16] Clyde Report, para 1.3.
[17] *Ibid*, para 1.10.
[18] *Ibid*, para 14.110.

individual agency members. Most tragic of all was the apparent failure to see the nine children involved as individual human beings.

While the Report made clear that the actual removal of the children was carried out with efficiency, criticism is levelled at various aspects of the children's treatment during the process and thereafter. In particular, the following matters caused concern: the prohibition on the children taking personal possessions with them; the failure to explain their rights, at least to the older children; failure to get from the parents written consent to medical examination of the children; confusion over the medical examinations; separate placement of siblings; prohibition, without review, on access by the parents to the children and the children to each other; inadequate attention to the religion of some of the children; and a lack of planning for the educational needs of the children placed in Strathclyde.

The interviewing of the nine children, after their removal, received special attention. Again, the picture is one of confusion and ineptitude. No specific decision to interview the children was taken, nor was there a clear idea of the purpose of the interviews. There was a lack of co-ordination between agencies, the facilities and aids used in the interviews were not always fully understood by the interviewers and, perhaps most seriously of all, not all of the interviewers were adequately trained for the task in hand, assuming they knew what that was in the first place.[19] Of greatest concern was the fact that the interviewers were working according to their own agenda, used leading questions and failed to keep an open mind, even in the face of persistent denials from the children that any abuse had taken place.

Nor did the conduct of the reporter escape criticism. He would have been entitled to continue with the case, but decided not to do so on the basis that the public statements of the sheriff who heard the case and the attendant publicity had so tainted the evidence as to make a fair hearing impossible. That decision was criticised for being taken precipitately, leaving the crucial matter of the truth or otherwise of the allegations unresolved.

So much for the conduct of those involved, but what of the law? Again, Lord Clyde was critical of the law in place at the time, not least ambiguity inherent in the place of safety order that authorised removal of children "on the basis of suspicion and uncertainty",[20] something

---

[19] Clyde Report, paras 14.60–14.101.
[20] *Ibid*, para 16.3.

Lord Clyde found to be undesirable in itself and in violation of the European Convention on Human Rights.

Not surprisingly, Lord Clyde made extensive recommendations designed to improve the training of the professionals involved in child protection, the procedures under which they should operate and the law on child protection. A particularly encouraging feature of the Report is that all of the recommendations are set in the context of the United Nations Convention on the Rights of the Child, which the United Kingdom had ratified only a few months before, and the European Convention on Human Rights which was to come to greater prominence as a result of the Human Rights Act 1998. Unlike so many of the inquiries into failures of the child protection since, this one produced very tangible results – the Children (Scotland) Act 1995 and revision of children's hearings rules and social work procedures.

Sadly, one crucial recommendation was not implemented. Recognising the specialist nature of child protection, in general, and investigation of allegations of multiple sexual abuse, in particular, Lord Clyde acknowledged the problems experienced by small social work departments like that in Orkney. He recommended that a central resource group be established to offer specialist advice to individual social work departments "in cases of particular complexity".[21]

No such body was established in the wake of the Report.[22] Had it been, three little girls, known only by the pseudo-names Alice, Barbara and Caitlin, in the Western Isles (Eilean Siar), might have been spared at least some of the physical and sexual abuse they experienced at the hands of the people to whom their parents made them available.[23] The local authority, Western Isles Council (Comhaire nan Eilean), had become aware of problems in the family almost as soon as they arrived on the island. Seventeen child protection case conferences in respect of them were convened between 1995 and 2001 and all three girls were referred to the reporter to the children's panel in 1997, resulting

[21] Recommendation 34 and paras 15.67–15.81.
[22] It was not until 2009 that the Multi Agency Resource Service (MARS), funded by the Scottish Government, was established at Stirling University to support professionals and agencies working in child protection by developing communities of expertise and sharing practice knowledge across Scotland. See further: http://www.mars.stir.ac.uk/.
[23] See *Inspection into the Care and Protection of Children in Eilean Siar* (2005), available at: http://www.cne-siar.gov.uk/socialwork/SWIAreport.pdf (hereafter "Eilean Siar Report").

in 24 children's hearings being arranged.[24] In 2003, 13 adults were arrested in Scotland and England in connection with the case and nine were charged subsequently with offences, including rape, lewd and libidinous and indecent practices and behaviour and making indecent images or pseudo-images of children on a computer, these offences relating to the three girls. In 2004, the Crown Office decided not to proceed with prosecution of any of these adults.[25]

The media

Extensive media coverage was a constant feature of the Orkney case. In part, this was because the parents of the Orkney children were very much more articulate and well educated than most parents accused of child abuse and some of them co-operated with the media in the belief that the world should know what was happening. That they felt powerless in the face of the authority of the state is, of course, quite understandable, but some were unhappy that their – and their children's – identities should become so widely known. While the law at the time sought to protect the identity of children involved in protection proceedings, legal provisions that have been strengthened since then, it was inevitable that anonymity would be compromised, given the very small community involved in this case.

Remember that the events in Orkney took place in a pre-Internet world, mercifully free from blogs, Twitter and tweets. Nonetheless, the case brought unprecedented publicity to the Scottish child protection system and the case, some of it introducing the sensational references to "satanic" or "ritualistic" abuse.[26] As the quotation at the beginning of this account illustrates, even publications as traditionally measured as *The Times* were not free from this sensationalism. Countless journalists and television crews descended on the island along with a media personality of the day, consumer advocate Esther Rantzen. Needless to say, the social work department was unhappy about the

---

[24] Eilean Siar Report, paras 24–30. 222 concerns over the girls' health and allegations of emotional, physical and sexual abuse were recorded between 1990 and 2000: *ibid*, para 32 and Appendix 2.

[25] *Ibid*, para 1.

[26] The Department of Health commissioned Jean La Fontaine, Professor Emerita of Social Anthropology at the London School of Economics, to examine allegations of satanic abuse in England. She concluded that the allegations were unfounded and based on myth: *Speak of the Devil: Tales of Satanic Abuse in Contemporary England* (Cambridge University Press, 1998).

media involvement, not least because it felt itself to be the victim of biased reporting to which it could not respond freely because of confidentiality considerations. While the media did not escape criticism from Lord Clyde,[27] it must be conceded that he endorsed many of the concerns first aired in newspapers and on radio and television.

In 1992, the Orkney parents were successful in preventing the BBC from broadcasting the taped interviews of their children by police officers and social workers while the children were on the mainland. They did not replicate that success in 1995, when they sought to halt the screening, again by the BBC, of Michael Eaton's play *Flowers of the Forest*, a fictional account of the handling of child abuse allegations in a small Highland community. In 2006, BBC2 aired a documentary, *Accused,* [28] examining the Orkney case and featuring a number of the key participants.

New legislation and procedures

Given the furore surrounding the events in Orkney, one might think that the legislative changes proposed by Lord Clyde and others would have been enacted swiftly.[29] Not so. Of course, there was no Scottish Parliament at the time and the proposed legislation had to compete, at Westminster, for one of the precious slots allocated to Scottish legislation. It seemed to many that this was an arena where Scotland mattered only a little and Scottish children mattered even less. That this was so had already been signalled earlier when Ian Lang, then Secretary of State for Scotland, rose to inform the House of Commons that he had received Lord Clyde's report. Such was the exodus from the House that the proceedings were interrupted by the noise of departing feet.[30] 1993 came and went with local government reorganisation being deemed more worthy of legislative time.[31] Indeed, it was only the collapse of plans to privatise the Post Office that allowed space for the Children (Scotland) Bill to be introduced in 1994.

[27] Clyde Report, paras 12.38–12.56.
[28] Blast! Films, 2006, directed by Ricardo Pollack. Further details at: http://www.blastfilms.co.uk/catalogue_detail.aspx?program=603.
[29] The White Paper *Scotland's Children: Child Care Law and Policy*, containing government proposals for reform, was published in 1993.
[30] *Hansard*, HC, 27 October 1992, col 865.
[31] Local Government (Scotland) Act 1994.

The Bill passed in 1995 and the Children (Scotland) Act 1995, Part II, made radical changes to the legislative framework for child protection in Scotland. The place of safety order, which required only a showing that there was reasonable cause to suspect that the child had been the victim of certain offences or "is likely to be caused unnecessary suffering or serious impairment of health" due to a lack of parental care,[32] disappeared. The whole thrust of child protection was set in a clear framework based on a triumvirate of principles: the paramountcy of the child's welfare, (usually) the right of the child to participate in the decision-making process and the requirement that no order be made unless it is better to make the order than that none be made.[33] Four new orders, designed to provide a wider range of responses to suspected abuse, were put in place. A showing of actual or likely "significant harm" is required to obtain either a child assessment order (authorising temporary removal of the child for further investigation of the allegations) or a child protection order (authorising removal, followed by referral to a children's hearing.)[34] A new order, the exclusion order, empowers the court to remove the suspected abuser from the family home, thus enabling the child to remain there as long as there is someone to look after him or her.[35] Of course, this order would have been of no help in the Orkney case, given the ambiguity about who the alleged abusers were. The fourth order, the parental responsibilities order, which effectively handed the parental role over to the local authority, has been replaced by the, rather more subtle and nuanced, permanence order.[36] The rules on how children's hearings must operate were also rewritten.[37]

Following the Clyde Report, the Secretary of State for Scotland and the Lord Advocate set up a working group to review the procedures adopted by police and social work procedures in their investigation of allegations of abuse, including sexual abuse.[38] As a result of that inquiry, new guidelines were issued. Social work procedures, more

---

[32] Social Work (Scotland) Act 1968, s 37.
[33] Children (Scotland) Act 1995, s 16.
[34] *Ibid*, ss 55 and 57.
[35] *Ibid*, s 76.
[36] Adoption and Children (Scotland) Act 2007, s 80.
[37] Children Hearings (Scotland) Rules 1996 (SI 1996/3261).
[38] *When Children Speak* … , Draft Report of Working Group set up by the Secretary of State for Scotland and the Lord Advocate, unpublished (Scottish Office, 1995).

generally, were revised.[39] A Social Work Inspection Agency was established to review local authority child protection services in the wake of the Orkney case.[40] While it always worked in co-ordination with other agencies, from 2009, the lead role in these reviews is now undertaken by HM Inspectorate of Education.[41]

While Childline (0800 1111) was established in 1986, the service it offers has developed and, in Scotland, it is now delivered by Children 1st, ironically, the reincarnation of the RSSPCC which, it will be remembered, received its share of criticism over its part in the Orkney case. A 24-hour, confidential, free telephone hotline (0800 022 3222) was set up in 2007 to enable members of the public to report concerns over child abuse or neglect and, following a review in 2009 of how well it was working, the decision was taken to staff it with qualified child protection professionals rather than trained call handlers.

After Orkney – the fate of some of the players

Since publicity was to follow many of the officials involved in the Orkney case, information about what happened to them after the case was over is available from press reports.

Paul Lee resigned as Director of Social Work for Orkney Islands Council while suspended pending disciplinary action over the case. Media reports refer to him receiving some £57,000 as part of his severance package. In July 1993, he was employed as senior social worker in the adult care team at Dumfries and Galloway Regional Council, failing to secure the post of Director of Social Work there a few months later.

Liz MacLean, one of the social workers involved in the case and criticised for the controversial interview techniques used, surfaced a couple of years later over her part in another case of over-zealous

---

[39] *Protecting Children – a shared responsibility: Guidance on Inter-Agency Co-operation* (Scottish Office, 1998), available at: http://www.scotland.gov.uk/library/documents-w3/pch-00.htm.

[40] For the most recent, overview report, see *How well do we protect Scotland's children? A report on the findings of the joint inspections of services to protect children 2005–2009* (HM Inspectorate of Education, 2009), available at: http://www.hmie.gov.uk/documents/publication/hwpsc.pdf.

[41] Services for Children and Inspection of Social Work Services (Scotland) Act 2006.

removal of children, this time in Ayrshire.[42] It was reported that she had set up a private consultancy in Edinburgh, counselling victims of child sexual abuse.

Sheriff Kelbie developed a brain tumour and died in 2001 at the tragically young age of 56.

Lord Clyde died in 2009 at the age of 77, again too soon, but after a glittering career in the law and public service.

His experience of working in Orkney may have been part of the reason that former police sergeant Malcolm Gilbert was appointed to a 1-year posting on Pitcairn Island in the wake of the child abuse cases scandal that so divided that small community.[43]

The Reverend Morris McKenzie died in Brechin, in 2003, after a long illness. He remained upset that he had been deprived of the opportunity to clear his name and was disappointed when the Church and Nation Committee of the Church of Scotland concluded that there was no basis for the claim that his human rights had been infringed. His concern proved somewhat accurate since newspaper reports of his death referred to his being implicated in the Orkney child abuse case, usually failing to mention that he was never charged with anything, far less convicted.

Little is known of what happened to the Orkney parents. However, showing a remarkable desire to bring something constructive out of his experience, one of the fathers in the Orkney case is reported to have applied to become a member of the children's panel.

May Willsher, one of the W children who had been removed from home some months before the Orkney children and whose family experiences triggered the Orkney case, has forgone anonymity. She lives in York with her partner and little boy. Having obtained qualifications in social health studies and psychology, she went on to study performance dance. In 2008, it was reported that she had been granted legal aid to pursue her damages action for compensation in respect of the removal and abuse that she allegedly suffered later while

---

[42] L, Petitioners (No 1) 1993 SLT 1310 and L, Petitioners (No 2) 1993 SLT 1342.

[43] Thirteen residents of Pitcairn Island (pop 47), located in the south Pacific and populated by descendants of Fletcher Christian and the other mutineers from The Bounty and indigenous Pacific islanders, were sentenced to terms of imprisonment (to be served on the Island) by the Pitcairn Supreme Court for rape and other sexual offences committed against girls and young women. The Privy Council had determined that English law applied to the island: Christian v The Queen [2007] 2 WLR 120.

in foster care. She has given a number of press interviews, detailing her experiences, and has denied media reports that she is suing for as much as £100,000.[44]

The people about whom we know least are the nine children. That is as it should be. Through no fault of their own, they were taken from their homes, sent to live with strangers and cut off from all contact with their parents and siblings for 5 weeks. Then, just as mysteriously (as it must have seemed to them), they were returned home. One can only hope that their parents had the personal resources to reinstate some sense of security in the children because the very officialdom that removed them did nothing further. Of course, further assistance from the state may have been the last thing the children or their parents wanted. We can only hope that they Orkney children are now happy, well-functioning adults.

Child protection in Scotland – the way ahead

For child protection in Scotland, this was far from the end of the story. In the years since the Orkney case, information came to light about, sometimes long-past, abuse in child care institutions. Marie Theresa Docherty, also known as Sister Alphonso, was convicted, in 2000, of abusing four children in her care in homes run by the Little Sisters of Nazareth. There was something of an outcry when she was admonished since she was a first offender and due to her age (she was only 57) and state of health. Attempts by some of the now-adult children who had lived in homes operated by the Order to obtain damages for the abuse they had suffered were found by the courts to be time barred.[45] The impact of child abuse raises special problems in terms of the victims pursuing their legal remedies and encouraging signs that the courts are getting to grips with the subtleties involved was signalled in a more recent case.[46]

Information began to surface about abuse of children in Kerelaw residential school and secure unit in Ayrshire, which had been operating since the 1970s. The school was closed in 2004, as was the secure unit in 2006. Two former staff members were convicted of abusing children

---

[44] See, eg, M Tierney, "May Willsher was snatched from her family in the Orkney child abuse scandal. And that's when she says the real abuse began", *The Herald* (Magazine), 28 October 2006, p 16.

[45] *B* v *Murray (No 2)* 2008 SC (HL) 146.

[46] *G* v *Glasgow City Council* 2009 Rep LR 74; [2009] CSOH 34, Lord Malcolm, 5 March 2009.

who had lived there and imprisoned and an independent inquiry was set up.[47] Recognising its moral, if not necessarily legal, responsibilities, Glasgow City Council made *ex gratia* payments to some of the former residents.

Then a wholly different group of cases began to emerge – modern cases of children who were left with their parents despite the authorities being well aware that there were problems in the family. Three-year-old Kennedy McFarlane was released from hospital to her mother's care just 12 days before she was killed by her mother's boyfriend in 2000.[48] Two-month-old Caleb Ness was on the Child Protection Register when he was killed by his father in 2001.[49] Similar fates befell 13-month-old Carla-Nicole Bone and 5-year-old Danielle Reid in 2002.[50] The list goes on and the latest in this catalogue of children failed, not only by their parents, but also by the system in place designed to protect them, is Brandon Muir. Brandon was almost 2 years old when he died of injuries resulting from a massive blow from his mother's boyfriend in 2008.[51] Social workers were well aware of concerns about Brandon and had scheduled a case conference for 2 days after his death.

The inquiries into these failures make depressing reading, of course, but perhaps most depressing of all is their similarity. Each catalogues the same shortcomings – overstretched social workers struggling to cope with their caseloads; defective procedures and failure to follow those in place; lack of communication between agencies; and accommodation of parental needs, sometimes at the price of child welfare. On each occasion, we are assured that procedures have been revised or that this is soon to happen and everything goes quiet – until the next time.

[47] *Independent Inquiry into Abuse at Kerelaw Residential School and Secure Unit* (Scottish Government, 2009), available at: http://www.scotland.gov.uk/Resource/Doc/271997/0081066.pdf.

[48] Dr H Hammond, *Child Protection Inquiry into the Circumstances Surrounding the Death of Kennedy McFarlane* (2000), available at: http://www.dumgal.gov.uk/Dumgal/Documents.aspx?id=11832.

[49] S O'Brien, QC, with H Hammond and M McKinnon, *Report of the Caleb Ness Inquiry* (2003), available at: http://www.edinburgh.gov.uk/internet/social_care/carers_introduction_to_services/CEC_the_report_of_the_death_of_caleb_ness.

[50] Dr J Herbison, *Danielle Reid: Independent Review into the Circumstances Surrounding Her Death* (2005), available at: http://nescpc.org.uk/uploads/dr-finalreport-8thsept-bkmarked.pdf.

[51] J Hawthorn and P Wilson, *Significant Case Review: Brandon Lee Muir* (2009), available at: http://www.dundeeprotects.co.uk/documents/SCR_Report_Brandon_Lee_Muir.pdf.

Conclusions

There is absolutely no doubt that the system of child protection in place at the time failed the Orkney children. No court has ever pronounced on what "really happened" to them. Either they were sexually abused, and received neither protection nor counselling, or they were not, and they were deprived of their liberty without the reasons for that ever being justified in a court.

After the case, it was widely believed that child protection law and procedures were improved dramatically. But were they? Have the legal tests for removal of children from their homes become too stringent and respectful of parental rights, leaving children at risk? Do social work guidelines discourage removal when that might be the prudent course of action? Does the memory of the Orkney case and the public pillorying they received over how it was conducted make social workers reluctant to intervene? Are these the explanations for the system continuing to fail children like Kennedy, Caleb, Carla-Nicole, Danielle, Brandon and so many others?

Yet another round of reform of child protection law is under way and it, along with modifications in social work practice, will bring further changes to the way child protection operates in Scotland. If this leads to greater intervention, the pendulum may have swung back to a pre-Orkney era. Let us hope this does not result in a repetition of the Orkney case.

Chapter 2

A FLAG IN THE WIND
MacCormick v *Lord Advocate*

Gavin Little

MacCormick v *Lord Advocate*[1] is a remarkable case. Although it took place nearly 60 years ago and the petitioners lost, it is the best-known Scottish case on constitutional law.[2] And while it raises interesting legal issues, its main significance is as an event in the tangled skein of Scottish constitutional debate.

To 21st-century eyes, the subject-matter of *MacCormick* appears quixotic. John MacCormick, the high-profile leader of the campaign for Scottish home rule (or self-government within the United Kingdom), challenged the Queen's adoption of the title "Elizabeth the Second of the United Kingdom of Great Britain and Northern Ireland" on her accession to the throne in 1952. There has never been an Elizabeth the First of Scotland. Nor has there been an Elizabeth the First of the United Kingdom, which was created in 1707 by the union of Scotland and England under the Treaty and Acts of Union.[3] There was, of course, an Elizabeth the First of England. Many in Scotland felt that the choice of the title "Elizabeth the Second" was provocative and offensive. The clear inference was that the union of 1707 had assimilated Scotland into England.

Along with his co-petitioner Ian Hamilton, a young supporter, MacCormick argued that the Queen's title breached the Treaty and Acts

---

[1] *MacCormick* v *Lord Advocate* 1953 SC 396 (hereafter "*MacCormick*").

[2] N Walker, "Fundamental Law" in N Whitty (ed), *The Laws of Scotland: Stair Memorial Encyclopaedia, Reissue Service, Constitutional Law* (2nd edn, 2002), paras 47, 57 and 62–65.

[3] That is, the "United Kingdom of Great Britain". In 1801 it became the "United Kingdom of Great Britain and Ireland"; "Northern Ireland" was substituted for "Ireland" in 1952.

of Union. This was felt by some to be disrespectful and even disloyal to the Queen. In the early 1950s, the institution of monarchy was viewed with a degree of deference which would seem strange today. More significantly, however, MacCormick used the subsequent assent by Parliament to the Queen's title in the Royal Titles Act 1953 as the peg from which to hang the argument that the established doctrine of the sovereignty of Parliament, as stated in its classic form by the 19th-century constitutional theorist A V Dicey,[4] was a feature of England's law and history and not that of Scotland.

MacCormick's argument against parliamentary sovereignty was straightforward. The Treaty of Union and its ratification by statutes of the Scottish and English Parliaments[5] created the United Kingdom of Great Britain. It also created the Parliament of the United Kingdom. This formally replaced the Parliaments of Scotland and England, which were abolished. For Dicey, it was axiomatic that the constitutional doctrine of the UK Parliament was that of the pre-union English Parliament. According to his theory of parliamentary sovereignty, which he derived from pre-union English common law, the UK Parliament possesses "under the English constitution, the right to make or unmake any law whatever; and further, that no person or body is recognised by the law of England as having a right to override or set aside the legislation of Parliament".[6] In terms of this doctrine, it is of key importance that Parliament has complete freedom to legislate as it pleases and that no Parliament can bind its successor: moreover, it is the courts that give effect to this legal sovereignty, or power, by upholding its statutes as the supreme law of the land. By the 1950s, Dicey's doctrine of parliamentary sovereignty had long been accepted as the dominant characteristic of the UK constitution.[7] Tellingly, it was also assumed that the "English constitution" applied in Scotland, notwithstanding its distinct constitutional history and separate legal system.[8]

MacCormick rejected this assumption, arguing that as parliamentary sovereignty was based on pre-union English common

---

[4] A V Dicey, *Introduction to the Study of the Law of the Constitution* (10th edn, 1959), p 39.

[5] The Union with England Act 1707 and the Union with Scotland Act 1706.

[6] Dicey (n 4 above), pp 39–40.

[7] See, eg, "Constitutional Law" in J L Wark and Viscount Dunedin (eds), *Green's Encyclopaedia of the Laws of Scotland* (1st edn, 1927), paras 944 and 950.

[8] *Ibid*; and *MacCormick* (n 1 above) at 403 per Lord Guthrie.

law it should not apply in Scotland. For him, the UK Parliament, as established in 1707, was not possessed of unlimited law-making power. Instead, he believed that the origin of its power to legislate is the Treaty of Union which, on ratification by Acts of the Scottish and English Parliaments, created the UK Parliament as a completely new constitutional entity. Thus, Parliament's law-making power is not, as Dicey would have it, sovereign and unlimited, but is subject to the Treaty. His argument was inter-linked with a belief that the pre-union Scottish principle of popular sovereignty, under which the people are the ultimate source of constitutional authority in Scotland, had continued after the union. According to MacCormick, the Scottish Parliament had no doctrine of parliamentary sovereignty to bequeath to the new UK Parliament, and the English Parliament had, by virtue of its ratifying legislation, surrendered its sovereign powers. Why, therefore, should it be assumed that the pre-union English theory of parliamentary sovereignty should prevail in Scotland, as opposed to indigenous doctrine?[9]

Importantly, MacCormick's arguments were heard on appeal by the First Division of the Inner House of the Court of Session, which was presided over by Lord President Cooper of Culross. Lord Cooper was the pre-eminent Scottish judge, legal historian and legal nationalist of the 20th century, and was also a substantial political figure. Crucially, although he rejected MacCormick's arguments on the matter of the Queen's title and hedged his opinion with important restrictions, Lord Cooper agreed in an *obiter* statement that the "principle of unlimited sovereignty is a distinctively English principle which has no counterpart in Scottish constitutional law".[10] He also left open the possibility that Acts of Parliament could be challenged in the courts if they were contrary to certain provisions in the Treaty and Acts of Union, which he accepted were "fundamental law".[11]

These ideas were, and still are, subversive of Dicey's doctrine of parliamentary sovereignty. They also stir the deep and sometimes stormy waters of Scottish constitutional debate. And, in human terms, the case had serious consequences for MacCormick, who paid a high personal price for daring to challenge the constitutional status quo.

[9] J M MacCormick, *The Flag in the Wind* (2nd edn, 2008), pp 187–190 (here-after "*Flag*").
[10] *MacCormick* (n 1 above) at 411.
[11] *Ibid* at 412.

The protagonists

John MacCormick

When he raised the action, John MacCormick was a 49-year-old solicitor and a partner in a Glasgow legal firm, which he had founded and built up through amalgamation.[12] He was also a well-known Scottish political figure and was the founder and chairman of the Scottish Covenant Association, a high-profile non-party-political organisation which campaigned for Scottish home rule. As such, he had recently been elected Lord Rector of Glasgow University. He was a small, tired-looking West Highlander with famously bad clothes sense, who suffered from a debilitating kidney condition. But he was also a charismatic orator and a remarkable politician, with a huge reservoir of commitment to the cause of Scottish home rule.[13]

As detailed in his political autobiography *The Flag in the Wind*, MacCormick's passion for politics took hold when he was a law student at Glasgow University in the 1920s.[14] Having become disenchanted with the Labour Party's lack of interest in Scottish home rule, he and some friends decided to form the Glasgow University Scottish Nationalist Association over cups of tea in a Sauchiehall Street café in late 1927. MacCormick went on to form the National Party of Scotland in 1928,[15] and played a leading role in creating the Scottish National Party ("SNP") in 1934.[16]

MacCormick's nationalism was, from the start, moderate and democratic. He deplored the anti-English extremism of some fellow nationalists, such as the poet Hugh MacDiarmid.[17] MacCormick also detested the form of nationalism emerging in Nazi Germany and by the late 1930s had become strongly sympathetic to the "united front" against fascism.[18] Although he continued to play a leading role in the SNP, he left the party in 1942. He had become convinced that what was important was the creation of a broadly based campaign for Scottish home rule within the UK.[19] He went on to found the Scottish

---

[12] N MacCormick, "Doubts about the 'Supreme Court' and reflections on *MacCormick* v *Lord Advocate*" (2004) 3 *JR* 237 at 238–240.

[13] I Hamilton, *A Touch of Treason* (2nd edn, 1994), pp 42–44.

[14] See *Flag* (n 9 above), Ch 2.

[15] *Ibid*, Chs 3 and 4.

[16] *Ibid*, Ch 13.

[17] *Ibid*, p 35.

[18] *Ibid*, p 88.

[19] *Ibid*, Ch 16.

Convention, which campaigned for home rule on a non-party-political platform[20] and joined the Liberal Party, standing without success as a candidate in a number of elections. Undaunted, he put forward the idea of a National Covenant for Home Rule, which was circulated around Scotland to gather signatures. Remarkably, around 2 million were collected by 1949. Despite MacCormick's jubilation, the Covenant was a political failure: home rule could come only through the ballot box.[21] MacCormick's high public profile in Scotland was, however, to continue. He was elected Lord Rector of Glasgow University by its students in 1951. He was also involved in the taking of the Stone of Destiny from Westminster Abbey by student supporters including Ian Hamilton and in the negotiations for its return – a bizarre escapade which has been dramatised recently as a feature film, with Robert Carlyle playing MacCormick.[22]

It was in the context of these extraordinary events that MacCormick, on hearing of the accession of the Queen as "Elizabeth the Second", saw an opportunity to draw public attention "in a most dramatic manner to the constitutional safeguards which ought to preserve something at least of the identity of Scotland".[23]

Lord Cooper of Culross

When *MacCormick* was appealed before the First Division of the Inner House of the Court of Session in the summer of 1953, the presiding judge was Lord Cooper of Culross, the Lord President of the Court of Session and as such the most senior judge in Scotland.[24] He was then 60 years old and was at the height of his professional powers, having had a distinguished career as a lawyer, civil servant, MP, Government Minister and judge. In his personal life, he was unmarried and devoted to his mother, who had died in 1951. Although he was a well-known public figure, he was by nature shy.[25] Apart from the law and politics, his main interests were (in no particular order) history, poetry, music, gardening, photography, golf, astronomy, the Church of Scotland and cats.[26]

[20] T M Devine, *The Scottish Nation 1700–2000* (1st edn, 1999), pp 565–568.
[21] *Ibid*.
[22] See *Flag* (n 9 above), Chs 23–25.
[23] *Ibid*, p 187.
[24] J M Cooper, "Biography" in Lord Cooper of Culross, *Selected Papers* (1957), p xi at pp xi–xxviii.
[25] *Ibid*, pp xxv–xxvi.
[26] *Ibid*, pp xix–xxiii.

A product of the Edinburgh bourgeoisie, the young Tom Cooper attended George Watson's College, before graduating MA from Edinburgh University and being called to the Scottish Bar in 1915. Rejected for military service in the First World War on medical grounds, he worked in the Civil Service in London, receiving an OBE at the war's end. He then returned to the Scottish Bar, taking Silk in 1927.[27]

Although legal commentators tend to focus on Cooper's achievements as a lawyer, it is important in the context of this discussion to appreciate that he also had considerable political experience. He was the Unionist Party (now Conservative Party) candidate for Banffshire in 1930 and was, as his personal papers show,[28] very active politically. Ultimately, he did not contest the seat, but he was later adopted as the National Government candidate in Edinburgh West and returned to Parliament in 1935. He immediately became Solicitor General for Scotland and was appointed Lord Advocate and a Privy Councillor shortly thereafter.[29] On the outbreak of war in 1939, Cooper served as Churchill's Lord Advocate and was a Joint Regional Commissioner for Scotland, while also dealing with the passage of emergency legislation in Parliament.[30]

Cooper was never robust physically and in 1941 he left the Government with much praise[31] to sit on the Scottish judicial Bench as Lord Justice-Clerk. Given the demands of serving as a government Minister in wartime, this was probably a relief for him.[32] He was appointed Lord President in 1946.

Lord Cooper was therefore no political ingénue when he presided over *MacCormick*. Moreover, although his brother described him as a "staunch unionist",[33] he also, as Hector MacQueen has argued,[34] exemplifies what Graeme Morton has termed "unionist nationalism".[35] This provided Presbyterian middle-class Scots of the

---

[27] J M Cooper, "Biography" in Lord Cooper of Culross, *Selected Papers* (1957), pp xii–xiv.

[28] Lord Cooper of Culross, National Library of Scotland, Manuscript Acc 6188/7.

[29] J M Cooper (n 24 above) p xvii.

[30] *Ibid*, p xvii.

[31] *Ibid*, p xviii.

[32] *Ibid*, p xvii.

[33] *Ibid*, p xiv.

[34] H MacQueen, "Legal nationalism: the case of Lord Cooper" in N M Dawson (ed), *Reflections on law and history* (2006), pp 83–98 at 89.

[35] See generally, G Morton, *Unionist Nationalism: Governing Urban Scotland 1830–60* (1999).

period with a dual identity which combined commitment to Scottish institutions with strong support for the union with England and rule from Westminster: unionist nationalists could develop Scottish institutions and interests domestically, while taking advantage of the opportunities made available by union and the Empire in particular.[36] Unionist nationalism was therefore strongly opposed to home rule but at the same time "explicit in its demands for the better government of Scotland".[37] Indigenous Scottish institutions such as the legal system, local government, the education system, and the Church of Scotland (which are *ex facie* protected by the Treaty of Union) provided the focus for unionist nationalist activity, to the great political advantage of the Scottish Unionist Party until the 1960s.[38]

As a leading Scottish Unionist, Lord Cooper was therefore fiercely opposed to the idea of a Scottish Parliament, while being wholly and without self-contradiction committed to Scottish institutions and the union. Indeed, his brother wrote that he "thought his services should be to Scotland, being a 'Nationalist' in the true sense of the word".[39] Lord Cooper's dislike of political nationalism was expressed in an undated note on Scottish home rule, possibly used as a speech, which is in his private papers.[40] Its hostile tone is apparent from the outset by his pencilled comment in the margin to "[f]righten the women":[41] the case for Scottish home rule was, he believed, a "[b]eggarly array of unconsidered and impracticable platitudes purloined from the common stock of political electioneering promises of the last thirty years".[42]

Lord Cooper's strong commitment to Scottish institutions was, however, reflected in his legal scholarship, which has been extremely influential. Most significantly, he was the creator in the 1930s and 1940s of what Ian Willock termed the "Cooper–Smith ideology" of Scots law, which was advanced subsequently by Professor T B Smith

[36] C Williams, "The United Kingdom" in T Baycroft and M Hewitson (eds), *What is a nation? Europe 1789–1914* (2006), p 286.
[37] *Ibid*.
[38] D McCrone, *Understanding Scotland – The Sociology of a Stateless Nation* (1992), p 159.
[39] J M Cooper (n 24 above), p xxv.
[40] Lord Cooper, National Library of Scotland, Manuscript Acc 6188/12.
[41] *Ibid*.
[42] *Ibid*.

and others. [43] According to this ideology, which can be characterised as a form of Scottish legal nationalism,[44] modern Scots private law is defined as a mixed legal system, in which the indigenous civilian tradition was subsumed by English common law after the Union of 1707.[45] Importantly, legal nationalism does not, as Lindsay Farmer and John Grant have argued, necessarily imply support for political nationalism:[46] indeed, as in the case of Lord Cooper, it can be consistent with unionist nationalism. A central tenet of the Cooper–Smith ideology is that the influence of English law has been largely damaging to Scots law. Crucially, Lord Cooper believed that for Scots law to survive it was necessary to build on its indigenous foundations and to look to developments in other mixed systems.[47] Viewed in this perspective, the challenge in *MacCormick* to the application in Scotland of Dicey's theory of parliamentary sovereignty – a doctrine of English common law – offered the opportunity for Lord Cooper to express his legal nationalism in judicial form.

The case and its context

As a result of the controversy surrounding the Queen's accession as "Elizabeth the Second", a number of Provosts of Scottish towns refused to read the official proclamation. More dramatically, a number of Royal Mail pillar boxes bearing the new title were defaced and a bungling attempt was even made to blow one up.[48]

Sensing a political opportunity, MacCormick thought that the situation offered the potential for the Covenant Association to mount a legal challenge to the application of parliamentary sovereignty in Scotland. Since his time as a law student, he had felt that Dicey's theory was permeated with the "arrogant assumption that the history

---

[43] I D Willock, "The Scottish legal heritage revisited" in J P Grant (ed), *Independence and Devolution: The Legal Implications for Scotland* (1976) pp 1–4; and H MacQueen, "Legal nationalism: Lord Cooper, legal history and comparative law" (2005) 9/3 ELR at 395.

[44] G Gretton, "The rational and the national: Thomas Broun Smith" in E Reid and C Millar (eds), *A mixed legal system in transition: T B Smith and the progress of Scots law* (2005), pp 32–33.

[45] MacQueen (n 43 above), p 396.

[46] L Farmer, "Under the shadow of Parliament House: the strange case of legal nationalism" in L Farmer and S Veitch, *The State of Scots law: law and government after the devolution settlement* (2001) at p 151; and J P Grant, "Introduction" in Grant (ed) (n 43 above), pp x–xi.

[47] MacQueen (n 43 above), pp 396–397.

[48] A Kemp, *The Hollow Drum: Scotland since the War* (1993), pp 90–91.

of the Kingdom of England has been continuous from the Norman Conquest until the present day".[49] This was, he believed, an affront to Scotland. He raised the matter at the Covenant Association, leading to uproar. MacCormick was accused of "downright disloyalty" to the Queen and a number of members resigned.[50]

The subsequent Royal Titles Act 1953 provided additional grist to MacCormick's mill. Under the Act, Parliament assented after the fact to the adoption by the Queen of such titles as she thought fit. MacCormick thought that it provided further potential for a legal action and discussed the possibility with Ian Hamilton, then a law student, and John Bayne, an advocate. Between them they drafted a petition, craving the Court of Session to interdict Ministers of the Crown from publishing a proclamation using the title "Elizabeth the Second of the United Kingdom" on the grounds that it was inconsistent with historical fact and political reality and involved contravention of Art I of the Treaty of Union and related legislation.[51]

The case was enrolled with MacCormick representing himself and Bayne representing Hamilton. The controversial nature of the case was apparent from the outset. Indeed, the petitioners struggled to find a solicitor who would lodge the petition with the Court of Session, and MacCormick's partners in his legal firm told him he must disassociate from them if he decided to proceed with the action.[52]

Three days before the Coronation, the petitioners appeared un-daunted before Lord Guthrie in the Outer House of the Court of Session. There was immense public interest and the courtroom was packed.[53] The basis of the petitioners' argument was that the Royal Titles Act 1953 was invalid on the ground that it was *ultra vires* for Parliament to pass legislation which contradicted those provisions of the Treaty of Union which, it was contended, were "fundamental" law, on the basis that they were intended[54] to have effect "in all time coming":[55] contrary to Dicey's theories, Parliament did not have unlimited sovereignty. More

---

[49] *Flag* (n 9 above), p 188. See, generally, N MacCormick (n 12 above), pp 240–242.

[50] *Ibid*, p 190.

[51] *Ibid*, p 191.

[52] N MacCormick, "Rights of a sovereign nation", *The Scotsman*, 20 December 1994.

[53] *Flag* (n 9 above), p 191.

[54] By its negotiators and the Parliaments of Scotland and England on ratification.

[55] Eg Treaty of Union, Arts I, II, VI, VII, XVIII, XXIV, and the annexed Protestant Religion and Presbyterian Church Act 1707.

specifically, the petitioners argued that if the Act sought to authorise the Queen to adopt the title "Elizabeth the Second", it was *ultra vires* on the ground that in the period since Article I of the Treaty caused the United Kingdom to come into existence in 1707 there had been no monarch named "Elizabeth" until the Queen's accession.[56]

It was clear that Lord Guthrie, who listened to the petitioners "somewhat stolidly"[57] and with few interruptions, would dismiss the action. His opinion was delivered the next day. It was, as MacCormick put it, "as complete a defeat as I could possibly have feared, with not one word of comfort in his findings":[58] in throwing out the case, Lord Guthrie affirmed *inter alia* that, notwithstanding the English law origins of Dicey's theory, parliamentary sovereignty was a basic principle of Scottish constitutional law.[59]

The only consolation for MacCormick was that Lord Guthrie produced a lengthy opinion, and it was on this basis that the petitioners appealed to the Inner House. The hearing was tabled to take place before the First Division and therefore Lord Cooper as Lord President (who was anxious to ensure that it did not take place during the forthcoming royal visit to Scotland[60]). Lord Cooper's involvement was a source of satisfaction for MacCormick, who was aware of his interest in Scottish legal history and the distinctiveness of Scots law. There was, however, no false optimism. As MacCormick wrote:

> "We had not the slightest expectation that the Court would now pronounce against the Queen's numeral but we hoped that something might emerge which would shake the monstrous notion that the Parliament of Great Britain was simply the Parliament of England to which a handful of Scottish members had been added."[61]

On the day of the hearing, MacCormick was in a state of acute depression and nervousness.[62] He had been warned against pursuing the case. Although he was an experienced solicitor, he had seldom appeared in even the lower courts. Had he not been a party litigant, he

---

[56] See, generally, *MacCormick* (n 1 above) at 397–402.

[57] *Flag* (n 9 above), p 192.

[58] *Ibid*.

[59] *MacCormick* (n 1 above) at 402–405.

[60] National Archives of Scotland, File 41191/819/1, Minute 6.7.53.

[61] *Flag* (n 9 above), pp 193–194.

[62] See, generally, *ibid*, p 194.

would not, as a solicitor, have had the right of audience in the Court of Session. He knew that he could make a fool of himself personally, professionally and politically. The financial risks of losing were also significant.[63] As MacCormick put it, he was going to advance a belief which he had held since his student days but which might seem "in the cold light of other people's reason to be merely a wild bee in my bonnet".[64]

At the hearing, there was again great public interest and the courtroom was crowded.[65] The judges on the Bench were Lord Carmont and Lord Russell, with Lord Cooper presiding. MacCormick's nerves were such that Bayne spoke first. MacCormick was then before the court for at least 2 hours. All three judges and Lord Cooper in particular interrupted continually, testing the arguments. MacCormick's nervousness left him as he proclaimed "in public in the Supreme Court of Scotland the disagreement with Dicey which long ago as a student [he] had wanted to express to [his] mentors".[66]

Although MacCormick was surrounded by congratulatory supporters at the end of the hearing, the appeal was, as expected, dismissed. Importantly, however, Lord Cooper took a very different approach to parliamentary sovereignty from Lord Guthrie.

With regard to the specific grounds of the appeal, Lord Cooper held that the petitioners had failed to make their case for a declaratory order specifying their rights in respect of the Queen's title with the required degree of precision (they had abandoned their attempt to secure suspension and interdict).[67] He focused immediately thereafter on their argument that the use of the enumeration "the Second" in the Queen's title was not only inconsistent with historical fact and political reality, but was in breach of the Treaty of Union and the subsequent implementing legislation. He held that the Royal Titles Act 1953 had no bearing on the case. It gave parliamentary assent to the title after the fact of accession and proclamation, rather than statutory authority. Moreover, the Act was incapable of being interpreted by a court, as it was not self-contained.[68] Lord Cooper did, however, agree with Lord Guthrie that Art I of the Treaty did not prohibit the adoption by the

[63] MacCormick (n 52 above).
[64] *Flag* (n 9 above), p 194.
[65] See, generally, *ibid*, pp 194–195.
[66] *Ibid*.
[67] *MacCormick* (n 1 above) at 409.
[68] *Ibid* at 409–411.

Queen of her title and that the petitioners did not have title to sue, as the case was concerned with public policy.[69]

If this was all that Lord Cooper had said in his judgment, *MacCormick* would be long forgotten. What makes the case significant, however, is Lord Cooper's *obiter* statement on the status of parliamentary sovereignty. MacCormick's hopes that Lord Cooper would understand and sympathise with his arguments on this key issue were realised, to some extent at least. Indeed, on reading Lord Cooper's comments on parliamentary sovereignty, there is the clear sense that he knew them to be controversial and that he wanted to express them publicly and judicially. They are different in style and tone from the rest of his opinion, which is almost perfunctory. In a passage which is worth quoting in full, Lord Cooper stated:

> "The principle of the unlimited sovereignty of Parliament is a distinctively English principle which has no counterpart in Scottish constitutional law. It derives its origin from Coke and Blackstone, and was widely popularised during the nineteenth century by Bagehot and Dicey, the latter having stated the doctrine in its classic form in his Law of the Constitution. Considering that the Union legislation extinguished the Parliaments of Scotland and England and replaced them by a new Parliament, I have difficulty in seeing why it should have been supposed that the new Parliament of Great Britain must inherit all the peculiar characteristics of the English Parliament but none of the Scottish Parliament, as if all that happened in 1707 was that Scottish representatives were admitted to the Parliament of England. That is not what was done. Further, the Treaty and the associated legislation, by which the Parliament of Great Britain was brought into being as the successor of the separate Parliaments of Scotland and England, contain some clauses which expressly reserve to the Parliament of Great Britain powers of subsequent modification, and other clauses which either contain no such power or emphatically exclude subsequent alteration by declarations that the provision shall be fundamental and unalterable in all time coming, or declarations of a like effect. I have never been able to understand how it is possible to reconcile with elementary canons of construction the adoption by the English constitutional theorists of the same attitude to these markedly different types of provisions."[70]

Lord Cooper went on to note that the Crown had conceded that Parliament could not repeal or alter the fundamental and essential

[69] *MacCormick* (n 1 above) at 413.
[70] *Ibid* at 411.

conditions of the Treaty, inferring that the Lord Advocate had been influenced by Dicey's views in his *Thoughts on the Scottish Union*.[71] In this, Dicey suggested that the Union had created an "absolutely sovereign Legislature which should yet be bound by unalterable laws": that is, although Parliament may repeal any laws, there are some, such as the fundamental provisions of the Treaty, which "cannot be changed without grave danger to the Constitution of the country".[72] This argument, did not, however, impress Lord Cooper, who noted that he had "not found in the Union legislation any provision that the Parliament of Great Britain should be 'absolutely sovereign' in the sense that that Parliament should be free to alter the Treaty at will".[73] He made a pointed rejection of Lord Guthrie's uncritical adoption of Dicey's theory, stating that the statements on the matter in his own judgment (which were concurred with by Lord Carmont and Lord Russell) "provide a necessary corrective to the extreme formulations of the Lord Ordinary".[74] Lord Cooper then went on to comment dismissively that the "academic logic" of Dicey's "earlier dogmas" had been encroached on by subsequent political realities, in particular the effect of the Statute of Westminster 1931,[75] which provided that Parliament should not legislate for the Dominions without their consent.

What were Lord Cooper's intentions in making these statements? Intriguingly, there is an unpublished, undated note in his private papers entitled "Dicey and the Act of Union".[76] It is unclear whether it was written by him, as it is initialled "A.H.C." in pen, and may therefore have been the work of Professor A H Campbell of Edinburgh University.[77] In any case, the note is a strong refutation of Dicey's theory of parliamentary sovereignty, and it is interesting to speculate whether, if it was not written by Lord Cooper, it influenced his thinking at the time of the case. Certainly, the underlying, critical theme of the note is similar to that of his *obiter dicta*. It starts with the remark "I

---

[71] *MacCormick* (n 1 above).

[72] See quotes *ibid* at 412.

[73] *Ibid*.

[74] *Ibid*.

[75] *Ibid*.

[76] Lord Cooper of Culross, National Library of Scotland, Manuscript Acc.6188/10/ xv.

[77] H MacQueen, "Two Toms and an ideology for Scots law: T B Smith and Lord Cooper of Culross" in Reid and Millar (eds) (n 44 above), pp 49 and at 69.

cannot without further argument accept Dicey's facile assumption based on his understanding of 'the English Constitution' that the Act of Union is merely an Act of Parliament like any other and may be modified or repealed by a subsequent Act or expressly by implication".[78] The Act of Union is seen as the "the constitution" of Parliament and the analysis of its fundamental provisions is particularly trenchant: even if Parliament has the power to legislate contrary to fundamental provision, "there must be a very strong presumption against it having the intention to alter such provisions as these".[79] The paper concludes with the statement that the issues are "much more complicated than Dicey makes out and, in particular, that anything in the Act of Union can be held to be repealed by mere implication from the terms of any subsequent Act is too sweeping and ill-considered".[80]

Whether or not these views had any bearing on Lord Cooper's thinking in *MacCormick*, it is important to note that his refutation of Dicey's theory in his judicial opinion was qualified carefully. There was, he pointed out, a "grave difficulty" for those seeking to raise an action in the courts on the basis of breach of the Treaty as fundamental law: could such a matter be determined as a justiciable issue by the courts? As he put it, "it is of little avail to ask whether the Parliament of Great Britain 'can' do this thing or that, without going on to inquire who can stop them if they do.".[81] How could the provisions of the Treaty be enforced, when the parties to it (ie the Kingdoms of Scotland and England) had ceased to exist? And while his opinion of the doctrine of parliamentary sovereignty was delivered in blunt terms, his views on the potential for the courts striking down an Act of Parliament on the ground of fundamental breach of the Treaty were much more circumspect. He simply reserved his opinion with regard to Arts XVIII and XIX of the Treaty (which provide respectively that no alteration can be made to laws concerning "private right" except when it is for "the evident utility of the subjects within Scotland" and that the existence of the College of Justice is to be protected).[82] A latent sympathy for some aspects of MacCormick's position was, however, more apparent in Lord Cooper's shielding of the petitioners from the accusation of

---

[78] Lord Cooper (n 76 above).
[79] *Ibid.*
[80] *Ibid.*
[81] *MacCormick* (n 1 above) at 412.
[82] *Ibid.*

disloyalty to the Queen,[83] and in his refusal of the Crown's application
for expenses on the ground that the petitioners had raised issues of
public importance.[84]

MacCormick was jubilant. The Lord President of the Court of
Session had supported the premise of his argument on parliamentary
sovereignty, albeit in *obiter dicta*. Lord Cooper had stated that the
doctrine of the sovereignty of Parliament had no counterpart in Scots
law and had inferred that Parliament's power to alter the fundamental
provisions of the Treaty of Union could potentially be restricted. In
MacCormick's eyes, though, what was "perhaps best of all"[85] was
that by reserving his opinion on the issue of whether the Court of
Session might challenge parliamentary legislation on the ground
of fundamental breach of the Treaty of Union, Lord Cooper had left
the door open for future legal actions. He concluded *The Flag in the
Wind* by deriving satisfaction from the idea that "[t]he law could never
again be stated in Scottish textbooks as though Scotland were a mere
appendage of England".[86] This, he believed, had justified the action in
full.[87]

The personal aftermaths

It is a matter for speculation whether the conclusion to *The Flag in the
Wind* was MacCormick presenting a brave face to a gathering storm
of personal adversity. As a result of pursuing the case, his partners
removed him from his legal firm. Perhaps in part motivated by his
experience of appearing before the Court of Session, MacCormick
sought admission to the Faculty of Advocates after spending a
year devilling. Although he lacked a pass in one professional
examination, the Dean of Faculty had the discretion to give an
exemption. MacCormick expected that this would be granted as he
was an experienced solicitor. It was, however, refused and he was
told that he would have to attend classes before he could sit the
examination. To his friend and co-petitioner Ian Hamilton, now a
distinguished retired Queen's Counsel, this was a deliberate attempt
at humiliation. Whether or not this was so, MacCormick was ruined

---

[83] *MacCormick* (n 1 above) at 413–414.
[84] See National Archives of Scotland (n 60 above), Minute 14.10.53.
[85] See, generally, *Flag* (n 9 above), p 195.
[86] *Ibid*.
[87] N MacCormick (n 12 above), pp 242–243.

professionally.[88] His kidney condition and other illnesses were causing him considerable pain, which his son, the late Professor Sir Neil MacCormick, recorded he bore with great courage.[89] MacCormick's health deteriorated and latterly he resorted to alcohol as a means of dulling the pain. He died in 1961 from a combination of kidney and liver disease at the age of 56.[90] In Hamilton's uncompromising view, "The great and the good feared him as a danger to their own mediocrity. They smothered him to death".[91]

Time was even shorter for Lord Cooper. Indeed, *MacCormick* was his last major judgment. In September 1954 he reached the apex of his career on being raised to the peerage, but was struck down shortly thereafter by a cerebral thrombosis, from which he did not recover. He resigned as Lord President later that year and died in July 1955, aged 62.

MacCormick v *Lord Advocate*: the consequences

Enforceable legal rights

In terms of establishing enforceable legal rights, *MacCormick* is an interesting case, but little more than that. Following on from Lord Cooper's *obiter dicta*, a number of challenges to legislation have been made in the Scottish courts on the ground that it is in breach of the Treaty of Union. In *Gibson* v *Lord Advocate*, the Lord Ordinary, Lord Keith, adopted Lord Cooper's approach by reserving his opinion on whether the court could strike down legislation in significant breach of Arts XVIII and XIX of the Treaty. He also reserved his opinion on the issue of whether legislation to abolish the Church of Scotland could be in breach of the Treaty.[92] Subsequent actions brought on similar grounds have sought to establish that legislation concerned with the poll tax and Skye Bridge tolls was invalid. None has been successful.[93] As in *MacCormick*, the courts held the alleged Treaty breaches to be irrelevant on their facts, while leaving open the possibility that an

---

[88] See, generally, I Hamilton in *Flag* (n 9 above), pp vi–vii: see also N MacCormick in *Flag* at p xix.

[89] N MacCormick, *ibid*, p xiv.

[90] *Ibid*.

[91] I Hamilton in *Flag* (n 9 above), p vii.

[92] *Gibson* v *Lord Advocate* 1975 SC 135 at 144.

[93] See *Murray* v *Rogers* (24 July 1990, unreported) (1st Div); *Pringle, Petitioner* 1991 SLT 330; and *Robbie the Pict* v *Hingston (No 2)* 1998 SLT 1201 (HCJ).

action could be brought competently against legislation for breach of the Treaty's fundamental conditions.

Moreover, the fundamental Treaty conditions specified by the courts which, if breached by statute, might give rise to competent challenge are extremely narrow. One may wonder why, after more than 300 years of union, Westminster would seek to abolish the Church of Scotland or the Court of Session, or attempt to replace Scots private law with English law. And looming over the whole issue is Lord Cooper's question of whether such matters are justiciable, or suitable for adjudication by the courts. Justiciability is, of course, a difficult concept.[94] But in simple terms, it is unlikely that Scottish judges would feel themselves to have the necessary constitutional authority to overturn the UK Parliament's legislation in the event of a fundamental breach of the Treaty. Technical potentialities aside, the courts have not provided practical, legally enforceable rights: in this respect, at least, they are a juristic Brigadoon, emerging occasionally from the constitutional mists when Westminster is felt to be encroaching on Scottish *amour propre.*

Constitutional debate

MacCormick is, however, of greater significance when set in the broader context of constitutional debate, particularly in Scotland. In academia, it has influenced the development of a distinctive and important approach to constitutional theory, in which the issue of sovereignty is central. This is due in large part to the immense scholarly contribution of Sir Neil MacCormick, who, as Regius Professor of Public Law at Edinburgh University, developed his father's ideals in a series of major publications.[95]

In one of his seminal works, *Questioning Sovereignty*, Sir Neil expanded on the idea that sovereignty cannot be seen as a single, indivisible entity. Rather, it should be conceptualised as compromising multiple, inter-related and overlapping sovereignties, as in the European Union.[96] Seen from this perspective, sovereignty is a

---

[94] See L Fuller, "The Forms and Limits of Adjudication" (1978) 92 HLR 353 at 365–368, 393–395 and 397–398: and Walker (n 2 above), para 65.

[95] N MacCormick, *Questioning Sovereignty* (1999); "Does the United Kingdom have a constitution?" (1978) 29 Northern Ireland Legal Quarterly 1; "The English constitution, the British state and the Scottish anomaly" (1998) *Proceedings of the British Academy: Lectures and Memoirs 101* 289; and "Is there a constitutional path to Scottish independence?" 53/4 (2000) Parliamentary Affairs 721.

[96] MacCormick, *Questioning Sovereignty* (n 95 above), pp 131–136.

pluralistic, multi-faceted phenomenon. But in the more parochial world of UK constitutional doctrine, an important distinction can also be made between *political* sovereignty, or power, and the narrower, *legal* doctrine of parliamentary sovereignty. For Dicey, the former is vested in those who have effective overall influence on Parliament – that is, the electorate, which periodically determines the composition of Parliament, if not the detail of its actions. The latter is concerned with the purportedly unlimited legislative power of Parliament.[97] Importantly, however, it should be appreciated that, although they are distinct concepts, they are also inter-related and co-dependent. Thus, the electorate's political sovereignty (and therefore democracy) is given effect, albeit indirectly, through the exercise of Parliament's legal sovereignty in the form of legislation. On this basis, Parliament can lay claim to being the most important political institution in the UK. The political sovereignty of the electorate and the institutional status of Parliament are reinforced by the judiciary performing the subordinate, deferential role of giving effect to Parliament's legal sovereignty through the upholding of its statutes as the supreme law of the land, and observing the inter-related doctrines that Parliament has the freedom to legislate on whatever matter it pleases and that no Parliament can bind its successor. Crucially, though, the authority of Dicey's classic parliamentary sovereignty as constitutional doctrine requires that Parliament's supposedly unlimited power to legislate is upheld without qualification by judges and the courts and also that it reflects political reality.

It is within this theoretical context that it can be argued that *MacCormick* has influenced the constitutional status of parliamentary sovereignty. In the early 1950s, the unchallenged centrality of Dicey's doctrine of parliamentary sovereignty in the UK constitution was such that the authority of Westminster's legislation was accepted without question.[98] Lord Cooper's *obiter dicta* in *MacCormick* inferring that, at least in principle, Acts of Parliament may be challenged competently in the courts on the grounds of breach of the Treaty of Union was therefore directly subversive of the doctrine and the orthodox view of the constitution. Jeffrey Goldsworthy has argued that underlying the debate over parliamentary sovereignty is the "location of ultimate decision-taking authority – the right to the 'final word' – in a legal

---

[97] MacCormick, *Questioning Sovereignty* (n 95 above), p 68.
[98] See n 7 above.

system".[99] Lord Cooper's reservation in his *obiter dicta* left open the possibility that, in the limited context of fundamental breaches of the Treaty of Union by legislation, it could be the judiciary that should have the last word, rather than Parliament. It is remarkable that subsequent decisions of the Scottish courts (which are not generally viewed as hotbeds of radical judicial activism) have maintained his position. Moreover, Lord Cooper blazed a trail by pointing out bluntly that the political limitations placed on Dicey's parliamentary sovereignty by the Statute of Westminster were rendering it anachronistic and inconsistent, a process which has continued as a result of, *inter alia*, UK membership of the European Union[100] and Scottish devolution.[101]

With these points in mind, Lord Cooper's *dicta* in *MacCormick* are perhaps best viewed as one of a number of significant judge-led constitutional events, along with *R v Transport Secretary, ex parte Factortame Ltd*[102] (in which the House of Lords decided that EC law overrides inconsistent UK legislation), and the ongoing development by a number of senior English judges of the concept of "common law constitutionalism" (which postulates among other things that as parliamentary sovereignty is a doctrine of English common law, its exercise may potentially be subject to the authority of the courts).[103] These events are part of an extended process of judicial activism, in which senior judges are chipping away at the inherent inconsistencies of Dicey's unlimited parliamentary sovereignty in decisions, *obiter dicta* and extra-judicial statements. In so doing, they are contributing to the doctrine, which is essentially monist in nature, gradually losing authority. Particularly in Scotland, *MacCormick* and the subsequent decisions of the Scottish courts can therefore be seen as part of a long-term, judge-led deflation of the authority of parliamentary sovereignty as constitutional doctrine.

This is not, however, to claim that parliamentary sovereignty has ceased to be of relevance in the UK constitution. Arguably, it remains

---

[99] J Goldsworthy, *The Sovereignty of Parliament* (1999), p 3.

[100] See Sir William Wade, "What has happened to the sovereignty of Parliament?" (1991) 107 LQR 1.

[101] G Little, "Scotland and Parliamentary Sovereignty" (2004) 24/4 Legal Studies 540.

[102] [1990] 2 AC 85 and (*No 2*) [1991] 1 AC 603.

[103] See, eg, Sir John Laws, "Law and Democracy" (1995) PL 72; Lord Woolf, "Droit Public English Style" (1995) PL 57; and Sir Stephen Sedley, "Human Rights: A Twenty-First Century Agenda" (1995) PL, 386. See also *Jackson v Att Gen* [2005] UKHL 56; [2006] 1 AC 262 per Lords Steyn and Hope.

intact formally as legal and constitutional doctrine – H L A Hart could still categorise it as a "rule of recognition" in the UK legal system.[104] If, as a matter of pure law (rather than political reality), Parliament were to pass legislation to abolish the Scottish Parliament without public consent, the courts would doubtless seek to give effect to it, irrespective of public and political opinion in Scotland. But no matter how doggedly it is maintained by Parliament,[105] Dicey's classic doctrine is a shadow of its former self after decades of contradictory political realities and waning judicial support.[106] In the latter context, *MacCormick* can be said to have played a distinctively Scottish part in its decline.

Moreover, the issues raised in the case – the Treaty of Union, sovereignty, the authority of Westminster and the monarch – are controversial topics in the rough and tumble world of Scottish constitutional politics, which is dominated by the so-called "national question", or the competing merits of Westminster rule, devolution and independence.[107] Parliamentary sovereignty also has political as well as legal connotations in Scotland: the adoption as doctrine by Parliament and the courts of Dicey's theory, which was derived from pre-union English common law and constitutional practice, gives legal and constitutional form to the political fact that, for all practical purposes, the post-1707 UK Parliament has indeed been the continuation of the pre-union English Parliament with a small number of additional Scottish representatives. Thus, to those Scots who are committed to the idea that the union of 1707 was a mutually respectful international agreement rather than assimilation, and to the belief that Scotland has a special national status within the UK, Dicey's doctrine of parliamentary sovereignty may appear at best inexplicable and at worst arrogant. To supporters and opponents of Scottish independence alike, it has also been symbolic of Westminster's political hegemony in Scotland.[108]

Seen in this context, MacCormick was using the challenge to the Queen's title as a high-profile platform from which to launch a fundamentally political re-assertion of Scottish identity. Given his political experience, it can be assumed that Lord Cooper would have

---

[104] H L A Hart, *The Concept of Law* (1st edn, 1961), pp 145–146.
[105] As in the Scotland Act 1998, s 28(7).
[106] MacCormick, *Questioning Sovereignty* (n 95 above), pp 70–75.
[107] Walker (n 2 above), para 61.
[108] Little (n 101 above), pp 553–559.

been aware of the wider implications of his *obiter dicta*. Notwithstanding his qualifications and caveats, and the obvious fact that he found against MacCormick, he would have understood that, by doubting the validity of Dicey's classic doctrine of parliamentary sovereignty in his capacity as Lord President, he was giving the legitimating authority of the Scottish courts to the idea that Scotland has a distinct and protected constitutional status within the UK, which should be treated with respect. Importantly, however, although nationalist and political in a generic sense, his adoption of this position would not have implied support for political nationalism: rather, it is entirely consistent with Scottish unionist nationalism and, more specifically, legal nationalism.

In concluding, it is intriguing to speculate whether the broad nationalism inherent in Lord Cooper's *obiter dicta*, stressing as it does the "otherness" of Scotland and the rejection of an alien encroachment from south of the Border, may have had an indirect, unquantifiable influence on subsequent constitutional debate (of which, it is safe to assume, he would not have approved).

MacCormick has, since the mid-1950s, been taught to generations of Scots law students as the pre-eminent Scottish case on constitutional law. Many of the senior figures in the Scottish constitutional reform movement over the past 50 years, such as Winnie Ewing, John Smith, Donald Dewar, Gordon Wilson, David Steel, Menzies Campbell and Jim Wallace, have been Scots lawyers, who would have studied the case at law school. Indeed, Donald Dewar[109] and Jim Wallace[110] made reference to *MacCormick* in parliamentary debate during the passage of the Scotland Act.[111] John Smith[112] (who, when a student, knew MacCormick) supported Lord Cooper's central assertion of Scottish nationhood, but felt that, as a matter of *realpolitik*, Scots had to settle for devolution rather than independence.[113] Did discussion of *MacCormick* in the lectures and tutorials of Scottish law schools in the 1950s, 1960s and 1970s and, more generally, the exposure of students to the Cooper–Smith ideology of Scots law influence constitutional developments decades later? This is indeed a sobering possibility

[109] Then Secretary of State for Scotland and subsequently First Minister of Scotland.
[110] Subsequently Deputy First Minister of Scotland.
[111] HC Deb, vol 305 cols 400, 358–359 and 369, 28 January 1998.
[112] MP and Leader of the UK Labour Party, 1992–94.
[113] Kemp (n 48 above), pp 90 and 93.

for legal academics to ponder. But it is arguable that MacCormick's high-profile challenge to Westminster's authority and articulation of a distinctive Scottish constitutional identity entered the collective consciousness of the Scottish body politic and took root in the constitutional reform movement of the 1980s and 1990s (in which Sir Neil MacCormick was a major figure[114]). Certainly, MacCormick's ideal of popular sovereignty was fundamental to the political authority of the Scottish Constitutional Convention,[115] the cross-party pressure group modelled on his earlier Convention, which led the successful campaign for devolution, culminating in the opening of the Scottish Parliament in 1999. It is also, for obvious reasons, of central political importance for the SNP, which remains committed to Scottish independence and is now the devolved Scottish Government.

Conclusion

In *The Flag in the Wind*, John MacCormick wrote: "Flags as well as straws show the way the wind is blowing. Movements of the spirit, springing from the most deeply rooted sentiments of the people, can never be denied their goal."[116] Although it did not establish readily enforceable legal rights, *MacCormick* was such a flag in Scottish constitutional debate. Just as those who carry the colours into battle often fall, MacCormick was to pay a heavy personal price as the principal standard bearer. But his flag remains aloft nearly 60 years later and still flies in the direction he would have wished.

---

[114] Sir Neil was a distinguished SNP Vice-President and MEP: see also C Harvie, *Scotland and Nationalism* (2nd edn, 1994), p 141.

[115] See ,eg, its 1998 *Claim of Right* (NB Sir Neil MacCormick was a co-author); and its 1995 *Final Report of the Scottish Constitutional Convention*.

[116] *Flag* (n 9 above), p 198.

Chapter 3

A GREAT MISCARRIAGE OF JUSTICE
Oscar Slater

Clare Connelly

Known as one of the "great" miscarriages of justice in Scottish legal history, the 1909 trial of Oscar Slater for the murder of Miss Marion Gilchrist continues to fascinate readers and authors of "real crime" literature. Allegations of police and prosecution involvement in a miscarriage of justice are accompanied by the suggestion that this was motivated to "cover up" the involvement of others of greater social standing in a horrific crime. As is often the case, the passage of time sheds greater light on cases of this sort. Access to official papers provides insight into both what was known by the relevant authorities and the discussions and decisions that were taken in private. There is a substantial body of literature and an even greater archive of official documents relating to the murder of Marion Gilchrist and the prosecution of Oscar Slater, held in the University of Glasgow Forensic Medicine Archives Project,[1] the Mitchell Library in Glasgow and The National Archives of Scotland.[2]

At the time of Miss Gilchrist's murder, Glasgow was a heavily stratified city. The Industrial Revolution had placed Glasgow as the second most important city of the Empire. With its thriving shipbuilding port, Glasgow was a modern and prosperous city, known for

---

[1] University of Glasgow, Forensic Medicine Archives Project, Case Against Oscar Slater:http://www.fmap.archives.gla.ac.uk/case%20Files/Slater/Case_File1.htm.

[2] National Archives of Scotland, 100th anniversary of a notorious Glasgow murder: http://www.nas.gov.uk/about/081214.asp. Scottish Record Office Sources held by the National Archives of Scotland: AD. 21/5, AD. 21/6, HH. 16/109, HH. 16/110, HH. 16/111, HH. 16/112. Selection of newspaper cuttings held by the National Archives of Scotland: HH. 16/111/37/21, 27, 35, 48, 54, 57.

its wealth and importance. The grime, overcrowding and unsanitary living conditions of the poorest sectors of society were in sharp contrast to the magnificent homes occupied by the middle and upper classes. This prosperous city also contained a seedier aspect, involving gambling clubs, music halls and prostitution. Those who embraced the Presbyterian values of the Reformation disliked both the frivolity of the rich and the popular pursuits of many of the less well-off, for example drinking, gambling etc. Like much of Europe and elsewhere in the world at that time, Glasgow was not cosmopolitan, and anti-Semitism was rife. Indeed, Slater had described himself as the "Scottish Dreyfus", referring to the French national, of Jewish descent, who was convicted of being a German spy. In the years prior to the Great War, fear and dislike of Germany and its nationals were growing.

In terms of the legal system, murder was a capital offence resulting in the death penalty in Scotland until reform by the Murder (Abolition of Death Penalty) Act 1965. At the time of the Gilchrist murder, there were three other significant differences from today, namely: legal aid was not available to secure legal representation; the Court of Criminal Appeal had yet to be created; and the prosecution was not compelled by the rules on disclosure which now compel it to share information with the defence, even if that information is useful to the defence but detrimental to the prosecution case.

The personal stories

Marion Gilchrist

Miss Marion Gilchrist was a spinster before her death at the age of 83. She lived the last 27 years of her life at 15 Queens Terrace (which forms part of West Princes Street) in Glasgow. Miss Gilchrist had relations living nearby but is recorded as having limited contact with them because of a family rift after she was left the largest share of her father's estate. She was known, at the time of her death, to be particularly close to a 47-year-old servant, Maggie Galbraith Ferguson, who was a frequent visitor.[3] Some recent commentators have suggested that this woman was Miss Gilchrist's illegitimate daughter.[4]

Police records reveal that members of Miss Gilchrist's family were suspected of involvement in her murder in the early stages of the

---

[3] J House, *Square Mile of Murder* (Richard Drew Publishing Ltd, 1984).

[4] T Toughill, *Oscar Slater: The Immortal Case of Sir Arthur Conan Doyle* (Sutton Publishing, 1993; 2006).

investigation. These suspicions were encouraged by a number of largely anonymous communications from members of the public that stated that a family member was responsible for the murder.[5] Commentators are divided over which members of the family were involved (those suspected include Wingate Birrell, Francis Charteris and Archibald Charteris), and it has been suggested that the police did not pursue this line of enquiry to avoid the scandalous nature of such a revelation. One of the factors of the case that certainly point to Miss Gilchrist having known her killer is her habit of not admitting anyone unknown to her flat. Her fear of being attacked by a man was spoken to by her maid, Helen Lambie, and also her downstairs neighbour, Arthur Adams, who had been asked on occasion to search her flat for assailants who might be in hiding. The fear of an intruder most probably stemmed from the fact that Miss Gilchrist had inherited between £40,000 and £80,000 from her father and, at the time of her death, had jewellery that was valued at £1,382-12s, but the shop value could have been double that. Miss Gilchrist's collection is described as being of 60 or so precious stones collected over 20 years and comprising rubies, emeralds, sapphires and diamonds which were set in bracelets, brooches and earrings. Statements made by Helen Lambie, the maid, suggest that, while Miss Gilchrist had few visitors, she did receive businessmen and, during those visits, Lambie was to make herself scarce. Later commentators on the Slater case have suggested that these businessmen may have been selling stolen gems to Miss Gilchrist.[6] Toughill (2006) suggests that one of these "businessmen" was Hugh Cameron, an acquaintance of Slater's who had a romantic link with Helen Lambie.

Oscar Slater

Oscar Slater was born Oscar Leschziner, in Oppeln, Germany, in 1872. Slater left Germany 20 years later to avoid military service and to see the world. He moved around Europe and America, making his living, gambling and dealing in jewellery. Using a number of different identities, he claimed various professions includ-ing "dealer in diamonds and precious stones", "gymnastics instructor" and "dentist". Slater first visited Glasgow in 1894. When he returned in 1901, he

---

[5] These are held in the Forensic Medicine Archives Project, University of Glasgow: University of Glasgow, Forensic Medicine Archives Project, Case Against Oscar Slater:http://www.fmap.archives.gla.ac.uk/case%20Files/Slater/Case_File1.htm.

[6] Note 4 above.

met and married May Curtis. They separated 4 years later. Slater
claimed that he used aliases because she continued to pursue him
and demand money. Following his separation, Slater returned
to London and met Andrée Juno Antoine, a 20-year-old Parisian
woman. They travelled together and lived in New York, where Slater
managed a gambling club. In 1908, they spent the summer in France,
the autumn in London and then journeyed to Glasgow. During this
time, Antoine worked as a prostitute under the name "Madame
Junio" from the homes she shared with Slater. She had a maid,
Catherine Schmalz, who accompanied them to Glasgow and returned
to London when they departed for New York. Slater was known to
the Glasgow police as "a disreputable foreigner, an associate of
prostitutes, thieves, burglars, and resetters. They also had reason to
believe he was an illegal gambling-den operator".[7] Prior to arriving
in Glasgow, Slater had been charged with malicious wounding and
assault in London and disorderly conduct in Edinburgh.

Helen Lambie

Helen (Nellie) Lambie was Miss Gilchrist's 21-year-old maid. She
came from Holytown in Lanarkshire. She appeared to get on well with
her mistress and was a companion to the elderly lady. Helen Lambie
found her mistress bludgeoned to death on 21 December 1908. She
gave evidence at Slater's extradition hearing and his trial.

Arthur Adams

Arthur Montague Adams, a professional musician, lived with his
mother and five sisters in the main-door flat under Miss Gilchrist's
flat. Adams was known to have assisted Miss Gilchrist by searching
her flat on those occasions when she suspected that a man had hidden
himself with the purpose of robbing her. Miss Gilchrist had arranged
that the Adams family would come to her assistance upon hearing
her signal of three knocks on the floor. It was indeed this signal that
summoned Arthur Adams on 21 December 1908.

Mary Barrowman

Mary Barrowman was a 14-year-old message girl for a shoemaker
located on Great Western Road. Mary lived with her adoptive parents

---

[7] National Archives of Scotland: http://www.nas.gov.uk/about/081214.asp.

on Seamore Street in Glasgow. Mary's identification evidence was crucial in the extradition and trial of Oscar Slater.

The investigating police officers

The head of the Criminal Investigation Department (CID), John Ord, led the investigation with the assistance of Superintendent William Douglas, Detective Inspector John Pyper and Detective Inspector John Thomson Trench. At that time, Chief Superintendent John Orr was John Ord's superior. The Gilchrist investigation proved to have lasting effect on the reputations of all of these men, but particularly in respect of John Thomson Trench.

The prosecution and defence teams

Based on information provided by the police, the decision to charge and prosecute a suspect for the murder of Miss Gilchrist was under the watch of James Neil, the Procurator Fiscal for Lanarkshire. The prosecution was conducted by the Lord Advocate, Alexander Ure KC, assisted by Advocates-Depute T B Morrison KC and Lyon Mackenzie. Slater was represented by A L McClure KC, the Sheriff for Argyll, who was assisted by John Mair, an Edinburgh advocate. Slater's solicitor was Ewing Spiers of Messrs J Shaughnessy & Son of Glasgow.

The murder of Marion Gilchrist

Miss Marion Gilchrist was murdered in her home in West Princes Street, in the West End of Glasgow, on 21 December 1908. Miss Gilchrist's maid, Helen Lambie, had left her mistress at 7 pm to purchase an evening paper from a nearby shop. A few minutes later, Marion Gilchrist's downstairs neighbours, the Adams, heard a thud followed by three bangs on their ceiling. As this was the pre-arranged signal to be given if Miss Gilchrist required help, Arthur Adams was dispatched by his sister to investigate. Adams left his main-door flat, entered Miss Gilchrist's adjacent close door and ran upstairs. At her front door, he rang the bell three times but there was no answer. He heard noises which sounded like sticks being chopped for the fire, which he assumed was being done by the maid. He returned to his own flat, where his sisters, having heard further strange noises, told him to investigate further. When he returned to Miss Gilchrist's front door, he was soon joined by Helen Lambie who was returning from the newspaper shop. The time was approximately 7.10 pm.

When Adams reported having heard strange noises, Helen Lambie suggested it was the kitchen pulley, which was used to dry clothes. She opened the front door and entered the hall. A well-dressed man appeared from the larger bedroom and walked across the hall to the front door. Helen Lambie stared but said nothing and neither she nor Adams made any attempt to challenge the man. Once outside the front door of the flat, the man ran at great speed down the stairs and out into the night. Helen Lambie first entered the kitchen and then the larger bedroom. When Adams asked where her mistress was, Helen Lambie entered the dining room and found Miss Gilchrist's body lying by the hearth, with the upper body covered by a rug. Adams and Lambie then made chase after the man who had been in the flat, but he had disappeared. Helen Lambie left West Princes Street to alert Miss Gilchrist's niece, Margaret Birrell, who lived nearby in Blythswood Drive. Adams sought the assistance of a passing police constable, William Neil. When he examined Miss Gilchrist, he found her still to be breathing. Arthur Adams then summoned a neighbour, Dr Adams (no relation), who confirmed on his examination that Miss Gilchrist had died.

The police investigation

Initial police investigations revealed no evidence of entry having been forced to Miss Gilchrist's flat. In the larger bedroom, from where the man had emerged when Lambie and Adams entered the flat, detectives found three wooden boxes on the floor – all had been forced open. Two of these boxes held personal effects (gloves and hairbrushes) and the third contained papers which were now scattered over the floor. The gas lamp in this room had been lit by the intruder who had left his box of "Runaway" matches behind. On the same table, below the lamp, a soap dish containing a number of items of jewellery was untouched. It was never established whether any papers had been taken from the wooden box, but the fact that only one item was known to have been taken from the flat, namely a crescent-shaped diamond brooch, has given rise to suspicion, at least retrospectively, that the motive in this crime was to obtain certain of Miss Gilchrist's papers. The fact that Miss Gilchrist's substantial and valuable jewellery collection was left untouched has been cited as evidence of this supposed motive.[8] No

---

[8] J Hamilton, *Scottish Murders* (2009); Toughill (n 4 above); R Whittington-Egan, *The Oscar Slater Murder Story. New Light on a Classic Miscarriage of Justice* (Neil Wilson Publishing, 2001); H Hodge, *Famous Trials* (1941).

murder weapon was found in the flat. A search of the back green the following morning, by an Inspector Rankin, discovered a large iron auger or screw-bit which had brown and grey human hairs stuck on the underside and staining which could have been rust or blood. This was submitted to the Western Police Office, where the hair was found to match that of Miss Gilchrist in length, colour and diameter.

Miss Gilchrist's body was examined in the dining room by detectives and a number of doctors. As noted above, Dr Adams was first to examine the deceased and declared that the dining chair found adjacent to the body had been used to inflict the multiple fractures found on Miss Gilchrist's head and that the assailant had stamped on the body while wielding the chair, thereby fracturing her ribs. Dr Hugh Galt and Professor John Glaister carried out the post-mortem examination at Glasgow Royal Infirmary on Wednesday, 23 December 1908. They concluded that the cause of death was extensive wounds and fractures of the bones of the face and skull, fractures of the breast-bone and ribs, together with shock and bleeding. Their opinion was that these injuries were inflicted using a blunt instrument and that the violence was applied with considerable force.

The main focus of the police investigation was on the various witnesses who claimed to have seen the assailant leave Miss Gilchrist's flat and also another man who had been seen watching the premises in the days prior to the murder. The first description of the suspect, issued by the police, was an amalgamation of the descriptions given by Adams and Lambie. Adams was short-sighted and not wearing his glasses, but he believed he had a better opportunity from the front door of seeing the man leaving Miss Gilchrist's flat than Lambie, who was already inside the flat. Lambie claimed not to have seen the man's face, but was able to describe his overcoat as light or fawn and three-quarter length, and that he wore a cloth cap. This description of the assailant's clothing closely resembled Adams' who said the man wore an overcoat which was either light grey or fawn, dark trousers and a felt cap. Adams added that the man was clean shaven and very dark. He was like a type of a clerk or a commercial traveller and between 25 and 30 years old. He subsequently stated that the man was sharp featured and, at a later date, that there was nothing special about him or about his nose. On the basis of this information, Inspector Pyper issued a report on the murder wherein he described the suspect as "a man between 25 and 30 years of age, 5 feet 8 or 9 inches, slim build, dark hair, clean shaven and dressed in light-grey overcoat and dark cloth cap". Thereafter other witnesses came forward. On 23 December, Rowena Adams, the sister of Arthur Adams, described to the police the man she had seen waiting outside Miss Gilchrist's flat, just before the murder, as slightly built, with a pale complexion and a peculiar dip in his long nose. He was dressed in a heavy brown- or fawn-coloured coat and a brownish tweed cap. On the same day, 14-year-old Mary Barrowman gave a statement describing the man she had seen around 7 pm on 21 December running out of Miss Gilchrist's close. He was 28–30 years of age, tall and slim, clean shaven, had long features with his nose slightly turned to the right, and was dressed in a fawn overcoat and dark trousers, brown boots and a tweed cloth cap.

On 25 December 1908, the following descriptions were issued by the Glasgow police, to police officers only, of the two men sought in connection with the Gilchrist murder. The first, a man from 25 to 30 years of age, 5 feet 7 or 8 inches tall, thought to be clean shaven, wore a long grey overcoat and dark cap. This man was seen leaving the flat. The second man, who had been seen descending the steps leading to the flat and running away, was 28–35 years of age, tall, thin, clean shaven, had his nose slightly turned to the right side, and wore a fawn-coloured overcoat, dark trousers, a dark tweed cloth hat and brown boots. On the same day, the second description, given by Mary Barrowman, was published in three Glasgow newspapers. Press speculation accompanied these descriptions, with reference being made to the assailant having been known to Miss Gilchrist, and promises of a sensational arrest, which has been interpreted by subsequent commentators to support a theory that Miss Gilchrist had been murdered by a relative. Indeed, both anonymous and sourced correspondence at this time, addressed to the police, also suggested that a relative was responsible for Miss Gilchrist's death, albeit that no-one appears to ever have been named in this correspondence.

A suspect

A major breakthrough for the police followed the printing of Mary Barrowman's description in the late editions on 25 December 1908. Having read the description, Allan McLean, a bicycle dealer and member of the Sloper Club, visited the Central police station and made a statement which described Oscar Slater as a German Jew of about 30 years of age, 5 feet 8 inches, clean shaven, with a lightly twisted nose. He claimed that he had not seen Slater at the Sloper Club since the night of the Gilchrist murder when Slater had been offering a pawn ticket for a valuable diamond brooch for sale. It was alleged that the brooch had been pledged for £50 on the day of the murder. McLean accompanied Detective Inspector Powell to Slater's flat at 69 St George's Road and later, around midnight, Powell returned to the flat, and was told by the maid that her mistress was out and that no man lived in the flat. Police officers who visited the Sloper Club were told that Slater had been introduced to the club by a man called Hugh Cameron. Cameron was located at his address around 2 am and confirmed that Slater had given him a pawn ticket on 22 or 23 December for a brooch that was in Liddell's pawn shop. Cameron had been unable to sell the pawn ticket and had so returned it to Slater on 24 December when he had accompanied him to the Cunard Line shipping offices in Jamaica Street to book a passage to New York. He also told the police that Slater had informed him a fortnight previously that he was going to San Francisco on the invitation of a friend.

Enquiries later that morning established that the pawned brooch had never belonged to Miss Gilchrist. It was a different brooch that had been pawned by Slater some time before Miss Gilchrist's murder. This fact did not change the focus of the police investigation. The police returned to Slater's flat where the former maid, Miss Schmalz, confirmed that Slater and his companion Antoine had left the previous evening. The police issued a detailed description of Slater and his companion. Schmalz herself arrived in London on 27 December and, when she was interviewed by the London police, she told them that Slater and Antoine had travelled to America via Liverpool. At 6.17 pm that evening, Chief Inspector Ord, who was heading the inquiry into the Gilchrist murder, received a telegram from Liverpool informing him that a man matching Slater's description and his companion had left Liverpool on 26 December bound for New York on the *Lusitania*, travelling under the names of Mr and Mrs Sando. The man had told shipping officials that he was an American citizen who had travelled from Glasgow and had stayed at the North-Western Hotel in Liverpool. On further enquiry, it was established that Slater and Antoine had indeed stayed at that hotel, registering under the name of "Oscar Slater, Glasgow". They had discussed their proposed trip to New York with the hotel chambermaid.

Arrest and extradition

The Glasgow police sent a telegram to New York, requesting that Slater be arrested on arrival and that he and his companion be searched for

pawn tickets. On their arrival in New York harbour, both Slater and
Antoine were searched and a pawn ticket was found in their possession
(for the brooch Slater pawned some time before the murder). Slater
was remanded in Tombs Prison, pending extradition proceedings, and
Antoine was sent to Ellis Island.

The extradition hearing took place on 26 January 1909. Arthur
Adams, Helen Lambie and Mary Barrowman had been accompanied
to New York to provide crucial identification evidence in the extradition
proceedings. A number of irregularities are recorded by subsequent
commentators on this case. Lambie and Barrowman had shared
accommodation on the journey to New York, which is suggested as
having facilitated collusion, despite the women denying this. On the
morning of the extradition hearing, Adams, Lambie and Barrowman
were accompanied by Inspector Pyper to the office of Mr Fox who was
acting as Crown Agent for the extradition proceedings. He showed
the witnesses photographs of Slater that had appeared in newspapers.
These individuals were also waiting outside the relevant courtroom
that was to hear the extradition application when Slater walked past
them, handcuffed to one of the two officials who were accompanying
him. The evidence of Adams and Barrowman was that Slater resembled
the man they had seen. Lambie told the court that she had not seen
the man's face but could identify him by his unusual gait. Despite this,
she was willing to positively identify Slater as the man she had seen
inside Miss Gilchrist's flat.

Lambie's and Barrowman's descriptions of Slater were now more
similar, with both citing that he was wearing a fawn-coloured coat
and a Donegal cap. In support of the oral testimony, Fox, who was
acting as Crown Agent, submitted two depositions. One of these
was from Gordon Henderson, who claimed that on the night of the
murder Slater had come to see him at 9.45 pm and asked him to cash a
cheque. Slater was wearing a fawn-coloured coat and a Donegal cap.
The deposition also stated that a German person had told him that
Slater had murdered a woman. A second deposition was submitted
from Agnes Brown, who stated that she saw two men running from
Miss Gilchrist's address at the time of the murder. Slater called one
witness, David Jacobs, a diamond dealer, who produced a letter sent
to him by Slater in late November intimating Slater's intention to
return to America in the near future. The extradition hearing was
adjourned on 28 January until 6 February. In the interim period, against
the advice of his lawyer, Slater volunteered to go back to Scotland.

He communicated his decision to his friend Hugh Cameron, who promptly gave the letter to the police. When the extradition hearing reconvened, Slater's decision was intimated to the court. He left New York to return to Glasgow on 14 February.

On his arrival in Glasgow, Slater's luggage was searched. Of note, the police found a soft hat and two caps, but not a Donegal hat and a fawn-coloured waterproof coat. Pyper found a small hammer later shown to have been purchased as part of a set from Woolworths. Slater's hat, coat and hammer were submitted for forensic investigation to the University of Edinburgh, but nothing of forensic interest was found on any of these objects.

An identification parade followed where Slater was placed among 11 Scottish men, nine of whom were police officers (undoubtedly of a height greater than 5 feet 8 inches) and two railway officials. Of course, by this time images and photographs of Slater had appeared many times in Scottish newspapers. Slater, having not yet engaged a legal representative, may not have been aware of the impact of these matters on the legitimacy of the identification parade and the evidence that was subsequently led at his trial.

The results of the identity parade were that Arthur Adams confirmed that Slater was the man he had seen in New York. Helen Lambie and Mary Barrowman both identified Slater as the man they had encountered on the night of Miss Gilchrist's murder. After the identification parade, Duncan MacBrayne visited the Central Police Office and identified Slater as the man he had seen on St George's Road, standing at Slater's close door about one hour after the murder. Slater was the only person in the room at the police office when MacBrayne identified him. Agnes Brown, a school teacher, was also invited to identify Slater in the Central Police Office. She had given a statement to the police on 31 December 1908 that, on the evening of Miss Gilchrist's murder, she had seen two men running along West Princes Street. They had come from the direction of Miss Gilchrist's flat. In this statement, Agnes Brown said that she had not seen either of the men's faces, but she was able to describe their clothing (she had watched them run along West Princes Street and then turn off towards Great Western road). On Sunday, 21 February, Agnes Brown identified Slater as one of the two men who had run past her. She picked him out of an identity parade. In her statement of 21 February, she stated that she recognised Slater by his profile, but that she did not get a front view of his face. She further stated that his companion wore a cap like the one shown to her. She stated Slater had been bareheaded and was wearing a grey Melton overcoat with velvet collar. In her earlier statement, she had stated that the bare-headed man wore a navy coat with velvet collar and his companion wore a grey overcoat and a dark tweed cap.

On 22 February, Oscar Slater was indicted for the murder of Miss Marion Gilchrist, in which the charge was that "on 21 December 1908, in Marion Gilchrist's House at 15 Queen's Terrace, West Princes Street, Glasgow, you did assault the said Marion Gilchrist, and did beat with a hammer or other blunt instrument, and fracture her skull and you did murder her".

He was remanded in custody and appeared on petition before a sheriff 2 days later when he made a declaration as to his innocence. Following a pleading diet on 20 April, a trial diet was set for Monday, 3 May 1909.

The trial

Slater's trial lasted 4 days. In the absence of forensic evidence linking Slater to the scene of the crime or the murder weapon, the vital issue at the trial was one of identification. Slater was identified as the man who had left Miss Gilchrist's house with varying degrees of certainty by Helen Lambie, Arthur Adams, Mary Barrowman and an official at the subway station. He was also identified by neighbours as the man who had systematically watched the house for some time before the murder. Evidence was led from experts to establish whether the small hammer found in Slater's suitcase could have been the murder weapon. A considerable part of the prosecution case was concerned with Slater's alleged "flight from justice" to New York.

Denigration of Slater's character began by the prosecution calling three members of the Motor and Sloper gambling clubs, Barr, Henderson and McLean, who testified that they had not seen Slater after 21 December. Barr referred to Slater having a poor reputation. Henderson claimed that around 9.45 pm on the night of the murder, Slater had entered the Motor Club and asked him to cash a cheque. He testified that he declined the request and that Slater had appeared anxious to get the money. This evidence had also been referred to in the extradition proceedings. McLean stated that, on 21 December, he learned that a friend of his named Anderson had been offered the opportunity to purchase a pawn ticket for a diamond brooch. When he read the description of Miss Gilchrist's killer on 25 December and about the stolen brooch, he reported to the police that he thought Slater matched the description.

The trial heard conclusive evidence that the pawn ticket Slater was offering for sale did not relate to Miss Gilchrist's brooch. The pawnbroker with whom Slater had pawned a diamond brooch on 18 November, McLaren, gave evidence to that effect at the trial, and also that Slater had released an additional £30 on the pledged brooch at 12.30 pm on 21 December.

The prosecution witnesses were subjected to cross-examination by Slater's counsel, McClure, but transcripts of evidence suggest that vigorous cross-examination was sometimes absent. Slater was advised by his counsel not to give evidence. As the onus of proof rests with the prosecution in any criminal trial, the accused is not obliged to give evidence. The presumption of innocence means that the prosecution must prove guilt; the accused does not need to prove his innocence. Where a defence is being pled, for example, self-defence, provocation or, as in Slater's case, alibi, it is more common for an accused to give evidence. In Slater's case, his alibi was spoken to by two witnesses: his partner Antoine and Schmalz, their maid. Both women gave evidence that, on the evening of the murder, Slater ate dinner with both of them at 7 pm, as was his usual habit. Schmalz also confirmed that she had been given notice on 21 December.

Dr Robertson, who appeared for the defence, gave evidence predominantly about the auger that had been found in the back green on the morning after the murder. He stated that he thought the auger was a more likely instrument than Slater's hammer to have caused Miss Gilchrist's injuries, but said that he would have expected them to have been inflicted by a heavier object. Slater's friends and acquaintances gave evidence that he carried on in his usual manner after 21 December. Between 22 December and his departure on 25 December, Slater had spent a substantial amount of time with Hugh Cameron, including attempting to book a berth for his voyage to New York.

During his cross-examination of Cameron, the Lord Advocate asked him what Slater was. Cameron answered "a gambler" but when further pressed stated "I had it that the man, like a great number of those who came to Glasgow, lived on the proceeds of women". This statement was damning of Slater's character and also cast his two key alibi witnesses, Antoine and Schmalz, in a poor light by suggesting that they were prostitutes. The answer was not objected to by Slater's counsel, as it should have been, on the grounds that it was hearsay evidence and therefore inadmissible, it was irrelevant to the charge and it breached the rules on character evidence.

In his summing up, the Lord Advocate referred to Cameron's answer, stating that "the man who lives upon the proceeds of prostitution has sunk to the lowest depths, and all moral sense in him has been destroyed and has ceased to exist". In the defence summing-up, McClure warned against the dangers of convicting on the identification evidence that had been heard. He also stated that the issue of Slater's character should not have been admitted as evidence. The judge clearly disagreed and, when directing the jury, stated that it had been proved that Slater "maintained himself by the ruin of men and on the ruin of women, and he has lived in a way that many blackguards would scorn to live ... a man of that kind has not the presumption of innocence in his favour".

On 6 May 1909, the jury, by a narrow majority,[9] convicted Slater of murder. Slater protested his innocence without comment from the judge. Lord Guthrie donned his black cap and sentenced Slater to death by hanging in Duke Street Prison, Glasgow, on the morning of 27 May 1909.

Commentators on the case have suggested that sinister inferences can be drawn from the prosecution's failure to lead all of the evidence that was uncovered in the course of the investigation. In an adversarial system, however, it is the norm for the prosecution to construct and present a case that supports the charges that have been brought against the accused. The current duties of disclosure did not exist at the time of Slater's trial.

The reprieve

A petition seeking commutation of Slater's death sentence on the ground that his conviction was unsafe, signed by more than 20,000 people, was sent to the Secretary of State for Scotland, Lord Pentland, by Ewing Speirs, Slater's solicitor. Two anonymous letters, dated 18 and 24 May, were also sent to the Secretary of State. These letters[10] both proclaimed Slater's innocence and both implicated Hugh

---

[9] Nine jurors found him guilty, five not proven and one not guilty.
[10] Scottish Home and Health Department File HH.16/109, held in the National Archives of Scotland.

Cameron and William Birrell in the murder of Miss Gilchrist. Official records[11] show that Lord Pentland was not happy with Slater's sentence, and his communication with the trial judge, Lord Guthrie, resulted in the latter stating that he thought Slater should not be executed, but instead his sentence should be reduced to one of penal servitude. Lords Pentland and Guthrie and the Lord Chancellor shared the view that, if there was to be a reprieve, Slater should not be released after the usual period of 20 years. The opposing view, expressed by the Registrar General for Scotland, was that there was strong public support that Slater should hang. Nevertheless, Lord Pentland sought a commutation from King Edward VII on the basis that both the Lord Chancellor and Lord Guthrie, the trial judge, supported that course of action; Slater was convicted by a narrow majority of 9 to 6; the prejudice caused by the public discussion of the case and the consideration that the character of the man and his past moral conduct might have prejudiced the outcome. King Edward VII issued a pardon to Slater in respect of the murder conviction and the sentence of death passed by Lord Guthrie, upon condition of his being kept in penal servitude for the term of his natural life. Thirty-six hours before his execution, Slater and other relevant parties were informed of his reprieve. Slater was transferred from Duke Street Prison to Peterhead Prison to serve his sentence of penal servitude.

The secret inquiry

Following the reprieve, a prominent public figure, Sir Arthur Conan Doyle, reviewed Slater's conviction and in 1912 published *The Case of Oscar Slater* which outlined why he thought Slater was innocent. This followed the 1910 publication of *The Trial of Oscar Slater* by William Roughead, which contained a transcript of the trial and triggered public expressions of unease with the safety of Slater's conviction. Sir Arthur Conan Doyle led a campaign to have the Slater case re-opened. On 10 December 1909, McKinnon Wood, the Secretary of State for Scotland, stated in the House of Commons that there were no new considerations that would justify re-opening the case.

Detective Lieutenant John Thomson Trench, who had been involved in the initial investigation into the Gilchrist murder, revealed startling details about the police inquiry in 1914. Aided by David Cook, a Glasgow lawyer, and William Park, a journalist, this information

---

[11] Scottish Home and Health Department File HH.16/109.

was first shared with one of his Majesty's Prison Commissioners for Scotland, Dr Devon. He then contacted McKinnon Wood, the Secretary of State, and informed him of Trench's position. This included that, on the night of the murder, Helen Lambie had identified the man seen in her mistress's house and had named him to Margaret Dawson Birrell, Miss Gilchrist's niece whom Lambie visited immediately after discovering her mistress. Trench claimed that the man named was Dr Charteris, Miss Gilchrist's nephew.

McKinnon Wood ordered a "secret inquiry", originally to be led by the Procurator Fiscal, James Hart, who had been centrally involved in the Gilchrist murder inquiry. When Cook protested over this appointment, the Secretary of State eventually appointed an alternative commissioner to lead the inquiry, James Gardner Millar, the Sheriff of Lanarkshire. However, the limits of the inquiry, namely that it should be conducted in private, limited to questions of fact and in no way reflect on the conduct of the trial, were regarded by Cook, Conan Doyle and others to be too narrow. At the inquiry, police officers involved in the investigation gave evidence. Trench submitted a statement stating that, on 23 December, he had been instructed by Chief Superintendent Orr to visit Margaret Birrell and take a statement. Trench submitted the statement he said was given by Margaret Birrell to the inquiry. It stated that Helen Lambie told Miss Birrell that the man who had killed her mistress was Dr Charteris. When she was called as a witness to the inquiry, Margaret Birrell denied having ever made this statement and she denied that Helen Lambie had revealed the identity of the killer to her on 21 December. Helen Lambie denied having known the man she saw leaving her mistress's house. Each of the police officers who gave evidence to the inquiry denied knowledge of the information provided by Trench. Only one officer, Alexander Cameron, recalled Trench telling him of Miss Birrell's statement, but said that he regarded it as hearsay. Cameron also stated that Trench had informed Superintendent Ord, but that the latter had dismissed the information, saying that the matter had been cleared up and there was nothing in it. On 17 June 1914, the Secretary of State, replying to a question in the House of Commons, stated that the inquiry had produced no findings that would justify him in interfering with Slater's sentence. The publication of the findings of the inquiry never named Dr Charteris; instead, the man allegedly identified by Helen Lambie was referred to as "AB".[12]

[12] This was clearly to avoid an action for libel.

Trench paid dearly for his actions that led to the secret inquiry. He was suspended from duty on 14 July 1914 and was subsequently convicted, on 14 September 1914, for having communicated information acquired in the course of his duty with persons outside the police force without the express permission of the Chief Constable. He was dismissed from the police force. Cook, Slater's solicitor and Trench himself appealed to the Secretary of State. Trench referred to having perceived the invitation from the Secretary of State to send his information as ample protection against any breach of discipline. The Secretary of State never replied. The consequences for Trench did not end there. He and Cook were subsequently arrested on 13 May 1915 and charged with the reset of goods that had been stolen in January 1914. On 17 August 1915, the Lord Justice-Clerk, Charles Scott Dickson, directed the jury that there was no evidence upon which they could convict the accused. This effectively silenced both Trench and Cook who never again spoke publicly about the Slater case. Trench died in May 1919 at the age of 50, of natural causes, having served in the Great War until October 1918.

Liberation of Slater

In February 1925, Slater persuaded a fellow inmate, Gordon, who was due for release, to smuggle out a plea for assistance to Sir Arthur Conan Doyle. The note was smuggled out under Gordon's dentures. Conan Doyle's representations to the then Secretary of State were denied. Another book challenging Slater's conviction was published by William Park in July 1927 and attracted a high level of public interest. This was closely followed by the publication, on 27 October 1927, of Helen Lambie's admission that she had known and named the man whom she had seen leaving her mistress's house on the night of the murder. This man was not named in the article, no doubt to avoid an action for libel being brought against the newspaper. Lambie stated in the article that the police had scoffed at the notion that the man she had named had robbed and murdered Miss Gilchrist and that she was thereby persuaded that she was mistaken. While the man and Slater had similar profiles, she said the man was of a better station in life. Following the *Empire News* publishing this story, *The Daily News* published an equally alarming statement by Mary Barrowman, on 5 November, wherein she stated that the Procurator Fiscal, Mr Hart, rehearsed her evidence with her on at least 15 occasions and persuaded her to change her statement that Slater was "very like the

man" to an emphatic declaration that he was the man she had seen
on the night of the murder. Around the same time, Sir Arthur Conan
Doyle had been in correspondence with the former Prime Minister,
Ramsay MacDonald, who was by then the Leader of the Opposition.
Ramsay MacDonald was in turn in correspondence with the then
Scottish Secretary, Sir John Gilmour. On 7 November, Slater's release
on licence after 18½ years was announced by Gilmour. Slater was
released from Peterhead Prison on 14 November 1927.

An appeal

On 13 November, Sir Arthur Conan Doyle sent a letter to the Prime
Minister and a circular letter to every MP containing the facts of the
Slater case and stating the need for an inquiry. On 15 November, the
Scottish Secretary announced that an amendment to the Criminal
Appeals (Scotland) Act 1926 would be made to allow Slater to appeal.
The amendment was necessary, as the legislation that had created the
Court of Criminal Appeal only provided for the appeal of convictions
or sentence recorded after 31 October 1926.

Slater's appeal was funded in part by donations made by the public.
The additional costs of securing legal representation were guaranteed
by Sir Arthur Conan Doyle. The grounds of appeal focused on the
failure of the Crown to disclose evidence to Slater and to the jury that
was favourable to Slater;[13] that the conduct of the prosecution was to
the material prejudice of Slater as his character was attacked by the
Lord Advocate; and that the judge had misdirected the jury that the
presumption of innocence applied with less effect to Slater than to a
man of good character. The court held[14] that the judge had misdirected
the jury in law as to the presumption of innocence and confirmed
that the presumption of innocence applied equally in all cases and
could only be displaced by evidence to prove the crime charged. The
court further held that, looking to the possibility that the jury were
influenced against Slater by taking his bad character into account, a
substantial miscarriage of justice had occurred and the conviction was
quashed.

The aftermath

Despite the conviction being quashed, Slater was frustrated that he
had not been declared innocent, which was beyond the competency of

---

[13] The current rules regarding disclosure were not in force at this time.
[14] *Slater v HM Advocate* 1928 JC 94; 1928 SLT 602.

the appeal court. Slater was offered and accepted £6,000 compensation from the Government. Sir Arthur Conan Doyle had suggested that more could be secured, but Slater ignored this advice. Slater, however, was reluctant to settle his debt incurred with Conan Doyle in respect of the costs of his legal representation. Relations soured between the parties. Finally, after a civil action was raised by Conan Doyle against Slater, a settlement was reached between the parties.

Slater lived the remainder of his life in Ayr. He married Lina Wilhelmina Schad in 1936. During the Second World War, the Slaters were interned as aliens. Slater died on 31 January 1948, aged 76.

In 1999, the Chief Constable of Strathclyde Police unveiled a plaque in the police museum in the presence of Mrs Nancy Stark, the last surviving child of John Thomson Trench. The plaque states that Trench acted "in the interests of truth and justice".

Conclusion

Despite Slater's conviction being quashed, no further police investigation took place to identify who was responsible for Miss Gilchrist's death. Those who have studied Slater's case and related papers agree that the wrong man was prosecuted for the murder of Marion Gilchrist, but there is some disagreement over who was responsible. What is certain is that this case casts a dark shadow over the integrity of those who investigated, prosecuted, judged and gave evidence in Slater's trial. The case highlights that those who are agents of the criminal justice process must discharge their responsibilities honestly and ethically. The case also highlights the importance of access to a skilled advocate to represent the interests of those charged with criminal offences. Such access to justice should not depend on the availability of private financial means.

Chapter 4

BRINGING UP CATHERINE
McFarlane v *Tayside Health Board* [1]

Kenneth McK Norrie

The sexual revolution that took place in the 1960s changed everything. Hormonal contraception was introduced in the United Kingdom in 1961 (though originally it was available on the National Health Service only to married women); abortion was made legal in 1967,[2] and sterilisation techniques became both socially acceptable and practically simpler. The development of these, and other, methods of birth control gave people the power to indulge in sexual activity without the threat of pregnancy, a freedom previously enjoyed only by gay and lesbian people. Women were the great beneficiaries, of course, and birth control gave them a power over their own bodies, and their own lives, that they had never had before as it freed them from the tyranny of excessive fertility. Pregnancy has now been effectively divorced from sexual behaviour and is, by and large, a matter of choice rather than the price women have to pay for being sexually active. The law now regards as a legitimate exercise of autonomy a person's choice to be sexually active without the risk of becoming pregnant. Birth control is today seen not only as a legitimate but also as a socially responsible choice. For those in stable long-term relationships who already have children, a commonly chosen method of birth control is sterilisation. A simple laparoscopic operation involving the occlusion of the fallopian tubes will prevent a woman's eggs moving down these tubes for fertilisation; even simpler is vasectomy, the cutting of the *vas deferens*, which prevents sperm from entering a man's seminal fluid.

---

[1] 1997 SLT 211 (Outer House); 1998 SLT 307 (Inner House); 2000 SLT 154, 2000 SC (HL) 1, [2000] 2 AC 59 (House of Lords).
[2] Abortion Act 1967.

However simple these operations are, they always depend for their success upon the skills and abilities of the medical team that provide them. Any health care provider who is careless, or negligent, runs the risk of causing physical and other injuries to the patient. A sterilisation operation is no different but it does have this unique feature: a consequence of the doctor's failure to exercise reasonable skill in performing such an operation is that the patient may remain fertile. And, because the patient is likely to be unaware of this, (hetero) sexual activity without other contraceptive precautions might lead to pregnancy – the very thing that the sterilisation operation was designed to prevent. Now, pregnancy and childbirth are of course entirely natural things, and usually the cause for celebration. For some sections of society they are for politico–religious reasons always to be regarded as a good thing. For others they are in practice a disaster, for a host of different reasons. If that disaster is a direct and natural result of the doctor's negligence in carrying out the sterilisation operation, the parents who suffer that disaster might be tempted to sue the doctor for reparation. But can the natural processes of pregnancy and childbirth ever be something that the law would regard as being loss, injury or damage for which reparation can be sought and, if so, to what extent?

These questions can only be properly understood within the economic context in which they are asked. Medical treatment, including sterilisation, is for the most part provided in the UK under the auspices of the NHS. One of the great challenges that that Service has faced since its inception is the appropriate allocation of limited resources across all areas of need. As the population has become healthier so, paradoxically, have our calls upon the NHS become greater. We want to be kept healthier, through screening programmes and the like, and we want to live longer. The fulfilment of these desires increases, rather than reduces, our reliance on NHS resources, and the older we get, the more demanding we become. New and expensive treatments are developed, and wonderful new machines are invented. In short, health care costs increase unceasingly. Adding to the huge costs of treatment and prevention of illness are the facts that we expect more of our health care providers, and we are less willing to thole their mistakes, and we sue them when things go wrong. As we should, for the most part. The underlying reality exposed by the case being discussed here is that every penny of compensation paid to a patient injured in the course of medical treatment is a penny less available for the NHS's primary purpose – the provision of health care to those who need it. This in itself is a factor that has to be taken into account in determining which injuries must be left to lie where they fall, and which injuries justify reparation on normal principles of delictual liability. These socio–economic considerations are at the heart of this case and, indeed, are more crucial for understanding its outcome even than strict legal doctrine.

The facts

Mr George McFarlane and his wife, Mrs Laura Helen McFarlane, lived a happy and fulfilled family life in the east of Scotland. They had been married for some years and been blessed with four lovely children. In 1989 they moved to a larger house, taking on a larger mortgage, and to help pay for this Mrs McFarlane returned to work. They considered their family complete and, in order to ensure that it grew no larger, they decided that Mr McFarlane should undergo a vasectomy. This was carried out on 16 October 1989 under the auspices of the NHS by a surgeon, Mr Irving, who was employed by Tayside Health Board. The operation itself was carried out with due care and attention and Mr Irving showed an appropriate level of professional competence, as NHS employees nearly always do.

Now, operations of this nature, even when competently performed, are never guaranteed to be successful, due to the human body's remarkable propensity to repair itself. A vasectomy can be reversed, through no fault of anyone, by the body itself reuniting the parts of the tubes that have been cut. This does not happen often, but its occurrence is well-enough known for hospitals always to advise patients to continue after the operation with contraceptive precautions until at least two samples of the patient's semen have been tested and proved negative for living sperm. Mr McFarlane provided samples for testing in January and February 1990, and in March of that year he received a letter from Mr Irving stating that both samples had proved negative, that he was consequently infertile, and that he and his wife might now cease using contraceptive precautions. Mr and Mrs McFarlane, pleased that the operation had achieved its aim, were happy to follow this advice.

However, unbeknown to the McFarlanes, there had been some mix-up (never fully explained) at the laboratory that tested the sperm. Either Mr McFarlane's records had been confused with those of another patient, or a semen sample given to the laboratory in March 1990 had been wrongly attributed to him. However it came about, a mistake had been made. Mr McFarlane had not been rendered infertile by the operation. He discovered this some 18 months later, when Mrs McFarlane fell pregnant. On 6 May 1992, after a normal pregnancy with no complications, Mrs McFarlane was delivered of a beautiful baby girl, healthy and happy. The McFarlanes named her Catherine, and they loved her dearly.

Notwithstanding that Catherine was welcomed as an unplanned (as most of us, in truth, are) but delightful addition to the family, the fact remained that her birth was caused by a mistake for which Tayside Health Board was responsible and which might amount to legal negligence, and this was a mistake that cost the McFarlanes dear. Mrs McFarlane had suffered the physical discomfort of pregnancy and the pain of childbirth. She had had to give up her job and the family struggled financially. The McFarlanes were put to expenses inevitably accompanying the birth of any child – baby clothes, cots, push-chairs and the like – and in addition there was the significant matter of the ongoing long-term costs of bringing up Catherine, which were no less economically burdensome for their being so willingly borne.

In an attempt to recover their losses, which were caused directly and foreseeably by the alleged negligence, the McFarlanes sued Tayside Health Board. Two separate claims were made. The first, by Mrs McFarlane alone, was for £10,000 in compensation for the pain and suffering she had endured during pregnancy and childbirth and for the consequential costs associated with these physical injuries, such as lost earnings and baby clothes. The second claim was made jointly by both Mr and Mrs McFarlane and was much larger: they sought £100,000 in compensation for their future expenditure in bringing up Catherine. At first instance, in the Outer House of the Court of Session, the claim was dismissed as irrelevant. On appeal by the McFarlanes to the Inner House, the Second Division overruled the Lord Ordinary and allowed a proof before answer on both claims. On appeal by the Health Board to the House of Lords, the Inner House was in its turn overruled, but the Lord Ordinary's interlocutor was not restored. Instead the House of Lords confirmed the relevancy of Mrs McFarlane's individual claim for pain and suffering, but rejected the joint claim for the costs of bringing Catherine up. The decision changed the existing law, and left many questions unanswered.

The existing law

McFarlane v *Tayside Health Board* was by no means the first case in which damages had been claimed by people who had become parents after having previously undergone a sterilisation operation. Indeed, to begin with, the case seemed destined to be no more than a Scottish example of a type of claim that had created a fairly consistent line of authority in the English courts where the settled law seemed to be that damages for both the pain and suffering (the pregnancy and childbirth) and the economic losses (including the costs of upbringing) were recoverable.

The earliest reported English decision was *Scuriaga* v *Powell*,[3] which was a claim for breach of contract to terminate a pregnancy by abortion. The abortion had been carried out negligently and it did not achieve its purpose. The court awarded damages for pain and suffering, for actual and prospective loss of earnings and for diminution of marital prospects, but not for the maintenance of the child which, it would appear, was not claimed. A rather more significant case, and not just because it was raised in tort rather than contract, was that of *Udale* v *Bloomsbury Health Authority*[4] where Jupp J dismissed the claim on the ground that it was contrary to public policy to award damages for the costs arising from the coming into being of a normal healthy child. This decision, however, was expressly disapproved by the Court of Appeal in *Emeh* v *Kensington and Chelsea and Westminster Area Health Authority*,[5] and in *Thake* v *Maurice*[6] Jupp J's policy reasons for rejecting the claim in *Udale* were carefully dismantled by Peter Pain J and public policy has not been decisive since. In *Emeh* the sterilisation operation upon the mother had been carried out negligently and, very sadly, the child was born with severe congenital abnormalities. (This was one more tragedy to add to this mother's life that had been full of misfortune – read the case and grieve for the woman.) Park J at first instance had held that damages should be denied for all injuries arising after the mother discovered she was pregnant because, on being offered an abortion at that point, she had declined to consider that option – effectively, the judge held that she was author of her own misfortune in deciding to carry on with the pregnancy. This approach, however, was emphatically rejected by the Court of Appeal and, again, the argument has never since been explicitly raised though it is often rejected by the judges. Importantly, *Emeh* was the first case in which the Court of Appeal allowed damages for both the mother's pain

[3] (1979) 123 SJ 406.
[4] [1983] 1 WLR 1098.
[5] [1985] QB 1012.
[6] [1984] 2 All ER 513 (QBD).

and suffering and for the cost of maintaining the child in the future. Puchas LJ, however, cited with approval an American decision[7] to the effect that the costs of rearing an unplanned child might be subject to offsetting the value of the child's aid, comfort and society during the parents' life expectancy.

Thake v *Maurice*[8] then reached the Court of Appeal. The claim in this case was very similar to that made by Mr and Mrs McFarlane, for here too a vasectomy had been carried out properly but it had subsequently failed due to the patient's own body restoring his fertility by natural regeneration. But the doctor had failed to warn the Thakes of this possibility and that failure was held to be an act of negligence which led directly and foreseeably to the pregnancy and childbirth. The damages awarded included the costs of bringing up the child (subject to the deduction of statutory benefits). But Peter Pain J, the judge at first instance, picking up the offsetting point mentioned by Purchas LJ in *Emeh*, had disallowed claims for the disappointment experienced by the parents on learning of the pregnancy, and for the mother's pain and suffering in the course of pregnancy and labour, on the basis that these matters were cancelled out by the birth of a healthy child. The Court of Appeal allowed the plaintiffs' cross-appeal against the refusal of these damages. The joy of having a child should be set off only against the trouble of bringing her up – the emotional advantages gained by being a parent could not be used to offset any physical or economic losses that parenthood involves.

The only Scottish case that had been decided before *McFarlane* v *Tayside Health Board* was the Outer House decision of *Allan* v *Greater Glasgow Health Board*.[9] Here the action failed on its merits, though Lord Cameron of Lochbroom saw no reason why damages should not be allowed for the pain and suffering associated with pregnancy and childbirth, and for the costs of bringing up the child.

So, costs of upkeep had been affirmed by the Court of Appeal twice in the mid-1980s, and had been awarded frequently since.[10] Though

[7] *Sherlock* v *Stillwater Clinic* 260 NW 2d 169 (1977).

[8] [1986] QB 644 (CA).

[9] 1998 SLT 580. Though reported after the Outer House decision in *McFarlane*, this case had in fact been decided 5 years previously.

[10] *Salih* v *Enfield Health Authority* [1991] 3 All ER 400; *Robinson* v *Salford Health Authority* [1992] 3 Med LR 270; *Allen* v *Bloomsbury Health Authority* [1993] 1 All ER 651; *Fish* v *Wilcox* [1994] 5 Med LR 230; *Walkin* v *South Manchester Health Authority* [1995] 4 All ER 132; *Crouchman* v *Burke* (1997) 40 BMLR 163.

this seemed to be an inevitable consequence of the application of traditional principles of delict, not all judges were happy. Ognall J said this in an unreported case:

> "I pause only to observe that, speaking purely personally, it remains a matter of surprise to me that the law acknowledges an entitlement in a mother to claim damages for the blessing of a healthy child. Certain it is that those who are afflicted with a handicapped child or who long desperately to have a child at all and are denied that good fortune, would regard an award for this sort of contingency with a measure of astonishment. But there it is: that is the law."

This was cited by Lloyd LJ in the Court of Appeal in *Gold* v *Haringey Health Authority*[11] and, he added, "many would no doubt agree with this observation". This judicial discomfort was substantially increased by the decision in *Benarr* v *Kettering Health Authority*,[12] where applying the law without qualification led to what many saw as an overly generous award. The family who sued in *Benarr* were very comfortably off and part of the costs that they claimed for bringing up the unexpected child was school fees. Discomfiting perhaps, but there is nothing conceptually odd in this. Just as the defender who, by inflicting devastating injuries, ruins the earning capacity of a successful entrepreneur must pay vastly more damages than the defender who does the same thing to a beggar, so the negligent Health Authority in *Benarr* was obliged to pay costs of upkeep substantially greater than those faced by economically modest families like the Thakes (or, for that matter, the McFarlanes). But in failed sterilisation cases damages will usually come from the National Health Service and, in the words of Lord Bingham in a subsequent case,[13] "the spectre of well-to-do families plundering the NHS" has haunted these cases ever since.

However, notwithstanding these occasional expressions of judicial misgivings, the law seemed to be both clear and settled by the time Mr McFarlane was undergoing his operation. Damages were claimable for both physical injuries and economic costs, including the future costs of upbringing, if it could be shown that a doctor's negligence either in the performance of a sterilisation operation or in the advice and information given to the patient led directly to pregnancy and

---

[11] [1988] QB 481 at 484F.
[12] (1988) 138 NLJ 179.
[13] *Rees* v *Darlington Memorial Hospital NHS Trust* [2004] 1 AC 309 at para 8.

childbirth. There was considered to be no reason of public policy to deny such a claim and the joys associated with parenthood were not to be used to offset the economic losses that were otherwise claimable. The law was so clear indeed that when the defendant in *Thake* v *Maurice* sought leave to appeal the decision in favour of the Thakes to the House of Lords, the Court of Appeal refused to grant that leave, and the House of Lords itself subsequently dismissed a petition for leave to appeal.[14]

But *Thake* was an English case. One of the major procedural differences between Scots and English law is that litigants in Scottish cases do not need leave to appeal from the Court of Session to the House of Lords, which is why it had to be a Scottish case that would finally make its way to that ultimate court on this issue. Thus it is that a Scottish case, once again, changed the course of legal development in both Scotland and England.

McFarlane in the Court of Session

The Lord Ordinary, Lord Gill, like all the judges to follow, dealt with the two claims separately. In relation to Mrs McFarlane's claim for pain and suffering caused by the pregnancy and childbirth, he said this:

> "Pregnancy causes discomfort, pain and sickness. Labour is acutely painful and distressing. But these are natural processes resulting in a happy outcome. They are the natural sequelae of conception and that is an event that in this case can hardly be considered as a physical injury *per se*."[15]

In any event, even if pregnancy and labour could be regarded as an injury, they could not be dissociated from their outcome, which in this case was the happiness brought by the existence of a healthy child. In other words, though pregnancy and childbirth were uncomfortable and painful, they were not "injury" as the law understood that term. So Mrs McFarlane's individual claim was irrelevant for the simple reason that she had suffered no loss recognisable to the law.

Lord Gill also found the claim for financial losses to be irrelevant. Even given that the McFarlanes were financially worse off, they had the benefit of a child, Catherine, who would bring them joy and happiness. To fail to take that joy into account would be "contrary

---

[14] See [1986] 1 All ER at 512H.
[15] 1997 SLT 211 at 214I.

to the principle that the purpose of damages is to effect *restitutio in integrum*, so far as money can. This purpose cannot be achieved if the parents receive the benefits of both the damages and the child".[16] This is really the "offsetting" approach that had been mentioned in a few of the earlier English decisions. But there was an insuperable difficulty in operating such an offset, and that was the impossibility of assessing, in financial terms, the value of the joy that Catherine's existence would bring to Mr and Mrs McFarlane. "In these circumstances", said Lord Gill, "I am of the opinion that this case should be decided on the principle that the privilege of being a parent is immeasurable in monetary terms; that the benefits of parenthood transcend any patrimonial loss, if it may be so regarded, that the parents may incur in consequence of their child's existence; and that therefore the pursuers in a case such as this cannot be said to be in an overall position of loss".[17] The whole claim, therefore, was dismissed as irrelevant.[18]

On appeal to the Inner House, the Second Division overruled the Lord Ordinary.[19] It pointed out that the right to raise an action for negligence in Scotland requires a concurrence of *iniuria* (the doing of a wrong, or the invasion of a legal right) and *damnum* (the suffering of prejudice in respect of an interest that the law recognises as worth protecting). If Mr and Mrs McFarlane were to receive skilled advice as to the former's fertility, it was their right not to receive advice that, as a consequence of the negligence of those giving it, was materially inaccurate and misleading. An infringement of that right, such as was clearly averred in this case, amounted to *iniuria*. The *damnum*, equally clearly averred, occurred when, as a consequence of the McFarlanes acting upon that negligently given advice, Mrs McFarlane became pregnant, for at that stage her deliberate choice to avoid pregnancy (an interest recognised and protected by the law) had been frustrated. The normal principles of causation and remoteness are, the Second Division held, the only limitations on the damages that can be claimed, and the unrealistic task of placing a monetary value on the benefit of the child can be avoided simply by holding that that benefit should

---

[16] 1997 SLT 211 at 215L.

[17] *Ibid* at 216B.

[18] Lord Gill's decision was not followed in an Outer House case decided shortly thereafter and before *McFarlane* reached the Inner House: in *Anderson* v *Forth Valley Health Board* 1998 SLT 588 the Lord Ordinary preferred to follow the English precedents.

[19] 1998 SLT 307.

not accrue to the relief of the wrongdoer. Mr and Mrs McFarlane had therefore made out a relevant claim and there were no public policy reasons to deny that result. The Second Division, therefore, remitted the case to proof to determine whether the error at the laboratory amounted, in law, to negligence. If it did, full recovery of everything the McFarlanes claimed for would be awarded.

Before that happened, however, the defenders, Tayside Health Board, appealed against the Second Division's decision to the House of Lords.

The House of Lords decides

Four of the five judges in the House of Lords rejected both of the results reached in the courts below.[20] Neither full recovery, as suggested by the Second Division, nor the complete denial of recovery, as suggested by the Lord Ordinary, was the correct approach.

The basic flaw of the judgments below was that they applied the classic test of liability for negligence to both types of claim, but these types were very different. The judges in the Court of Session had failed to take account of developments in the law of negligence subsequent to the English cases that had permitted full recovery, like *Emeh* and *Thake*. In particular, the Second Division had been in error in following the now discredited approach to new types of claim set down by the House of Lords in *Anns* v *Merton London Borough Council*,[21] that is to say applying the normal test for negligence and then examining whether there are policy reasons to reject liability. For in *Murphy* v *Brentwood District Council*[22] the House of Lords had overruled its decision in *Anns* and the approach in *Caparo Industries plc* v *Dickman*[23] was approved instead. *Murphy* and *Caparo* had confirmed that there was a distinction to be made between claims for personal injury and claims for economic loss, and that with the latter something more than the normal test of foreseeability needs to be satisfied before a duty of care could be found to exist. Mrs McFarlane's sole claim for her pain and suffering was unexceptional and could be allowed to go to proof since pregnancy and childbirth were foreseeable physical consequences of the Health Board's alleged negligence. But the joint

20 [2000] 2 AC 59.
21 [1978] AC 728.
22 [1991] 1 AC 398.
23 [1990] 2 AC 605.

claim by Mr and Mrs McFarlane for the costs of bringing up Catherine
was in a quite different position: this was a claim for pure economic
loss.

Lord Hope of Craighead quoted Lord Oliver in *Murphy*:

> "In the straightforward case of the direct infliction of physical injury
> by the act of the plaintiff there is, indeed, no need to look beyond the
> foreseeability by the defendant of the result in order to establish that
> he is in a 'proximate' relationship with the plaintiff ... the infliction of
> physical injury to the person or property of another universally requires
> to be justified. The causing of economic loss does not. If it is to be
> categorised as wrongful it is necessary to find some factor beyond the
> mere occurrence of the loss and the fact that its occurrence could be
> foreseen. Thus the categorisation of damage as economic serves at least
> the useful purpose of indicating that something more is required."[24]

That something more, it is plain from *Caparo Industries*, is the satisfaction
of the "fair, just and reasonable" test. In other words, in order to
show that there was a duty by a defender not to cause a pursuer pure
economic loss, the necessary "proximity" between the two needs to be
established by showing not only that the loss sued for is reasonably
foreseeable but also that it would be fair, just and reasonable to
impose liability in these circumstances. This is unashamedly a control
mechanism – a matter of legal rather than public policy – designed
to ensure that liability for economic loss does not exceed the bounds
of what is either socially acceptable or structurally feasible to the
economy as a whole. All five judges in the House of Lords held that
it would exceed these bounds to allow the joint claim by Mr and Mrs
McFarlane to recover the costs of bringing up Catherine, though they
expressed their understandings of what was fair, just and reasonable
in a variety of ways.

For neither Lord Slynn nor Lord Clyde would it be fair, just or
reasonable "to impose on a doctor or his employer liability for the
consequential responsibilities, imposed on or accepted by the parents
to bring up a child. The doctor does not assume responsibility for
those economic losses".[25] Lord Steyn, after referring to the "judicial
scepticism" that has prevailed since *Murphy* about the existence of an
overarching principle for the recovery of new categories of economic

---

[24] [1991] 1 AC 398 at 486–487.
[25] [2000] 2 AC per Lord Slynn at 76; per Lord Clyde at 105.

loss,[26] held that instead of corrective justice, where the court's aim is to transfer loss from the person who suffered it to the person who caused it, the "vantage point of distributive justice" is preferable in cases of economic loss. This approach seeks to ensure that losses are fairly distributed across society as a whole. "If the matter is approached this way", he said,

> "it may become relevant to ask commuters on the Underground the following question:'Should the parents of an unwanted but healthy child be able to sue the doctor or hospital for compensation equivalent to the cost of bringing up the child for the years of his or her minority, i.e. until about 18 years?' My Lords, I am firmly of the view that an overwhelming number of ordinary men and women would answer the question with an emphatic 'No'".[27]

There are numerous reasons why the answer would be "No":

  (i) many people cannot have children, while others have the sorrow and burden of disabled children;
  (ii) parents would have to argue in court that an unwanted but now loved child is more trouble than it is worth;
  (iii) instinctively people feel that the law has no business providing remedies for the birth of a healthy child "which all of us regard as a valuable and good thing" and, in particular;
  (iv) distinctions would have to be made between children from poor families and children from rich families.[28]

Here most clearly is the fear being expressed that to award damages to this modest family would necessitate in the future awarding much larger amounts to families whose need was much less. This fear is picked up, from a slightly different angle, by both the Scottish judges, Lord Hope and Lord Clyde. They worried that awarding damages would be disproportionate to the minor nature of the error. Especially when the child was born to a very wealthy family, the child's upbringing might lead to a very substantial award, which would be disproportionate to the duties which were undertaken and consequently to the extent of

---

[26] [2000] 2 AC 59 at 79.

[27] *Ibid* at 82. In *McLelland* v *Greater Glasgow Health Board* 2001 SLT 446 Lord Morison at para 6, after quoting this, rather tartly noted that his own perception of what the traveller on the Underground would think would invariably be what he thought himself.

[28] *Ibid*.

the negligence.[29] Additionally, they were concerned by the fact that Mr and Mrs McFarlane, as well as suffering losses, did get a real benefit in the shape of Catherine herself. This reality meant that it would not be fair, just or reasonable, in any assessment of the loss caused by the birth, to leave that benefit out of account: "otherwise the pursuers would be paid far too much".[30] But (without directly admitting as much) Lord Hope agreed with the Lord Ordinary, Lord Gill, that the value of the benefit of Catherine's existence was incalculable, with the result that it cannot be established whether, overall and in the long run, the cost of upkeep would exceed the value of the benefit.[31]

Lord Millett was the fifth judge and, while he agreed that the joint claim for economic loss should be dismissed, he disagreed with his brethren that Mrs McFarlane's individual claim for pain and suffering should nevertheless be permitted to succeed. He followed precisely the approach of the Lord Ordinary, that the law has to take the birth of a normal healthy baby to be a blessing and not a detriment – in other words, that there is no loss at all. This had to apply to both claims because, unlike his brethren, Lord Millett was not persuaded by the distinction between economic and non-economic losses: "the only difference between the two heads of damages claimed is temporal. Normal pregnancy and delivery were as much an inescapable precondition of Catherine's birth as the expense of maintaining her afterwards".[32] It followed that, since the joint claim for economic losses had to be rejected, Mrs McFarlane's claim for pain and suffering had to be rejected too.

However, Lord Millett did not want the pursuers to go away empty handed. He accepted that they both suffered loss, though not the loss that they had identified themselves as having suffered (and not the loss, therefore, they were suing upon). Instead, Lord Millett found that the alleged negligence of the Health Board had denied the McFarlanes the freedom to limit the size of their own family. This he saw as an important aspect of their personal autonomy, and its denial as a loss that the law should recognise and provide compensation for. This entirely depersonalised loss had nothing to do with the existence or otherwise of Catherine as an individual and so a "conventional sum" of modest proportion, in the order of no more than £5,000, should be

[29] [2000] 2 AC 59 per Lord Hope at 91; per Lord Clyde at 106.
[30] *Ibid* per Lord Hope at 97; per Lord Clyde at 105.
[31] *Ibid* per Lord Hope at 97.
[32] *Ibid* at 114.

awarded in cases such as this. None of the other judges in the case took this approach, or even mentioned it – perhaps because it had not been argued by the pursuers. But it was this approach which, as we will see, was to have an afterlife.

The end result for the McFarlanes was that Mrs McFarlane's claim for her pain and suffering was regarded as relevant but her and her husband's claim for costs of upkeep was rejected. The law reports do not tell us whether a proof was ever heard to determine whether Mrs McFarlane's claim was in fact made out. The likelihood is that Tayside Health Board settled by paying the £10,000, which was probably cheaper than arguing the case any further. An appropriate use of NHS resources, perhaps.

The aftermath

Now, of the nine judges who heard *McFarlane*, six rejected the claim for the costs of upkeep. Many of the judges in the House of Lords emphasised that this decision was in accordance with the approaches in most other jurisdictions to which they had been referred, but the fact that a wide variety of reasons is apparent from these jurisdictions suggests that this is an area in which judges struggle to find consensus. Even when they think the answer is obvious (as, for example, Lord Steyn clearly did), the way to the answer is not. Some influential courts have concluded that the House of Lords gave the wrong answer in *McFarlane*. The High Court of Australia, for example, was faced with the same question a mere 4 years later. In *Cattanach* v *Melchior*[33] negligent advice was given by a doctor to a patient that, following her sterilisation operation, she was now infertile, while in fact only one of her fallopian tubes had been tied. After giving birth to a healthy baby boy she sued her surgeon, and by the time the case reached the High Court of Australia (the highest court of appeal in that country) the only issue was whether the costs of upkeep were recoverable – and the argument turned on whether Australian law should follow the House of Lords in this Scottish case. By a majority of four to three, the High Court of Australia declined to follow *McFarlane* and awarded damages to cover the costs of bringing up the child. It is interesting to note, however, that some states in Australia have taken the political decision that this is an inappropriate use of health care funds (the "distributive justice" approach of Lord Steyn) and so,

[33] [2003] HCA 38; (2003) 215 CLR 1.

by legislation, have subsequently prevented courts from awarding damages for costs of upkeep in the future.[34]

And even in the United Kingdom, the limitations to the application of *McFarlane* were soon tested and that case was certainly not the last to exercise the minds of our higher judges. Every one of the judges in *McFarlane* had emphasised that Catherine had been born healthy and whole, and many expressed the view that, while childbirth is normally an occasion for rejoicing, this might not necessarily be so if the child is born disabled in some way. The hint was clear: the decision in *McFarlane* might have been different had Catherine been born disabled. And this hint was not long in being picked up and used as the basis for a new claim. In *Parkinson* v *St James and Seacroft University Hospital NHS Trust*[35] the English Court of Appeal held that, while the ordinary costs of rearing a child are not recoverable, *McFarlane* did not preclude the recovery of any *extra* costs attributable to the child's disability. A disabled child is likely to need extra care, and the provision of that care is likely to mean extra expenditure. This extra expenditure can, it was held, be recovered from the health care provider whose negligence led to the pregnancy.

But there is a flaw here. These extra costs are caused by the child's disability, not by the child's very existence. There is a clear causal connection between the doctor's negligence and the child's existence (and the costs referable thereto, which are, standing *McFarlane*, irrecoverable), but a doctor who is negligent in the performance of a sterilisation operation, or in the advice he or she gives following such an operation, does not cause the child's disability and so does not cause any of the extra costs incurred as a result of that disability. This flaw was spotted by Lord Morison in his dissenting judgment in *McLelland* v *Greater Glasgow Health Board*,[36] a case also involving a disabled child, though it differed crucially from both *McFarlane* and *Parkinson* in that the negligence lay in the failure to diagnose the disability before birth and, therefore, to offer the pregnant woman an abortion. The

---

[34] This is the case in Queensland (where *Cattanach* v *Melchior* originated) and in New South Wales: see, respectively, s 4 of the Justice and Other Legislation Amendment Act 2003 (QLD) and s 71 of the Civil Liability Act 2002 (NSW). Note that the former is limited to costs "ordinarily associated" with rearing a child, while the latter talks of "costs associated with". This makes a difference in the circumstances about to be discussed in the text.

[35] [2001] EWCA Civ 530; [2002] QB 266.

[36] 2001 SLT 446.

damnum, in other words, was not the failure to prevent pregnancy but the failure to prevent the birth. It had been conceded in *McLelland* that the additional costs of bringing up a disabled child were recoverable, but Lord Morison[37] could not see why that concession should not also apply in a case like the present to the normal costs, given that both were caused (as they were not in *Parkinson*) directly by the doctor's negligence.

Yet another fact scenario presented itself in *Rees* v *Darlington Memorial Hospital NHS Trust*.[38] The claimant in this case was effectively seeking an extension of the exception to *McFarlane* identified in *Parkinson*, for it was not the child who was disabled in *Rees* but the mother. She was blind. The reason she underwent a sterilisation operation was her fear that her own disability would make bringing up a child too difficult for her. But the operation was carried out negligently, Ms Rees remained fertile and a year after the operation she became pregnant, giving birth in due course to a healthy son. She would be entitled to claim a modest solatium similar to that which Mrs McFarlane recovered, but the decision in *McFarlane* would prevent her from claiming the costs of upkeep. *Parkinson* suggested a route to allow Ms Rees to claim more. She sought to recover the extra costs referable to her blindness. These extra costs were no more – nor, in truth, any less – caused by the doctor's negligence than the extra costs in *Parkinson*. But *Parkinson* was thin ice upon which to build a claim, even if it was truly in point, and so her counsel adopted the courageous tactic of mounting an all-out attack on *McFarlane* itself. He asked the House of Lords to overrule its own decision, issued barely 4 years earlier. An unusual Court of Seven Judges was convened to re-examine *McFarlane* and its application to cases such as *Rees*.

All seven judges in the House of Lords agreed that *McFarlane* could not be overruled just because a differently constituted court would decide that profoundly controversial case differently, and indeed four of them explicitly approved the decision (and another two, Lords Hope and Millett, gave no indication that they had changed the views they expressed in the earlier case). So the question revolved into whether the rule in *McFarlane*, that upbringing costs were not recoverable, applied when the mother was disabled, or whether the rule in *Parkinson*, that the extra costs referable to the child's disability, should be extended to

---

37   2001 SLT 446 at para 7.
38   [2003] UKHL 52; [2004] 1 AC 309.

include the extra costs referable to the mother's disability. The Judicial Committee was deeply split on that question. A majority, composed of Lords Bingham, Nicholls, Millett and Scott, held that to award damages in the present case would not be a legitimate extension of *Parkinson* but an illegitimate gloss on *McFarlane*. In *Parkinson*, the extra costs were referable to the child's disability, and could be traced, via the child, to the doctor's negligence. But in *Rees* the extra costs were referable to the mother's disability which had nothing to do with the doctor. There was, in other words, no causal link between the negligence and the costs claimed. It might, of course, be argued that the causal link is equally non-existent between the negligence and a child's disability, but only Lord Scott went so far as to say that *Parkinson* had been incorrectly decided.[39] In any event, the majority held that, as in *McFarlane*, it would not be fair, just and reasonable to allow recovery for the costs of bringing up the child, even the extra costs in this case referable to the mother's blindness.

But Ms Rees did better in the end than the McFarlanes, for Lord Millett finally got his way. Lords Steyn and Hope, who like him had sat on *McFarlane*, had not then approved his idea of a "conventional sum" to recognise the McFarlanes' loss of autonomy and they liked it even less now. But, with Lord Hutton, they were dissenters in *Rees*, on both the outcome and this point. Lords Bingham, Nicholls and Scott all accepted Lord Millett's revived suggestion that such a conventional sum should be awarded in recognition of the fact that Ms Rees had lost the opportunity to live her life in the way that she wished and planned. But instead of the £5,000 he had suggested in *McFarlane*, all four agreed that the figure should appropriately be set at £15,000.

And in the greater scheme of things, who is to say that they were wrong in doing so? Cases involving sterilisations undertaken solely to limit family size, which generated for a few years at the turn of the millennium a huge amount of litigation, have now been killed stone dead.[40] If a sterilisation operation fails as a result of a mistake for which

---

[39] [2003] UKHL 52; [2004] 1 AC 309 at para 145. Lord Hope explicitly approved it (para 57).

[40] The only cases that come to court nowadays are those where the child is born handicapped and there is some negligence claimed in, eg, genetic counselling or antenatal care that denied the claimants the opportunity of abortion. See, eg, *Farraj* v *King's Healthcare NHS Trust* [2006] EWHC 1228; [2008] EWHC 2468; [2009] EWCA Civ 1203; *Whitehead* v *Searle* [2008] EWCA Civ 285; [2009] 1 WLR 285; and *FP* v *Taunton and Somerset NHS Trust* [2009] EWHC 1965 (QB).

a health board is responsible, it is far cheaper for that board to write a cheque for £15,000 than to employ lawyers to argue the case in court. This is distributive justice in action, though some (like Lord Hope) might well question whether it is for the courts rather than Parliament to make the choices upon which that distribution is made.

Chapter 5

THE SNAIL IN THE GINGER BEER FLOAT
Donoghue v *Stevenson*

Elspeth Reid

Contrary to popular belief, the pages of the law reports are packed
with high drama – collisions at sea, floods, explosions, loss of life
and limb, and the collapse of business empires. But in *Donoghue* v
Stevenson,[1] a minor misadventure led to a court case which went
all the way to the House of Lords in London and subsequently
became "probably the most famous case in the whole Commonwealth
world of the Common Law".[2] On the evening of 26 August 1928, Mrs
May[3] Donoghue stepped through the doors of the Wellmeadow Café
in Paisley and on to the pages of learned legal treatises for many
decades to come. That fateful evening, the café proprietor served May
with ginger beer which turned out to have been contaminated with
the remains of a decomposing snail, and she was understandably
aggrieved. The incident might well have passed without notice as
a trivial consumer complaint, but instead it became the subject of
litigation that transformed the law and even prompted a "Pilgrimage

---

[1] Proceedings in the House of Lords are reported in 1932 SC (HL) 31; 1932 SLT
317; [1932] AC 562 (references are to the SC report throughout). Proceedings
in the lower courts are noted in 1930 SN 117 (Outer House of the Court
of Session) and 1930 SN 138 (Inner House), and reproduced in full at the
special website devoted to the case by the Scottish Council for Law Reporting
at http://www.scottishlawreports.org.uk/resources/dvs/donoghue-v-stevenson.
html.

[2] A Rodger, "Mrs Donoghue and Alfenus Varus" (1988) 41 Current Legal Problems
1 at 2.

[3] The *Session Cases* report notes her name as "Mary", while *Scots Law Times*
uses "May". However, "May" is correct, and her maiden name was spelled
as "McAllister": see Rodger (n 2 above) at 4.

to Paisley"[4] 62 years later by legal luminaries and supreme court judges from Scotland, England, Canada and Australia. How did this apparently unremarkable Scots law story come to such a momentous conclusion?

The facts of the case

26 August was a Sunday. The weather had been fine[5] and May had travelled to Paisley from her home in the east end of Glasgow, an excursion which would have taken her through pleasant countryside, not the urban sprawl of today. Towards nine o'clock in the evening, she had stopped off with a friend for refreshments at the café, near Paisley town centre on Wellmeadow Street.[6] May's friend ordered a pear and ice cream for herself and a ginger beer float for May. The name and gender of this generous friend, who paid for both of them, has never been established beyond doubt, but it is thought that she was female.[7]

The proprietor of the café, Francis Minghella,[8] served the pair himself. He placed ice cream into a glass for May and poured over it some of the contents of a bottle of ginger beer. The bottle was sealed with a metal fastener and made of opaque dark glass, as was common for ginger beer bottles; this concealed the yeasty sediment often found in the mildly alcoholic brew of that era. After May had drunk some of this delectable concoction, her helpful friend poured more of the liquid from the bottle. To their horror, the decomposing remains of a

---

[4] See P T Burns and S J Lyons (eds), *Donoghue v Stevenson and the Modern Law of Negligence* (1991), a collection of essays which celebrates the case and tells the story of the Pilgrimage and conference in Paisley Town Hall, 28–30 September 1990.

[5] See W W McBryde, "The story of the case", in Burns and Lyons (n 4 above), 25 at 37. (An earlier version of this text had appeared in A J Gamble (ed), *Obligations in Context: Essays in Honour of Professor D M Walker* (1990), p 13.)

[6] The report of the case refers to Wellmeadow Place, but McBryde confirms the correct street name in "The story of the case" (n 5 above) at p 30.

[7] There is speculation that May was with a male friend, but the only clear indication of the gender of her companion is the reference by Lord Macmillan in his speech in the House of Lords to "she" (1932 SC (HL) 31 at 61). This possibly reflected references earlier in proceedings, but it might have been conjecture. May had recently separated from her husband, and the sequence of events, including the friend paying and pouring the drink for May, might, in those days, have suggested that the acquaintance was male.

[8] The written pleadings name him as Minchella, but his birth certificate has him as Minghella. "Francis" was a corruption of Francesco, his name given at birth. See McBryde (n 5 above) at p 32.

snail tipped into the glass. May was shocked by the sight of the snail and by the realisation that her drink had been contaminated, and she claimed that she was made so ill by gastro-enteritis that she later required treatment at Glasgow Royal Infirmary. As a result, she was absent from her work and lost wages.

In the furore which followed the appearance of the snail, May's resourceful friend took note of the label on the bottle. This indicated that it had come from "D Stevenson, Glen Lane, Paisley". May, a shop assistant, was a woman of little formal education, but she lost no time in taking legal advice and on 4 April 1929 she raised an action in the Outer House of the Court of Session in Edinburgh, claiming £500 in damages from David Stevenson, the proprietor of the firm that had manufactured the ginger beer. Either by good fortune or on good advice, she had instructed Walter Leechman to act for her, an able and energetic Glasgow solicitor who had already built up a successful practice in reparation cases.[9]

May Donoghue's claim

Had May paid for her drink herself that evening, legal history would probably have passed her by. She would have had a contract with Minghella. She could have sued him in terms of that contract for providing her with goods that were unfit, and her story would have ended there. But the contract had been made between Minghella and her friend, and her friend had not suffered any shock or illness from consuming her own pear and ice cream. So, instead, May brought an action against Stevenson in delict, that branch of the law which is concerned with compensating those who have been injured by the wrongful conduct of another, even when they have had no contract or other prior agreement with that person. More specifically, her case was argued under the law of negligence, that part of the law of delict which addresses unintended harm caused by the defender's carelessness, rather than intentional or malicious injury. These were the days before a European Directive[10] and a UK statute[11] imposed rigorous safety standards on the manufacturers and suppliers of consumer products.

[9] See J F Leechman, "Mrs Donoghue's Solicitor" in Burns and Lyons (n 4 above) at 273.
[10] Council Directive 85/374/EEC of 25 July 1985 on the approximation of the laws, regulations and administrative provisions of the Member States concerning liability for defective products.
[11] Consumer Protection Act 1987.

However, May contended that the common law imposed a duty of care on manufacturers like Stevenson to make products safe and to prevent harm to the consumer, even though there was typically no contractual relationship between manufacturers and the ultimate consumers, and no specific statutory obligations.

More specifically, May claimed that this duty of care obliged Stevenson to provide a system of working in his factory that would have prevented snails from getting into his ginger beer bottles. She alleged that his empty bottles were stored in places to which it would have been obvious that snails had access (in that snails and their slimy trails would have been observed). Stevenson ought to have had a system for inspecting the bottles before they were filled and sealed. Furthermore, Stevenson ought to have sold his drinks products in clear bottles so as to allow the contents to be checked for contamination before being consumed. Had he fulfilled those duties, the snail would not have got into the bottle or, if it had, its presence would have been detected. May would not therefore have been made ill. As a result of his negligence, she had suffered injury for which she now claimed compensation.

Minghella, the café proprietor, was also a party in the court action at an early stage. May sued him as well as Stevenson in delict, but she quickly dropped this part of the case, presumably because Minghella's conduct could not be classed as wrongful even if the facts were proved. The ginger beer had been sold to him in opaque bottles so that it would have been impossible for him to detect that this particular bottle was contaminated. Moreover, the metal seals placed on the bottles meant that the snail could not have gained entry after the bottle left Stevenson's factory.

May's prospects of success in this litigation cannot have seemed very hopeful. She was a woman of little means whereas her opponent was an established and successful businessman. Moreover, recent authority in the Court of Session seemed to be against her, as discussed further below.

The defence

In response, Stevenson contended that the case against him should be dismissed as irrelevant; in other words, even if the facts were proved as stated by May, he maintained that there was no legal basis for the remedy which she claimed. Stevenson did not dispute the specific content of the duties listed by May – taking care to keep bottles free of snails and so on – but his argument was more fundamental. His case was that he owed no such duty of care to persons like May. Duties of this nature might arise from certain types of relationship where there was a degree of proximity between the parties. Stevenson did not deny that manufacturers owed contractual duties to the retailers to whom they sold their goods, and that the retailers in turn owed contractual duties to their customers. However, he insisted that manufacturers could not reasonably be required to answer for the safety of their products to the ultimate consumer in all cases – all the unknown persons into whose hands goods eventually might fall. The imposition of a general duty vis-à-vis such a wide circle of potential litigants would be far too onerous.

In his support, Stevenson invoked a very similar recent case, *Mullen* v *Barr & Co*,[12] in which a father had brought an action against another drinks manufacturer after a mouse had been found in a bottle of ginger beer from which his children had already drunk. Mullen had brought his action in the local sheriff court. The sheriff-substitute had allowed the case to go to trial, but on appeal to the sheriff and then to the Court of Session the action was dismissed. It was accepted that the mouse had indeed been present, but Mullen was unsuccessful because the facts as alleged did not necessarily show that the drinks manufacturer had been negligent in its working practices. An important feature of the case, however, was the discussion of whether manufacturers owed a duty regarding their products to any persons except those with whom they had entered into a contractual relationship – an issue upon which the Court of Session Bench was divided but upon which the majority appeared to take a negative view.[13]

The Court of Session

Since the parties were in dispute on the relevancy of May's case, the first step in proceedings was a hearing before a single judge in the Outer House of the Court of Session: the Lord Ordinary, Lord Moncrieff. His role was not at this point to adjudicate on the facts, but to determine whether her claim had sufficient legal merit to justify

---

[12] 1929 SC 461; 1929 SLT 341. This report also notes the case of *M'Gowan* v *Barr and Co* in which the pursuer alleged that she had become ill after discovering a mouse in ginger beer bought for her by her son.

[13] Of the four judges sitting in the case only Lord Hunter was for recognising such a general duty. Lord Ormidale and Lord Anderson were against it, and Lord Justice-Clerk Alness reserved his judgment on this point since Mullen had in any event failed to prove that Barr and Co had been negligent.

the remedy sought if it were brought to trial. Lord Moncrieff delivered his judgment on 27 June 1930. He opened his judgment by stating the general rule that such cases required three elements: a general duty owed by defender to pursuer; some kind of relationship between the parties that brought the pursuer "within the consideration of the discharge of the duty"; and, finally, a causal connection between the breach of duty and the injury claimed. Certain English cases might indicate that, except in relation to dangerous items, manufacturers owed a duty to see that their products were safe only to those parties with whom they had a direct contractual relationship. However, counsel for Stevenson[14] conceded that there was no authority for adopting this as a doctrine in Scots law. The discussion in *Mullen* v *Barr* of course required to be taken into consideration, but this did not persuade Lord Moncrieff to dismiss the action in *Donoghue* since negligence was not proved against the manufacturer in *Mullen* and judicial opinion had in any event been divided on the scope of duty.

In conclusion, therefore, Lord Moncrieff declared that it was a

"wrongful act to sell, in order that others may purchase and consume, articles which have been exposed through negligence to a practical risk of contracting a dangerous taint. More especially in cases in which the articles are distributed in sealed bottles, I regard this wrong as having been committed by the manufacturers against the destined sufferer, being none other than the consumer, for whose use the product was in fact prepared".

On that basis his Lordship found in May's favour and allowed the case to go forward to "proof" (ie trial) to determine whether the facts could be proved.

Stevenson, however, appealed to the Inner House of the Court of Session, where the Second Division delivered its opinion on 13 November 1930. Unfortunately for May, the composition of the Second Division Bench was the same as that which had heard the appeal in *Mullen* v *Barr* only a short time before. Rather predictably, and delivering judgments much shorter than that of Lord Moncrieff in the Outer House, they found against her by a majority, on the basis that the case was indistinguishable from *Mullen*.

---

[14] W G Normand, later to become Lord Normand, Lord President of the Court of Session from 1935 to 1947 and Lord of Appeal in Ordinary (House of Lords judge) from 1947 to 1953.

The House of Lords

Three months later, on 25 February 1931, May launched her appeal to the House of Lords, and the case was heard over two short days on 10 and 11 December 1932. The Scots courts had from earliest times operated a system of legal aid enabling the very poor to litigate, but it appears that May had not availed herself of such assistance in the early stages of her case. By the time of the House of Lords appeal, however, with legal costs mounting, she made a successful application to continue the case as a "pauper", swearing that her total assets did not exceed £5.

No transcript of the proceedings remains to us, and the supplementary statement lodged by May's counsel in the House of Lords[15] is brief. The essence of their argument was that "where anyone performs an operation, such as the manufacture of an article, a relationship of duty independent of contract may in certain circumstance arise, the extent of such duty in every case depending on the particular circumstances of the case".

As was customary in House of Lords appeals, May's appeal was heard by a committee of five Law Lords. Two were Scots[16] (Lords Thankerton and Macmillan); two were English (Lords Buckmaster and Tomlin); and one was Welsh–Irish (Lord Atkin).[17] Often in House of Lords cases, the speeches of the Law Lords varied in length, and it was not unusual for some simply to state in one or two sentences that they agreed with the opinion of one of their "noble and learned friends". Not so in *Donoghue* v *Stevenson*, where all five members of the committee rendered speeches of some substance. Lord Buckmaster, the most senior judge in the case, delivered the first speech,[18] in which he

---

[15] G Morton and W R Milligan. The statement is reproduced in the section devoted to the "Appellant's Case" at http://www.scottishlawreports.org.uk/resources/dvs/donoghue-v-stevenson.html.

[16] Lord Gordon was in 1876 the first judge from the Scots courts appointed to the House of Lords (although the Lord President, Lord Colonsay, had been sent to assist with Scottish appeals some years earlier, in 1867). Thereafter Lords of Appeal from Scotland were regularly appointed and it became customary to have two Scots lawyers in the House at any given time.

[17] Lord Atkin was born in Australia of Irish and Anglo–Welsh parents, but brought up in Wales and thought of himself as Welsh (see G Lewis, "Atkin, James Richard, Baron Atkin (1867–1944)", *Oxford Dictionary of National Biography* (2004, online edn 2008)).

[18] Although it was in fact read for him by Lord Tomlin.

expressed a "vigorous, almost violent"[19] opposition to the arguments
advanced by May's counsel. Reviewing the English authorities on this
point, as well as *Mullen* v *Barr*, he concluded that it would be "little
short of outrageous" to make manufacturers liable to all who might
buy their products. Lord Tomlin agreed with him, but Lords Atkin,
Thankerton and Macmillan did not. They found in favour of May,
which meant that she had won by a majority of three to two. Of those
three, the speeches of Lords Atkin and Macmillan merit particular
attention.

Lord Atkin

Lord Atkin's speech – perhaps the most often cited in the case –
glimpsed the major significance the case was to assume. He began with
the reflection "I do not think a more important problem has occupied
your Lordships in your judicial capacity, important both because of
its bearing on public health and because of the practical test which it
applies to the system under which it arises".[20] He went on to observe
how difficult it was to find in the English authorities statements of
general application defining the relations between parties that give
rise to a duty of care in the law of delict (or, as the English call it,
tort). Typically, the courts concerned themselves with the "elaborate
classification" of duties rather than the fundamental rules underlying
the duty to take care in dealings with others. The duty to take care was
established in a variety of specific situations, therefore, but there was
no consideration of unifying principle. The latter was what mattered
in this case.

The search for authority to substantiate those general principles
took Lord Atkin back to the Book of Luke, Chapter 10, and to the
discussion between Jesus and the lawyer on the meaning of the legal
imperative to "love thy neighbour as thyself".[21] In the Gospel, the
lawyer's question "Who then is my neighbour"[22] does not elicit a crisp,
precise definition, but instead the parable of the Good Samaritan. The

[19] As described by Lord Macmillan in his memoirs, *A Man of Law's Tale* (1952) at
p 151.
[20] At 43.
[21] Sir Frederick Pollock had stated in one of the leading English texts, *The Law of
Torts* (1st edn, 1889), at p 12: "'Thou shalt do no hurt to thy neighbour.' Our law
of torts, with all its irregularities, has for its main purpose nothing else than the
development of this precept."
[22] Luke 10:29.

biblical parable thus demonstrates the "positive spiritual imperative to show mercy".[23] In contrast, Lord Atkin's reply to the lawyer's question was more "restricted". In a passage that was to become known to generations of law students as the "Atkin *dictum*" he declared:[24]

> "You must take reasonable care to avoid acts or omissions which you can reasonably foresee would be likely to injure your neighbour. Who, then, in law, is my neighbour? The answer seems to be – persons who are so closely and directly affected by my act that I ought reasonably to have them in contemplation as being so affected when I am directing my mind to the acts or omissions which are called in question."

Proximity between the parties and foreseeability of harm were thus of the essence in determining when one was legally obliged to take care for the safety of the other. Lord Atkin went on to reason that the "ordinary needs of civilised society and the ordinary claims it makes upon its members" required a remedy to be found for consumers where they were injured as a result of manufacturers' negligence.[25] If case law from the lower courts indicated that manufacturers did not owe any duty to the ultimate consumers of their goods, then Lord Atkin discerned a "grave defect in the law, and so contrary to principle" that he was not disposed to follow those authorities.[26] He was confirmed in his reasoning by the landmark judgment of Judge Benjamin Cardozo in the New York Court of Appeals some 15 years earlier in *MacPherson* v *Buick Motor Co*.[27] In that case the manufacturer was found liable to a customer injured when the wooden wheel on one of its cars disintegrated. It was no defence that the car had been bought, not directly from the manufacturer, but from a dealer, nor that the wheel itself had been made by another supplier. Where danger could be foreseen as a result of the manufacturer's negligence, Cardozo held, liability followed irrespective of the absence of a contract between the parties. By the same reasoning, Lord Atkin held it to be "sound common sense" that:[28]

> "… by Scots and English law alike a manufacturer of products, which he sells in such a form as to show that he intends them to reach the

---

[23] K Spiers, "Who is my neighbour" in Burns and Lyons (n 4 above), 279 at 282.
[24] At 44.
[25] At 46.
[26] At 46.
[27] 217 NY 382; 111 NE 1050 (1916).
[28] At 57.

ultimate consumer in the form in which they left him, with no reasonable possibility of intermediate examination, and with the knowledge that the absence of reasonable care in the preparation or putting up of the products will result in an injury to the consumer's life or property, owes a duty to the consumer to take that reasonable care".

It is possible that *Donoghue* v *Stevenson* afforded Lord Atkin a welcome opportunity to expound theories that he had been pondering upon the moral basis for the law of tort/delict. Only a few months previously, he had declared in a lecture delivered at King's College, London, on "Law as an educational subject":[29]

"British law has always necessarily ingrained in it moral teaching in this sense: that it lays down standards of honesty and plain dealing between man and man ... He is not to injure his neighbour by acts of negligence; and that certainly covers a very large field of the law. I doubt whether the whole law of tort could not be comprised in the golden maxim to do unto your neighbour as you would that he should do unto you."

And note here the use of the term "British law".

Lord Macmillan

The speech of Lord Macmillan, one of the Scots judges, is also of special interest, although it is perhaps less often cited than that of Lord Atkin. Lord Macmillan's speech as published in the law reports proceeded on the basis that there was "no distinction between the law of Scotland and the law of England in the legal principles applicable to the case" and presented a detailed review of English and American authorities. At the heart of his speech, however, was an appeal to first principles. The gist of Stevenson's defence was that May had no contract with him. But, citing one of the leading English textbooks of the day,[30] Lord Macmillan reasoned that the existence of a contract did not prevent another type of obligation arising between the same parties out of the relationship brought about by the contract. Moreover, there was no reason in principle why the same circumstances might not give one person a right of action in contract and another person a right of action in delict. In the case of a consumer, therefore, the contract for

---

[29] Lecture given on 28 October 1931, reproduced in (1932) Journal of the Society of Public Teachers of Law 27 at 30.

[30] F Pollock, *The Law of Torts* (then in its 13th edn of 1929) at p 570.

the sale of goods between manufacturer and retailer did not preclude a delictual claim by the consumer against the manufacturer.

Like Lord Atkin, Lord Macmillan also sought to set out the basis upon which one person was deemed to have assumed the duty to take care for the safety of another. Unlike Lord Atkin, however, Lord Macmillan took his lead not from the Gospels but from common sense and the standards of that mythical creature, the "reasonable man":[31]

> "What then are the circumstances which give rise to this duty to take care? In the daily contacts of social and business life, human beings are thrown into, or place themselves in, an infinite variety of relations with their fellows; and the law can refer only to the standards of the reasonable man in order to determine whether any particular relation gives rise to a duty to take care as between those who stand in the relation to each other. The grounds of action may be as various and manifold as human errancy; and the conception of legal responsibility may develop in adaptation to altering social conditions and standards. The criterion of judgment must adjust and adapt itself to the changing circumstances of life. The categories of negligence are never closed."

Applying this standard, it was clear, in Lord Macmillan's analysis, that a duty of care existed between Stevenson and those who drank his ginger beer. In the reasonable man's judgment, someone who manufactured foodstuffs owed a duty to consumers to take care that the goods remained "wholesome and innocent", and not "dangerous to life and health". He could foresee that, if he was careless about food safety, he might injure his consumers. Moreover, given that the ginger beer bottles were closed with a metal seal in the factory, and made of thick glass so that retailers could not inspect the contents, the presence of a snail in a bottle, if proved, would indicate that Stevenson had indeed been careless. The case should therefore go to trial to determine whether the facts set out by May could be proved.

In conclusion, Lord Macmillan reassuringly professed himself to be "happy to think that in their relation to the practical problem of everyday life which this appeal presents, the legal systems of the two countries are in no way at variance, and that the principles of both alike are sufficiently consonant with justice and common sense to admit of the claim which the appellant seeks to establish".[32]

[31] At 70.
[32] At 71–72.

Lord Macmillan's draft

Yet behind Lord Macmillan's speech there lies a story within a story. It may be recalled that the House of Lords heard May's appeal in December 1931, but did not publish its decision until late May 1932. It was originally scheduled that the judgment should be given on 14 April, but this date was postponed without explanation. The judgment therefore took an exceptionally long time to appear – nearly 6 months, when half that time was typical. An intriguing article by Lord Rodger of Earlsferry[33] gives an insight into what may have been going on behind the scenes.

An earlier[34] draft of Lord Macmillan's speech was among the papers he bequeathed to the Faculty of Advocates Library in Edinburgh on his death in 1952. Lord Rodger's article reproduced that draft in full and analysed the quite significant differences between it and the final version. The most obvious was that the draft was notably longer than the final version of the speech, and extensive discussion of Scots law was excised from the latter. After narrating the facts, the draft launched into several paragraphs considering the Scots authorities. The draft affirmed that the case was to be determined by the law of Scotland. It presented its conclusions on the English authorities tentatively, noting a close "approximation" between the Scots law of delict and the English law of tort, but also distinctions "both in origin and in principle" between the two systems.[35] The final version, on the other hand, relied mainly on English cases and, as mentioned above, presented its conclusions as equally applicable to both England and Scotland. In sum, therefore, the general principles which in the draft Lord Macmillan had identified as forming the foundations for the Scots law were repackaged in the final version and, as outlined above, they were presented in unequivocal terms as the law of both systems.

Lord Macmillan was to reflect in his memoirs that he never had any doubts that May's claim was relevant.[36] But why did he alter his speech so? Lord Rodger advanced several theories, but in his view the most likely explanation was that Lord Macmillan was persuaded to do so by

---

[33] A Rodger, "Lord Macmillan's speech in *Donoghue v Stevenson*" (1992) 108 *LQR* 236 (the author is now a Lord of Appeal in Ordinary, but in 1992 was Solicitor General for Scotland).

[34] Lord Rodger deduced that the draft had been written in March 1932.

[35] As reproduced in Lord Rodger's article at 248–249.

[36] *A Man of Law's Tale* (1952), p 151.

Lord Atkin.[37] The English authorities on this subject were equivocal. It will be remembered that the case was decided by a three-to-two majority, so that in effect Lord Macmillan had the "casting vote". If his speech had found in May's favour on the basis of Scots law but come to no definitive conclusion on the English law, the English law would have remained uncertain. As it was, his speech in the final version, coupled with those of the other two judges in the majority, set on a firm basis the law of both jurisdictions. In essence, the opportunity was seized to settle a branch of the law that had been unsettled on both sides of the border and was hugely important for the modern development of the law. If that was the intention, then the tactic was extraordinarily successful. The case of the snail in the ginger beer became the foundation for the modern law of negligence in both England and Scotland and, to the bemusement of Scots lawyers, has even come to be referred to as the most famous case in the *English* law of tort.[38]

The lasting impact of *Donoghue* v *Stevenson*

The broad terms in which the speeches in *Donoghue* v *Stevenson* were cast meant that the case could be read as authority for a number of important legal propositions, ranging from the particular to the general. It settled beyond doubt that manufacturers owe a duty of care to the ultimate consumers to ensure that their products are safe. It also put paid to the idea that "privity of contract" restricted the right of the injured party to claim compensation in this type of situation; in other words, where injury to A is caused by negligence in the performance of a contract between B and C, A is not precluded from bringing a claim in delict. It set out for the first time a general test for determining when one person owes another a duty to take care in terms of the law of negligence: namely, ought the former reasonably to have foreseen that his or her acts or omissions would be likely to result in damage to the latter.[39] Finally, the case established that the principles applicable in this central part of the law of negligence were the same in Scotland as in England.

---

[37] At 246–247.

[38] See, eg, N McBride and R Bagshaw, *Tort Law* (3rd edn, 2008), p 72.

[39] For discussion on the extent to which the "neighbour principle" is to be considered as part of the *"ratio"* of the case (ie the legal basis upon which it was decided), given that it appears only in Lord Atkin's speech, see R F V Heuston, *"Donoghue v Stevenson* in retrospect" (1957) 20 *MLR* 1 at 8.

The idea that duties of care might be extended to new situations simply by applying the general principles as expressed in *Donoghue* was not immediately embraced in the courts – perhaps the "neighbour" principle was perceived as dangerously broad But, after *Donoghue*, there was a clear move towards a more general approach and away from the restrictions of individual duties of care.[40] Two more Scots cases decided by the House of Lords in the ensuing decade gave further definition to the framework of negligence, and indeed "nearly everything you need to know about negligence is to be found in these three cases".[41] *Bourhill* v *Young*[42] confirmed that duty was owed only to those persons whom the defender could reasonably foresee as being within the range of injury if his or her conduct was careless. A short time later, *Muir* v *Glasgow Corporation*[43] established that the defender was to be judged as "free both from over-apprehension and from over-confidence"; he or she could not be expected to foresee *every* possible danger to the pursuer, only that which was reasonably foreseeable. The analysis of duty continues to evolve, for, as Lord Macmillan had presciently remarked, "the categories of negligence are never closed".[44] Nevertheless, *Donoghue* v *Stevenson* is universally acknowledged as marking the beginning of the "more modern approach of seeking a single general principle which may be applied in all circumstances to determine the existence of a duty of care".[45]

Scots law and English law

Since *Donoghue* v *Stevenson* was a Scots case, the decision of the House of Lords could not, strictly speaking, be binding upon the English courts. Nevertheless, one important feature of the case was the agreement by all concerned, the counsel for both sides and judges at all levels, that the law on this issue was the same on both sides of the Tweed. With the important amendments to Lord Macmillan's

---

[40] See D Ibbetson, *A Historical Introduction to the Law of Obligations* (1999), pp 191–192; A Beever, *Rediscovering the Law of Negligence* (2007), p 3.

[41] Rodger (n 2 above) at 9.

[42] 1942 SC (HL) 78; 1943 SLT 105; [1943] AC 92.

[43] 1943 SC (HL) 3; 1944 SLT 60; [1943] AC 448.

[44] *Donoghue* at 70.

[45] *Caparo Industries* v *Dickman* [1990] 2 AC 605 per Lord Bridge at 616. For discussion of the evolution of duty of care, see D Brodie, "In defence of *Donoghue*" 1997 JR 65.

speech, discussed above, the judges in the majority in the House of Lords had lost no opportunity to underline that they were setting out the principles common to both Scotland and England. *Donoghue* has since been credited with sealing the "convergence" between the Scots and English law of negligence,[46] and the principles stated there have been accepted as authoritative not only in the English courts,[47] but in other jurisdictions where the legal system has its roots in English law – in the Commonwealth as well as Ireland.[48] That is not to say, however, that the "intellectual superstructure"[49] of the Scots law of delict more generally has become indistinguishable from that of the English law of tort, but this is the subject for different Scots law stories.

Postscript

In the end, May never had her day in court. David Stevenson died on 12 November 1932, before the case went to proof in Court of Session, and it seems that his executors settled the action with May by paying out a sum to her which was probably £100.[50] So, the case never went to trial to establish whether the facts alleged by May – indeed the very existence of the snail – could be proved.[51] However, the following is known of the fate of the main protagonists in this story.

What of our heroine? At the time of her ill-starred visit to the Wellmeadow Café, May Donoghue had just turned 30 years of age. Born May McAllister on 4 July 1898 in Cambuslang in Glasgow, she was one of a large family of a steelworker. She left school before her 13th birthday,[52] and by the age of 17 she was married to Henry Donoghue, also a steelworker, by whom she was already expecting a child. The child, a son, also Henry, survived, but three subsequent children were all born premature and died in infancy. The marriage to Donoghue

---

[46] H MacQueen and W D H Sellar, "Negligence" in K G C Reid and R Zimmermann (eds), *A History of Private Law in Scotland* (2000), vol 2, 517 at 546–547.

[47] See Heuston (n 39 above) at 5–6.

[48] For an overview of the impact of *Donoghue* v *Stevenson* "Into the Common Law World", see M Chapman, *The Snail and the Ginger Beer: The Singular Case of Donoghue v Stevenson* (2009), Ch 7.

[49] MacQueen and Sellar (n 46 above) at 547.

[50] On the differing theories as to the amount actually paid, see M Chapman, *The Snail and the Ginger Beer: The Singular Case of Donoghue v Stevenson* (2009), 173.

[51] Accounts of the case going to trial and the existence of the snail being disproved have been shown to be unfounded: see, eg, McBryde (n 5 above), p 54.

[52] McBryde (n 5 above), p 35.

was not successful and the couple split up in 1928, so that, by August, May was living with her brother John in the east end of Glasgow. By the time of the court case, she and her son Henry had moved on once more to another address in the city centre. May eventually divorced her husband in 1945, but never remarried. Her son Henry was twice married and the second marriage produced grandchildren for May. The only available photograph of her pictures a proud grandmother, smiling as she holds her twin granddaughters on their Christening day in 1952.[53] May died of a heart attack aged 59 on 19 March 1958 in Gartloch Hospital in Glasgow.[54] It seems that her estate amounted to £364 18s 8d, in which the main asset was her savings bank account[55] – hardly a large estate, but she was certainly no longer the "pauper" that she had been in 1931.

The Stevenson family business had been providing "aerated waters" to the citizens of Paisley since the mid-19th century. The David Stevenson sued by May had taken the business over from his father, also David Stevenson. The family business was continued after the death of David Stevenson the younger, and it became a limited company in 1950. The family sold on in 1956 and eventually the business came under the control of Ind Coope (Scotland) Ltd, later joining with Allied Lyons plc, which more recently was taken over by Pernod Ricard. The premises in Paisley were, however, demolished in the 1960s.[56]

One intriguing issue that will now never be resolved was whether the snail, assuming it *did* exist, in fact drowned in Stevenson's ginger beer or that of another unidentified manufacturer. The practice in the drinks trade at the time was that manufacturers used their own marked bottles, for which they charged customers a small deposit. The bottles were returned to retailers after use and thence to the manufacturers to be cleaned and refilled. Unscrupulous traders, however, were in the practice of using the bottles of other manufacturers and filling it with

---

[53] Reproduced on the SCLR website described in n 1 above, at http://www. scottishlawreports.org.uk/resources/dvs/most-famous-litigant.html.

[54] Although Gartloch was primarily a mental hospital, it also housed a medical unit (see NHS Greater Glasgow and Clyde Archives at http://www.archives.gla. ac.uk/gghb/collects/hb1.html), and it is therefore possible that she was being treated there for a medical rather than a psychiatric condition.

[55] Rodger (n 2 above) at p 9.

[56] Information on the Stevensons' business taken from McBryde (n 5 above), pp 26–30.

their own brew.[57] The circumstance that Stevenson's name appeared on the offending bottle was not therefore conclusive evidence that the snail had come from his premises, as his counsel would no doubt have been at pains to argue had the case in the end gone to trial.

Francis Minghella, the café proprietor, had taken over the café a few years previously, and had come from a line of confectioners of Italian origins. After the famous court case, he soon gave up the business altogether in favour of a job as a labourer in the Paisley Burgh Roads Department. The building housing the Wellmeadow Café was taken over by the local authority and demolished in 1959.[58] Minghella family honour was vindicated at the closing ceremony of the 1990 Pilgrimage to Paisley described in the first paragraph of this story. Young Allan Minghella, the great-grandson of Francis Minghella, served ginger beer to the host of legal dignitaries visiting Paisley on that day. None discovered an unpleasant surprise in the bottom of the glass.

Perhaps the last word should go to the villain of the piece, however: the snail. (Rumours that the creature might in the end have been English have never been substantiated.[59]) Although only one grainy photograph remains to us of May Donoghue, artistic likenesses of the meandering mollusc, its shell glossily intact, have been preserved for posterity on the covers of student textbooks the world over. Few other images have ever exercised such a hold over the collective imagination of the legal publishing world.

---

[57] On the property law problems caused by such bottle swapping (another Scots law story), see *Leitch & Co* v *Leydon* 1931 SC (HL) 1.

[58] Information on Wellmeadow Café and the Minghella family taken from McBryde (note 5 above), pp 30–33.

[59] See T B Smith, *British Justice: The Scottish Contribution* (1961), p 52, citing a speech made by Lord Walker to the American Bar Association in 1960.

Chapter 6

LAWYERS, WHO NEEDS THEM?
Sheridan v *News International*

Alistair Bonnington

For many years, lawyers have regarded London as the libel capital of the world. England's old-fashioned libel laws have attracted Hollywood celebrities to the Royal Courts of Justice in the Strand. They come, allegedly, to restore their besmirched reputations. But some cynics believe it is rather to win the substantial damages which more modern defamation systems would deny them – all while achieving lots of no-cost publicity for the stars.

Scotland has never managed to rival England in this area, despite its libel regime being just as Jurassic as the one south of Hadrian's Wall. So it was something of a shock for English libel lawyers to have to admit in 2006 that the most celebrated case of that year had been fought in the Court of Session in Edinburgh between the Scottish Socialist Party leader Tommy Sheridan and the Rupert Murdoch-owned Sunday tabloid newspaper the *News of the World*.

To be able to understand this case, a short tutorial on the *dramatis personae* must precede the account of the trial itself. The pursuer (plaintiff) Tommy Sheridan was the young firebrand far-left politician who had been expelled from the Labour Party for being part of the neo-Communist Militant Tendency faction. He founded the Scottish Socialist Alliance in 1996, which became the Scottish Socialist Party 2 years later, and was elected under that banner to the Scottish Parliament in 1999. A charismatic orator, Sheridan had led protests against Margaret Thatcher's Government's hated community charge, or poll tax as it was commonly called, when it was introduced into Scotland in 1989. He also campaigned against Scotland's arguably out-of-date laws on the recovery of debt, which allowed the creditor to seize and sell most of the debtor's household goods. Such is his strength of feelings for the causes he supports that he went to prison three times, once for attending a warrant sale when ordered not to do so and twice for protesting at the Faslane Naval Base.

Whatever else the Scots look for in a politician, they assuredly look for passion and genuine belief. These Sheridan held in abundance, and so was an acceptable public figure to many Scots who held political views miles away from Sheridan's far-left beliefs. He was also a very good-looking young man and achieved the kind of sex-symbol status with the ladies which rather eludes most of us. His picture was pinned onto many a female journalist's computer screen. He foreswore alcohol and tobacco and claimed his only extravagance was his penchant for sun-bed parlours which he visited regularly, resulting in a fake tan. Prior to his marriage, he was never short of female company.

The *News of the World* is a very popular Sunday tabloid. Many of its stories centre on celebrities. It has a particular speciality in prurient tales. This has led to its nickname "News of the Screws". Its politics are right wing, like most of the Murdoch media outlets. So, Sheridan would be this newspaper's natural enemy. Perhaps his success as a politician irked the editorial staff.

In any event, in late 2004 and early 2005, the *News of the World* ran articles claiming that Sheridan, after his marriage to glamorous British Airways hostess Gail, had carried on an illicit affair with a "former" prostitute. As is often the case, the tabloid had paid the prostitute and other witnesses substantial sums for their stories. Inevitably, this hugely increases the chances that a court will disbelieve the evidence of such witnesses, something tabloid journalists seem to have the greatest difficulty comprehending.

There was immediate political fallout within Sheridan's party, the SSP. Sheridan was removed from the leadership of the party in November 2004 "due to allegations about his private life". What had occurred at the meeting which took this decision was to become crucial in the subsequent court proceedings. A motion to destroy the minute of that meeting was proposed by the SSP Cardonald branch – in effect, Sheridan himself. The *News of the World* was later to claim in court that this motion was drafted because Sheridan had admitted to his fellow SSP members at the meeting that the newspaper's allegations were true, and he did not want the record of that admission to feature in the court case.

The trial begins

So it was that Tommy Sheridan sued News International, the owners of the *News of the World*, for defamation. The trial before Lord Turnbull and a jury of 12 people opened in the Court of Session in Parliament Hall, Edinburgh, on 4 July 2006. Civil jury trials are very rare in Scotland: there are usually no more than 10 in one year, all other civil business being conducted by a judge sitting alone. Even if a jury trial is a possibility according to the procedural rules, the defender can usually avoid a jury by putting in a preliminary plea. This means that the fact-finding exercise takes the form of a "proof before answer" which can only be conducted by a judge sitting alone.

In the *News of the World* case, there was no legal point on which the newspaper could base a preliminary plea. It had no option but to peril its whole defence on the basis that what it had printed about Sheridan was true or substantially true (see the Defamation Act 1996); in short, a *veritas* defence, in England called "justification". Because a preliminary plea was not an option open to the defence, it fell to the pursuer, Tommy Sheridan, to decide if the fact-finding would take the form of a proof (before a judge alone) or a jury trial. He opted for the latter.

It is worth noting here that the presiding judge, Lord Turnbull, had just recently been appointed to the Court of Session Bench. He had had a tremendously successful career as an Advocate Depute, prosecuting many difficult high-profile cases for the Crown. Whether he rejoiced at his nickname "The Prince of Darkness", I cannot say; but that was assuredly his *nom de guerre* in criminal matters. He was one of the key prosecutors in the Lockerbie Trial at Kamp van Zeist in Holland. So his recent experience was as an expert criminal counsel. It is likely that he had done little, if any, civil work for some years. Tribute must be paid to him for his handling of this case. Although I take issue with a couple of his directions on the law of libel, he kept the case progressing along the right procedural lines, an especially hard task in the particular circumstances of this trial, for reasons we will soon examine.

At the opening of the *Sheridan* v *News International* trial, the two leading counsel in Scotland sat at opposite sides of the table; for Sheridan, Richard Keen QC; and for the newspaper, Mike Jones QC. Both are devastating examiners of witnesses, a key skill in a case of this sort where credibility is the key to winning or losing.

Because of the "reverse onus" in libel cases where *veritas* is the defence, it fell to the newspaper to lead by calling its evidence first.

So, the jury were to be treated to: (a) a procession of prostitutes (some claiming to be "retired"!), (b) SSP members, all of whom seemed to be strongly pro- or anti-Sheridan for political reasons – this group included the three women SSP members dubbed by the tabloids "The Three Witches"; and (c) Tommy Sheridan's female acquaintances, all of whom seemed to claim to have had sexual congress with him.

Immediately, any experienced lawyer will see the problem for the newspaper: most of these witnesses were likely to be treated by the jury as being of low credibility, either because they were generally thought to be dishonest (for example, prostitutes) or had a degree of bias and self-interest in the outcome. To exacerbate these problems, the newspaper had followed what in the UK is quite normal practice for a tabloid covering a sex scandal: it had paid the witnesses for their stories. So here was another weakness: many witnesses had a financial stake in giving lurid testimony about Sheridan's private life. Although tabloid newspapers seem to fail to understand why, the record of tabloids defending this kind of tale in the UK courts is one of juries regularly finding against tabloids. Juries find their methods reprehensible. They also, I think, find tabloid journalists in the witness box to be less than dependable. The kind of person who is employed as a tabloid journalist is generally unlikely to be an individual in whom anyone of judgement would place any trust.

So the battle commenced. Mike Jones called witness after witness to say either that they had had sex with Tommy Sheridan after his marriage or that they had seen Tommy Sheridan having sex after his marriage. The *News of the World* had alleged that Tommy Sheridan had had a 4-year affair with Fiona McGuire, an SSP activist and former prostitute. The newspaper had also claimed that Sheridan visited a sex club, had taken drugs and indulged in sexual activity with various women after his marriage. To prove its *veritas* defence to Sheridan's summons, it would be necessary for the newspaper to call witnesses who supported these allegations. Most important of all, the jury would have to find these witnesses to be credible and reliable before a verdict in favour of the *News of the World* could be the final outcome of these proceedings.

The newspaper's witnesses were a motley crew – an array of females who were either prostitutes or at best incredibly promiscuous was supplemented by embittered SSP rivals of Sheridan. Then there were the *News of the World* journalists – not a group likely to be viewed as truthful by any jury exercising reasonable common sense.

One of the important passages of evidence came in the early days when a witness for the newspaper, Ann Colvin, was recounting her tale of being invited to a party at the Moat House Hotel in Glasgow in June 2002. She claimed that she went to the hotel with two female friends and was met there by a Matt McColl. Mr McColl took the three of them to a suite in the hotel. When they entered the room, Ms Colvin claimed she saw Tommy Sheridan on a bed with a woman and a 6-foot-4 black man. All three were engaged with each other in sexual intercourse. This story is plainly astonishing and, had the jury believed it, the newspaper would have achieved a large part of its task of proof. But there were a number of problems with the tale. First, Mr McColl did not back up what Ann Colvin said. Secondly, the corroboration the newspaper had hoped to find for Ms Colvin's evidence (of Sheridan's unfaithfulness to his wife) in the evidence of one of their columnists, Anvar Khan, fell apart when Khan admitted that her story in the newspaper, to the effect that she had had an affair with a married MSP, was partly fabrication.

Sheridan dismisses his lawyers

It was during the cross-examination of the two women that high drama unfolded in court. Richard Keen, Sheridan's senior counsel, had a commitment to a House of Lords case and so, following normal practice, left his junior to conduct the Edinburgh trial. For some reason, the junior got his facts confused and put to Ms Colvin that she had a criminal conviction for fraud. This was quite wrong. Sheridan was furious at this error and responded by dismissing his entire legal team, advocates and solicitors, despite being counselled against this move by Lord Turnbull. So, from now on, it was to be Sheridan alone against one of the most able and combative counsel in Scotland. How could anything other than Sheridan's humiliation follow?

The dismissal of the lawyers happened on 14 July and the trial was to run until 3 August. During this time, Sheridan was assisted in the presentation of his case by John Aberdein, an SSP member to whom Sheridan paid tribute after the trial concluded. But the burden of standing up and cross-examining the newspaper's witnesses had to fall on Sheridan himself. Sheridan is a highly intelligent man, who also has a most courteous manner; staff members in the Scottish Parliament were very fond of him because of his courtesy and his lack of "airs and graces". Doubtless, these attributes played their part in facilitating Sheridan's able conduct of his case and in his ability to win over the jury.

Another major asset for the pursuer was his wife Gail, who turned up every day with her husband. The pictures of the two of them walking into Parliament House hand in hand became almost a stock front-page picture for the Scottish press. When she gave evidence, Gail made it clear that, if she thought that Tommy was cheating on her, she would be off out of the marriage and Tommy would be having a very hard time from her. Gail Sheridan is a fairly formidable (and glamorous) lady. The jury probably set great store by what she said. She claimed to have checked up from her diaries as to where she and her husband had been on the dates referred to in the *News of the World* articles. She stated that, from these diaries, she had discovered that it was impossible that the newspaper claims were true. She said that, like any wife, she was not naive and she wanted to check up on her husband in this way, rather than just accept his word.

A crucial passage of the newspaper's evidence came when it tried to prove that Sheridan had admitted his infidelity and also visited a sex club called Cupids, in Manchester, at an SSP meeting on 9 November 2004. We recall here that the minute of this SSP meeting had itself been the subject of ancillary proceedings in the Court of Session and that the SSP Secretary had gone to jail rather than hand over the minute to the court. Coupled with the move, which appeared to come from Sheridan, to have that minute suppressed, there was understandable interest in the jury hearing all about the meeting of 9 November. A number of attendees of that meeting stated clearly that Sheridan had admitted to everyone there that he had gone to Cupids in 1999 and 2002. The problem for the newspaper was that these witnesses were obviously Tommy Sheridan's opponents within the SSP and were, putting it bluntly, "out to get him" politically. So, their evidence might well be viewed as tainted by the jury. Steven Arnott of the SSP, called as a witness, stated that was precisely what was happening here: Sheridan's political enemies were "getting him" with no regard for the truth. Mr Arnott said that, on 24 November when he attended the next SSP meeting, there was no minute from 9 November in the terms now alleged.

Mike Gonzalez, a professor at Glasgow University, had also attended the SSP meeting of 24 November and supported Arnott that no minute from 9 November (in which Sheridan allegedly made admissions) was produced. Finally, an attendee on 9 November, Jock

Parma, stated that Sheridan had never made the admissions which were now being claimed by other SSP members.

Looking at all of this together, it is little wonder that the jury did not accept the evidence the newspaper put before them as proving the allegations printed "on the balance of probabilities".

One bright spot in the newspaper's evidence came with the calling of Katrine Trolle to the witness box. A Danish SSP member, she impressed many onlookers as the most credible of the *News of the World* witnesses. She said that she had had an affair with Tommy Sheridan. But when Sheridan's wife Gail gave evidence she claimed that Ms Trolle had told her that the *News of the World* had offered her money if she would say that she had had a sexual relationship with Sheridan after his marriage. Mike Jones QC recalled Ms Trolle at the end of the trial to have her deny that she had had such a conversation with Gail Sheridan.

In any defamation case, the evidence of the pursuer is crucial. Although, technically, he does not need to give evidence in a case such as this (where the onus is on the defenders), almost every pursuer will want to tell his or her story. In the final reckoning in this particular case, Mike Jones called Sheridan as a witness – which he is perfectly entitled to do – but the procedural niceties make no difference to the jury. What is vital is what the jury make of the pursuer's credibility. If they disbelieve him, then surely a verdict for the defence must follow.

Sheridan is a fine orator – a rabble-rouser, many would say. But he can also convey his thoughts and feelings in a much lower key. That is what he did in the courtroom. His courtesy never faltered. He came across as a man genuinely aggrieved by what the newspaper had printed about him. His support from his wife was plain by her evidence and her attendance at court (or else it was an Oscar-worthy performance). On this last point, Mike Jones asked Sheridan a question he probably has since regretted. "Why is your wife hanging about in the courtroom all day?", he challenged. Sheridan's devastating reply was: "My wife is a woman of considerable substance who doesn't hang about. Sometimes, unfortunately for me, she shops. Sometimes she works. Often recently she has been weeping because of the lies told in this court."

Drawing to a close

In closing speeches, predictably, Sheridan and Mr Jones asked the jury to interpret the evidence in radically different ways. Sheridan asked the jury to take the view that the *News of the World* hated him because of his left-wing political beliefs. He asked them to consider if he would be foolish enough to risk his reputation, career and family by taking part in sex orgies. In the opinion of many seasoned court reporters, this was an excellent closing speech – as good as, if not better than, what any lawyer could have done for Sheridan. It lasted just over an hour.

In reply, Mike Jones took 6 hours to go over the evidence he had brought before the jury for the newspaper. He claimed it was Sheridan's recklessness and ego which had landed him in court. Doubtless, such an able and eloquent QC will have good reason for the way in which he conducts a case; but 6 hours is a huge length of time to ask a jury for its attention.

So, by the end of the evidence, the jury had before them two quite different accounts of the life of the married Tommy Sheridan. One painted him as a serial philanderer who visited suspect "swingers" night-clubs; the other was of a man who was faithful to his wife.

Lord Turnbull's directions to the jury contained two points on which any libel lawyer would comment. First, he said that Sheridan, and indeed every citizen, was entitled only to the reputation he deserves. But that is not the law in either Scotland or England. So, too, he stated that, if the jury believed any of the 18 witnesses brought to court by the *News of the World*, then they must find against Sheridan. This is very difficult to follow. The law required that the newspaper prove that all its allegations were true or substantially true. One witness could not possibly speak to a sufficient percentage of the totality of the allegations to make the approach urged on the jury by Lord Turnbull sound in law. So, it seems that, had Sheridan lost, he would have had good grounds for appeal based on these misdirections.

But, as we all know, that was not necessary. The jury not only found in favour of Tommy Sheridan, but awarded him the full £200,000 he was claiming. Sheridan left the Court of Session hand in hand with his wife, to the cheers of the waiting crowd of supporters. Many journalists observed Lord Turnbull looking out of his window onto this scene, shaking his head sadly. It seemed pretty clear where his sympathies lay. One wonders too whether the fact that the Faculty of Advocates came out of this whole affair so badly might have been a factor in leading Lord Turnbull to be so anxious that perjury proceedings were considered by the Crown. A case which started off with the two leading QCs in Scotland had seen one of the legal teams sacked for an error made by the junior advocate and then the party litigant had won convincingly against the other senior counsel. The Faculty is nothing if not pompous and precious. So this must have been a huge blow to the enormous esteem it has for itself.

The verdict was greeted by the *News of the World* with astonishment. The Editor of the *News of the World* gave a mournful press conference at which he complained that the jury had not found any one of the 18 witnesses called by the newspaper to be credible. The newspaper appealed to the Inner House of the Court of Session a few days later, but that appeal has been shelved to await the outcome of the perjury prosecution against Tommy and Gail Sheridan.

Another Sheridan trial

At the end of the trial, Lord Turnbull said from the Bench that perjury (telling lies on oath) had clearly occurred in the trial and that it seemed to him that the prosecuting authorities should look into that aspect of the case. It seems odd, at least to this observer, that the Sheridan trial had been singled out for this comment. In such a case, at best one side is lying. The same is true of most criminal cases which go to trial in the Scottish courts. Perjury inquiries simply do not happen, even where the presiding judge expresses vehement disbelief in what was said by certain witnesses.

In England, the jailing of Jonathan Aitken, the Conservative MP, and of Jeffrey Archer, the novelist, on perjury charges showed that libel was perhaps a case apart where, for some unknown reason, the Crown would take an interest in perjury following on libel proceedings. Indeed, Oscar Wilde had gone to Reading Gaol for perjury as a result of his unsuccessful action against Lord Roseberry (Bosie's father) in the libel courts. So too, in the USA during the MacCarthy witch-hunts of the 1950s, Alger Hiss had been imprisoned not for un-American activities but for perjury. So, there is an established, if somewhat dishonourable, history for perjury proceedings in such circumstances.

In any event, Lothian and Borders Police, under instructions from the Crown, began an investigation which expended a huge amount of public money. In January 2009, Tommy and Gail Sheridan were indicted on charges of perjury arising out of their evidence at the libel trial, prompting Tommy to comment that "the streets of Lothian must be crime-free if the police can devote time to harassing a family". The criminal trial, starting in September 2010, will, no doubt, be another Scots law tale in its own right.

Conclusion

We can only speculate as to why the jury in the Sheridan defamation trial found as they did. I have already pointed out that, generally, juries place little faith in prostitutes ("retired" or not), tabloid journalists and witnesses who have been paid by newspapers to tell their story. But I wonder if this may not be one of these cases where the public, through that "mini Parliament", the jury, was telling lawyers something. Frankly, who has an interest in this whole sordid business other than the Sheridans themselves? If Gail Sheridan is happy to continue with her married life with her husband and child, why should the law interfere and tell her she is wrong to do so? Perhaps the jury thought it was none of their business to judge – and maybe they were right.

Chapter 7

ST NINIAN'S ISLE TREASURE
Lord Advocate v University of Aberdeen and Budge*

David L Carey Miller

The find in 1958 of a remarkable hoard of buried treasure by an Aberdeen University team on a Shetland summer dig led to litigation which clarified the basis of entitlement to discovered treasure in Scots law. The Court of Session opinions in the matter are the primary authority on the distinctive position of the common law of Scotland concerning finds of treasure. The story of the find and the University's claim to the splendid medieval objects discovered in the ruins of an ancient church on a beautiful island close to the Shetland mainland is already a fascinating one in its essential facts; taking account of the persons involved adds a dimension both interesting and revealing, for lawyers especially so, of a most notable figure of modern Scots law, Professor Sir Thomas Smith QC FBA FRSE (1915–88), one of two lead players in the St Ninian's Isle treasure saga. The case sheds light on this totemic individual, arguably the genius of a revival of the spirit and confidence of Scotland's legal culture and system, the critical development of which can so much be associated with his life and times.[1] The treasure dispute also illuminates the sometimes troubled relationships between the various constituent parts of the UK at a time when nationalism of the more traditional "political" variety was enjoying a rebirth.

---

* I am grateful to my wife Anne MacKenzie who, as an Edinburgh law student post-Smith but from a time in which his influence was growing, especially helped me come to a position on his role.

[1] See generally but especially K G C Reid's opening chapter in E Reid and D L Carey Miller (eds), *A Mixed Legal System in Transition: T B Smith and the Progress of Scots Law* (2005).

The find[2]

In the summer of 1955, with the consent of landowner James Budge, an Aberdeen University team began excavation in a project aimed at establishing the history of a medieval church on St Ninian's Isle, Shetland. Possibly hastened by the frequent storms which affected Shetland in the period, signs of the ruins had largely disappeared by the late 19th century. Professor of Geography Andrew C O'Dell FRSE led the University Geographical Society student team. There was no local tradition of treasure and the project's sole aim was to obtain information about the church which, probably because of its antiquity, was regarded as Shetland's mother church, but on which very little was known.[3] Relevant sources show that there was never a reformed minister and the church did not feature on the list of Shetland churches submitted to the General Assembly in 1586.[4]

The small, treeless St Ninian's Isle is connected to the mainland of Shetland by the transient feature of a slender tombola of sand of about a quarter of a mile. On a bright summer day, the white sand of the narrow connecting causeway stands out against the lapping blue Atlantic on either side, with contrasting green of mainland and isle at each end. But for much of the year this would be a wild and desolate place. Its atmosphere must have made an impression on Sir Walter Scott, who visited Shetland in 1814. Scott adopted St Ninian's Isle as the setting for a strange scene in *The Pirate* (1821) in which Ulla Troil, or Norma of Fitful Head, carries out a macabre search in the sand for the bones of her forebear Ribolt Troil.

In the project's fourth spell of summer excavating, on 4 July 1958, an unexpected find was made by Douglas Coutts, a Lerwick schoolboy who had been allowed by Professor O'Dell to join the dig. Near the nave of the church ruins, under an irregular sandstone slab, in a disintegrating larch-wood box, a hoard of treasure,

---

[2] My source in respect of the background is A Small, C Thomas and D M Wilson, *St Ninian's Isle and its Treasure*, Aberdeen University Studies Number 152, 1973, vol I; in subsequent references this work will be cited by referring to the name of the author of the particular chapter concerned in "Small *et al*". Vol II of this definitive work on the find contains drawings and photographs of the objects in the hoard and their relevant context.

[3] Alan Small in Small *et al* (n 2 above) at p 2.

[4] *Ibid.*

comprising 28 pieces of silver, was found. With the treasure pieces was a porpoise jawbone. The find turned out to be one of the most important for 20th-century Scottish archaeology.

The largest of the silver objects is a superb hanging bowl mounted on a three-armed base; there are seven smaller standard bowls, some with quite elaborate decoration. Six small objects in silver or silver-gilt, including a spoon, a pommel and two very fine chapes and 12 silver-gilt brooches make up the hoard. The collection of Pictish brooches, probably made in the late 8th century, is significant to the study of "one of the most ubiquitous antiquities of the early Christian period in Scotland".[5]

There can only be speculation as to the circumstances under which the treasure came to be assembled and buried in its box in a remote early church. Was the treasure laid down under threat of Viking attack in the 8th century? It has been suggested that the absence of coinage and the relative homogeneity of the hoard points to family ownership rather than spoils.[6] Adding to the mystery, the wood of the chest containing the treasure was larch. The larch is not found in Shetland and, indeed, the tree only came to Britain in the 18th century. If the box came from furth of Shetland, it seems likely that the treasure also did, even if as family property.

Why was a porpoise bone in the chest with this remarkable collection of 8th-century silver? It may be "that the mammal was important in the early Christian period" but "[t]he deeper meaning of the bone remains an enigma".[7] T B Smith, in an account published abroad under the pseudonym "Vulcan" not long after arguing the unsuccessful appeal, speculates with characteristic flair:

> "It has been conjectured that in an era when comparative anatomy was not closely studied the porpoise bone might have been venerated as the relic of a Pictish saint. Aeolus and the dolphin were, so to speak, brothers under their skin."[8]

---

[5] David M Wilson in Small *et al* (n 2 above) at p 81.
[6] At 146.
[7] At 123–124.
[8] "The St Ninian's Isle Treasure – A Legal Riddle of the Sands" 1964 *Acta Juridica* 187 at 188.

The University position[9]

Initial developments

The other lead player, perhaps the principal player, was Principal Sir Thomas Taylor QC (1897–1962) of the University of Aberdeen. The University's retention of the treasure – judged a matter of right and entitlement and perceived appropriate in terms of the public interest by the institution – caused the litigation which commenced in the Court of Session in September 1962. The Queen's and Lord Treasurer's Remembrancer (QLTR), in a letter of 21 October 1958 to Professor O'Dell, formally claimed the treasure for the Crown. The University Court – the executive governing body – in a minute of 11 November 1958, only some 4 months after the find, records its decision to assert a right to retain the treasure. This position was maintained consistently for some 4 years until four appellate court judges rejected all the arguments presented. Intimating that the QLTR was "claiming the articles in treasure-trove", the University Court decided that "the Principal be authorised to take such steps as he might deem necessary to ensure that the present custody of the articles be with the University". The Court minute reveals that at this early stage the treasure was "in the British Museum on exhibition", a position consistent with the Principal's statement that "the University's intention was to house the articles in the Museum at Marischal College until such time as a suitable museum was available in Shetland". But how did the treasure come to be in London at this early stage? Because of concern as to the unstable state of the treasure, it was sent, very soon after being found, to the British Museum Research Laboratory for restorative work.[10] On completion of this work, the University agreed that the treasure be exhibited at the British Museum for a period before being returned to Aberdeen. On 23 August 1958, the story of the find, with two pages of photographs of the treasure, appeared in *The Illustrated London News*.

---

[9] My source here is the range of material relevant to the St Ninian's Isle treasure held in the Special Libraries and Archives of the University of Aberdeen and in the T B Smith Papers held in the Centre for Research Collections of the University of Edinburgh. I am most grateful to reading room staff at both universities for their most helpful assistance in my quest for relevant materials.

[10] See E Meldrum, "St Ninian's Isle Treasure", part I, "Scotland's most important find of the century"; part II, "Who shall be the guardians?" *Glasgow Herald*, 22 and 23 December 1960.

Early in 1959, the treasure was back in Aberdeen and on display at a special exhibition in the Marischal Museum. The opening, attended by the Provost of Lerwick and his wife, was reported in the *Shetland News* of 3 March 1959. Both Principal Taylor and University Chancellor Thomas Johnston spoke at the opening of the exhibition. Their comments reflected frustration, if not anger, that the QLTR had a few months earlier asserted a claim to the treasure based on the public interest in its preservation. This position they clearly regarded as Edinburgh-centric bias.

University museum factor

That Principal Taylor was actively pursuing a museum custodian role is confirmed by a Court minute of 12 May 1959 acceding to a request from the Lord Lieutenant of the County of Zetland for a loan of the treasure for a Shetland exhibition to coincide with a visit of Her Majesty the Queen planned for 10 August 1959.[11]

While asserting a right to the treasure, the University was at the same time actively pursuing a negotiated settlement. A Court minute of 14 October 1959 reports that the Principal and Chancellor had held two meetings with the Secretary of State for Scotland. The record also refers to an informal agreement arrived at with the Scottish National Museum of Antiquities (SNMA) that the treasure "reside" at that museum for the greater part of the year but be displayed elsewhere in Scotland, and in Shetland, over the summer. That the University was urging the interest of Shetland emerges from the Court decision at this meeting to approve the provisional arrangements and to reaffirm the opinion "that the interests of Shetland be preserved".

In 1960, the University continued to seek a concession as to its formal entitlement in exchange for agreement that the treasure would be made available on loan to suitable museums. A Court minute of 8 March 1960 records a communication of Principal Taylor to the Chair of the Trustees of the SNMA, proposing arrangements "on the footing that the University was the lender and the Museum the borrower". The reported response was that the Trustees had no authority to make any arrangements "except upon the footing that the Crown was the owner". On 13 December 1960, the Court decided to authorise the

---

[11] A University Court minute of 14 October 1959 reported that the treasure was exhibited in Shetland in August notwithstanding cancellation of the Queen's visit.

Principal to indicate that an acknowledgement of Crown ownership
was unacceptable "and that the University would stand on its rights".

The significance of Marischal Museum would have been a factor in
Principal Taylor's museum role thinking. Founded in 1786, by the mid-
1950s the Museum's collection, at least in certain areas, was among
the most important in Scotland. A Marischal Museum role also comes
across in a foreword by the University Chancellor, the Rt Hon Thomas
Johnston, to an expensively produced 1960 Aberdeen University Press
book of photographs and drawings, apparently produced to publicise
the treasure.[12] The Chancellor wrote:

> "They were brought to light in 1958 by an archaeological expedition led
> by Professor A C O'Dell, our Professor of Geography; and the resolution
> of the University and generosity of the owner of the ground, Mr
> James Budge, having obtained for the people of the North of Scotland
> the opportunity of seeing in the Museum of Marischal College these
> magnificent relics from what we commonly regard as the Dark Ages."[13]

Supporting opinion

The University's uncompromising stance, in terms of the legal position,
may be explained by the fact that early in 1960 counsel's opinion
fortified the position which Principal Taylor and Professor Smith had
almost certainly already adopted. As they saw it, the Crown's right to
treasure trove derived from the sovereign's position as the ultimate
superior in the feudal tenure context; on this basis, it did not apply in
Shetland where udal tenure, giving an absolute right of ownership,
prevailed. The Principal advised the University Court on 9 February
1960 that "he had now received the Opinion of Counsel on the legal
position in relation to these articles, the gist of the opinion being that
the Crown had no right to them".

The memorial briefing counsel in 1959 emphasised the udal factor
which it took to rule out Crown entitlement, leaving the landowner
and the finder as the only potential claimants. Counsel's opinion
endorsed this position as an "attractive" and "powerful" argument
which could be "strongly supported". The opinion does not identify,
even if only to reject, any coherent alternative argument; certainly

---

[12] A University Court minute of 15 August 1960 approved publication of 1,000
copies and a contribution of £200 from general funds.
[13] A C O'Dell, *St Ninian's Isle Treasure*, Aberdeen University Studies Number 141
(1960) 3.

nothing capable of undermining the preoccupying udal factor premise and consequent assumption that, because Crown entitlement to treasure trove derived from feudal overlordship, it could not apply where udal tenure prevailed.

Counsel's opinion explains certain aspects of the University's position and strategy. On the basis of the possibility that the Crown be subject to the onus of proving that the objects meet a narrow definition of treasure – *a là* English common law – the opinion advised that "in any correspondence it would be advisable to avoid the use of the word treasure". This accounts for the colourless word "articles" appearing in the many relevant University Court minutes. The opinion urged the importance of an alliance with landowner James Budge. The thinking here was that the University faced competition for legal ownership more with Budge than the Crown. Finally, the opinion drew attention to something which became prominent in the University's public promotion of its quest to retain the treasure. The ultimate point noted that "the preservation of objects of antiquarian value for the public interest" is prominent in the Crown's claim. But, the opinion asked, does not the University have available "adequate facilities and resources, alone or in conjunction with others to achieve this end?". This was preaching to the converted in so far as, from the start, the University, with some justification, saw itself in a national museum role.

Campaign for public support

The University's concern to provide a benefit to Shetland from the St Ninian's treasure took tangible form some 3 years after the find. Three sets of replicas of certain of the objects had been made, at a cost of £300 to the University. On 16 June 1961, in Lerwick, Principal Taylor presented a set to the people of Shetland. A copy of his speech in the Aberdeen University Special Collections tells much of the University's perception of its role. Saying first that, had there been facilities in Shetland "to look after such fragile and precious things", he would be handing over the objects themselves rather than replicas, the Principal went on to say that

> "the University of Aberdeen which discovered these things has never asserted a right of exclusive ownership in them. All along we have taken the position that we hold them as depositaries and trustees and that, subject to the rights of Mr Budge the proprietor of the land on which they were discovered, we would hand them back to you, the people

of Shetland, whenever a suitable museum was provided to receive them".

Going on to say that the University held the treasure (not, however, using that word) "against all comers" but not in any "dog in the manger attitude" rather "continuously on public exhibition in our museum at Marischal College ... and on proper safeguards for exhibition in any of the museums in Scotland".

Moving on to the legal position, Taylor stated that the University's advice was that the Crown claim could succeed only if it could establish itself to be "the feudal superior of Shetland". Establishing this, the Principal went on to suggest, would undermine the structure of much of Shetland's private law and private rights; for this reason "in our interests and in yours" the University would resist the claim with "all our resources".

Questions in the House

On 27 June 1961, Mr Hector Hughes, MP for Aberdeen North, addressed questions in the House to the Chancellor of the Exchequer, Sir Edward Boyle, presumably on the basis of his ultimate responsibility for Crown property. The MP's questioning could hardly have been heavier in portraying the State as the villain of the piece. Sir Edward said that he was advised that, according to the law of Scotland, the objects belonged to the Crown. Hughes pressed him with the statement that the position of the Principal of the University of Aberdeen was that the Chancellor of the Exchequer and the Secretary of State for Scotland "without any legal right and in opposition to the relevant law and court decisions of long standing and authority, wrongly persist in claiming this treasure from Aberdeen University, which is its depository and trustee" and went on to ask whether steps would now be taken "to abandon these wrong, improper, unjust and dishonest claims?". Sir Edward, observing that he found it "venturesome" to discuss "even English law", declined "to indulge in a discussion of the Scottish law, not even with the encouragement of the Principal of Aberdeen University".[14] It would be speculative to contend that this powerful denouncement of the Crown claim mirrored Principal Taylor's position. However, an Aberdeen law student at the time, my colleague Emeritus Professor of Public Law Frank Lyall, has told me

[14] See *Hansard*, vol 643, no 135, Oral Answers, 27 June 1961.

that the Principal's serious concern as to the rights of the matter was very much evident.

Characterising the dispute

In a certain sense the St Ninian's Isle treasure dispute was an "in-house" difference. The University of Aberdeen, an ancient and reputable Scottish institution, wanted to retain legal control of the treasure and exercise a museum role via its Marischal Museum. The Crown was politely but firmly insisting that title and control had to be with it. A letter of 8 March 1961 to the University from the Secretary of State for Scotland reflects a firm but tolerant attitude to the University's intransigence. Submitted to the University Court on 14 March 1961, the letter started with an expression of regret that it had not been possible to arrive at arrangements generally acceptable. The letter went on to say that, while noting that the University's legal advice was that the Crown's claim was ill founded, both the writer and the Chancellor of the Exchequer were advised that the claim was sound. The Secretary of State for Scotland was willing to have another meeting; if, however, the University maintained its present position "the Crown would have no alternative but to obtain a judicial ruling on the ownership of the objects". The recorded Court decision simply remitted to the Principal to inform the Secretary of State for Scotland "that the University Court maintained its present position".

T B Smith, in his Hamlyn Lectures delivered in 1961 and published the following year, refers to the treasure "held in trust by Aberdeen University in berserker defiance of feudal claims" this being "a timely reminder of the Norse tradition in Scottish affairs". A footnote to "berserker defiance" states that the treasure is held by "Principal, Sir T M Taylor". *Chambers Dictionary* refers to the adjective "berserker" as rare, meaning "violent, frenzied or angry", with the noun "a Norse warrior who on the battlefield was filled with a frenzied and irresistible fury". Smith's allusion to the Norse factor in the St Ninian's treasure case can be understood, but the use of the word "berserker" has images which seem rather extreme. The metaphor may reflect T B Smith's tendency to colour if not embellishment but, that said, the Principal's statements do show a certain exasperation.

There can hardly be any doubt that fellow-lawyers University Principal Taylor and his vigorous appointee Professor T B Smith masterminded the decision that the University should reject the claim of the QLTR and assert a right to possession of the treasure. Having accepted appointment to the Edinburgh University Civil Law Chair in 1958, T B Smith moved from Aberdeen, but this would not have affected necessary contact.

The primary defence – that the Crown's normal entitlement did not apply because the udal land tenure dispensation of Shetland did not support it – was very likely a point immediately seen by both Taylor and Smith. The Professor of Conveyancing, Farquhar MacRitchie, would have agreed. The distinctive udal character of Shetland land tenure would have been trite to him.[15] It would be entirely predictable that his view would also be that the *quod nullius* principle vesting title to unowned goods in the Crown was another offshoot of feudal overlordship and so did not apply in Shetland.[16] That this represented an entirely plausible position suggests that these three lawyers would not have considered the University's retention of the treasure to be, in any sense, a flaunting of the law. As it turned out, Lord Hunter accorded serious consideration to this point; early in his opinion, the learned judge observed that "[t]he fact that the objects were found on udal land has been the cause of much legal research and has given rise to a number of intriguing and by no means easy legal questions".[17]

The litigation

Introductory remarks

The litigation involved two stages. After an initial hearing in the Outer House of the Court of Session, the Lord Ordinary (Lord Hunter) decided, on 10 September 1962, in favour of the Crown. Following a reclaiming motion heard over 25–28 June 1963, the Second Division of the Inner House of the Court of Session, on 2 August 1963, issued opinions rejecting the appeal. The court comprised Second Division judges Lords Patrick, Mackintosh and Strachan and Lord Guthrie of the First Division. Lord Guthrie sat instead of the Lord Justice-

---

[15] It is mentioned in the context of salmon fishings in Farquhar MacRitchie's fourth edition of Burns's *Conveyancing Practice* (1957) at p 337.

[16] The critical first part of this proposition is supported by Rankine's much respected *Law of Land-Ownership in Scotland* (4th edn, 1909) at p 249 where the Crown's right to treasure is seen as "very analogous to its caduciary right of inheritance as *ultimus haeres*". Lord Hunter did not see this as necessarily meaning that the right emanated from the feudal regime rather than royal prerogative: see 1963 SC 533 at 544.

[17] 1963 SC 533 at 538.

Clerk, Lord Grant, who in his former role as Lord Advocate had raised the action. The opinions in respect of both hearings are reported together.

Proceedings commenced when the Lord Advocate (William Grant) brought action for declarator that the treasure belonged to the Crown and for its delivery by the University. The basis of the claim was the *quod nullius* principle in terms of which the Crown was residual owner of all unowned moveable things which had been previously owned. The defenders, the University and landowner Budge, formally denied the claim in their pleadings and put the Crown to proof of entitlement. The essential facts were not in dispute. The udal factor was only raised at the debate stage. The Solicitor General, D C Anderson QC, appearing for the Crown with J P H Mackay – a future Lord Chancellor – as his junior, intervened early in the defenders' opening speech to concede that the treasure had been found on land subject to udal rather than feudal tenure.

The University and landowner presented a common case, with the Dean of Faculty, W I R Fraser QC, leading Kemp Davidson for the University, and T B Smith QC appearing for Budge, also with Kemp Davidson as his junior.

Case before the Lord Ordinary

The defence arguments before the Lord Ordinary involved a denial of the pursuer's claim to the treasure and a consequent assertion of entitlement; only in the reclaiming motion, after amendment of the pleadings, was a positive claim urged. This was based on the first defender's finding of the treasure on the second defender's Shetland land.

The main negative argument, consideration of which occupies the greater part of the opinion of Lord Hunter, was, of course, denial that the normal position of a find of apparently unowned things applied because its feudal tenure basis did not apply in the udal tenure context of Shetland. A second leg of this argument was that, as udal owner, the second defender had absolute *dominium* over his land and was accordingly entitled to anything and everything on it; more obviously so, anything buried in the land. The defenders' positive claim, only argued in the appeal stage, was that the finder and the landowner were entitled, with the Crown, to equal shares on the basis of a 13th-century Norwegian code; a second leg of this argument was that, as a matter of constitutional and international law, prerogative Crown rights did not apply to conquered or annexed territory until relevant domestic laws had been replaced.

All the defenders' arguments, in one way or another, derived from the historical position of Shetland as former Norwegian territory. Lord Hunter considered very fully the facts and implications of this history. Prior to 1468, the Shetlands and Orkney were part of Norway and naturally subject to the law of that state. In 1468 and 1469, King Christian I of Norway made over the sovereignty of the islands and their associated Crown property in security for a debt due to the Scottish Crown. The debt arose from the dowry of Princess Margaret of Norway in respect of her marriage to James III of Scotland. The pledge of the islands was never redeemed. The jurist Thomas Craig, writing almost a century later, presented the view that the right of redemption was renounced.[18]

Decision on udal issue

Turning to Lord Hunter's opinion, the learned judge recognised that, in so far as Shetland and Orkney became part of Scotland, they were subject to her law and legal system. At the same time, however, there was not any general replacement or revision of the law which applied before the change and, in consequence, it was accepted that residual elements remain extant. As to ascertaining what aspects of the law might be distinctive in the circumstances of this history, Lord Hunter suggested the following approach, being a development of a 19th-century *dictum* emphasising an essential position of difference unless departed from.[19]

> "As a practical matter, it is probably more accurate to say that the ordinary statute and municipal law of Scotland operates, except in so far as there is some speciality still extant in Orkney and Shetland which modifies it. But whatever may be the point of view from which one approaches the question, the important point is to discover what are the survivals."[20]

In any event, it was accepted that a udal land tenure regime applies as a surviving aspect of the distinct legal system of Shetland. Moreover, it was equally recognised that this form of tenure is fundamentally different from the feudal form which prevailed, albeit in increasingly diluted form, until its final abolition by legislation which came into

[18] *Jus Feudale* (1655) 1.15.14.
[19] *Bruce* v *Smith* (1890) 17 R 1000 at 1014.
[20] 1963 SC 533 at 538.

effect in 2004.[21] Under udal tenure, title is absolute in the sense of not being subject to the ultimate right of a feudal superior. While the tenure issue was not in dispute, the critical question was whether the basis of entitlement to treasure was the Crown's position as ultimate feudal overlord or, rather, a matter of royal prerogative unconnected with land tenure. Rights vesting in the Crown are either *regalia majora* or *regalia minora*; the former, held in trust for the people and inalienable, include rights to the sea, the foreshore and navigable rivers; the latter is a miscellaneous category of alienable rights, including the Crown's right to all unowned but formerly owned things. It was not in dispute that the right to treasure fell under *regalia minora* and could be disposed of by the Crown.

The institutional authorities of Scots law are not clear on the question whether the *regalia* rights concerned exist as matters of general sovereignty or as rights pertaining in consequence of the monarch's residual position in the feudal tenure structure. Lord Hunter considered that the authorities did not support the notion of a feudal system conceived of in terms of a distinction between the sovereign as ruler and as landowner. Even though "[t]he distinction was probably not clearly perceived even by Stair":

> "the great weight of the authority of Stair favours the view that although treasures found in the ground are *inter regalia*, in the sense of things which the law appropriates to princes and states, and exempts from private use, the right to treasure is a right belonging to the sovereign by virtue of his royal prerogative and as head of the national community rather than by virtue of his position as universal landlord".[22]

Lord Hunter considered it significant that neither institutional writer Stair nor Erskine treated treasure as a right pertaining to land, with Stair stating that even in the case of a barony title the right is not carried by implication; while Erskine classifies treasure as a *res publicae* rather than a land-related *regalia* right.

While the conclusion that the right to treasure was a matter of royal prerogative put paid to the defenders' primary argument, their contention remained that the absolute ownership of udal tenure meant that buried things vested in the landowner. By analogy, it was argued, the situation of a feudal right to the foreshore precluded Crown rights

---

[21] Abolition of Feudal Tenure etc (Scotland) Act 2000.
[22] 1963 SC 533 at 543.

under the common law.[23] But an obvious difficulty with that was that
concealed moveable treasure could hardly be seen as subject to the
right of a landowner by analogy to rights directly associated with
landownership such as otherwise unowned fish or game; moreover,
separate moveable things did not accede to the land by reason of being
concealed in the land rather than merely present on it. Lord Hunter
accordingly rejected this supplementary argument:

> "The idea that plenary ownership of land carries with it everything *a
> caelo usque ad centrum*, including even all moveable articles in or on the
> land, is, in my opinion, fallacious, and was certainly not supported by
> any convincing authority."[24]

Definition of "treasure"

Having rejected the defence submissions in support of its argument
that the Crown was not entitled, on the usual basis, in the circumstances of the location of the find, Lord Hunter proceeded to consider
the prerequisites of treasure. In the Scottish context, it may be
noted, this issue is, in a certain sense, a superfluous consideration.
All apparently unowned but previously owned property vests in the
Crown as *bona vacantia*. On this, Lord Hunter[25] quoted with approval
Bell's[26] statement of that rule:

> "Things already appropriated, but lost, forgotten, or abandoned, fall
> under a different rule from that which regulates things which have never
> been appropriated. The rule is, '*Quod nullius est fit domini Regis*'."

As a practical matter, in terms of the position of the finder, treasure
is indistinguishable from any other property in that, in principle,
anything taken into possession by a finder must be delivered to the
civic authority as Crown property. This position is provided for in
legislation concerned with lost property.[27]

Nonetheless, there is an important and obvious distinction between
treasure and lost property. What might be treasure on the basis of the
circumstances of the find could be a case of lost property if it were

---

[23] *Smith* v *Lerwick Harbour Trs* (1903) 5 F 680; see also *Lord Advocate* v *Balfour* 1907
SC 1360.
[24] 1963 SC 533 at 550.
[25] At 549.
[26] *Principles*, s 1291(3).
[27] Civic Government (Scotland) Act 1982.

apparent that what was found had an owner. The importance of distinguishing treasure from other property is in the procedure applied to deal with the find. While the relevant law relating to finds of treasure has not changed, the practice under which the law operates has been subject to development. The long-prevailing former position[28] remains essentially in place, but has been recently revised with particular emphasis on the role of the public in reporting finds.[29]

Lord Hunter's opinion is important as a legal authority on fundamental matters relating to treasure. As a matter of definition:

> "In order to qualify as treasure, articles must be precious; they must be hidden in the ground; and there must be no proof of their property or reasonable presumption of their former ownership."[30]

While Lord Hunter took the view that the precious aspect was not in issue and that there was no reasonable presumption of former ownership, he considered that the hidden aspect, relevant to treasure rather than mere *bona vacantia*, was not satisfied. But, of course, the issue of treasure was academic in the sense that a decision in favour of the pursuer was justified on the basis of the find as *bona vacantia* in any event vesting in the Crown.

While of no relevance to the St Ninian's treasure case, it may be noted that on the definition of "treasure" the common law of England and of Scotland are quite different. In Scotland, there is no limit on what might be classified as "treasure", nor does any minimum value apply. In England, a specific but narrow common law definition of "treasure" meant that the popular notion of "finders keepers" not infrequently prevailed. This was a factor behind legislative reform[31] which moved the law appreciably closer to that applicable in Scotland. It might be said that English law has come to reflect the long-standing policy position of Scots law that finds of treasure should vest in the Crown for the benefit of the nation.

University response to decision

A special meeting of the University Court was held on 26 September 1962. The Principal having died on 19 July, before the Lord Ordinary's

---

[28] See D L Carey Miller and A Sheridan, "Treasure Trove in Scots Law" (1996) 1 Art, Antiquity and Law 393.

[29] See www.treasuretrovescotland.co.uk/html/finders.asp.

[30] 1963 SC 533 at 548.

[31] Treasure Act 1996.

decision was handed down, the meeting was chaired by Sir William
Scott Brown, a graduate retired from the Indian Civil Service who sat
on the Court as Rector's Assessor. It was intimated to the meeting that,
on 10 September 1962, the Lord Ordinary gave judgment against the
defenders, ordaining the University to deliver the treasure to the Lord
Advocate and reserving the question of expenses.

It was decided by the Court that Vice-Principal Professor Wright
(acting Principal and subsequently Principal), Mr Maurice Cramb (an
Aberdeen law graduate and practising solicitor elected in 1960 to serve
as an Assessor on the University Court) and Dr Butchart (another
University law graduate, H J Butchart, University Secretary 1919–52,
continued to serve as University law agent after retiring as Secretary)
should meet with Mr James Budge and his law agent Mr Tait, to discuss
the matter. It was also decided that, provided timeous agreement was
reached with Mr Budge, junior counsel C K Davidson would be asked
to attend another special meeting of the Court on 5 October to discuss
a possible appeal.

That special meeting, chaired by Vice-Principal Wright, was attended
by C K Davidson; also present were H M Braine (of the University's
Edinburgh solicitors Gordon, Falconer and Fairweather WS), Professor
of Conveyancing Farquhar MacRitchie and Dr Butchart. Mr Cramb
submitted a report on the meeting with James Budge in which
agreement had been reached on a price to be paid by the University for
Budge's share in the treasure if he was found to be entitled. A joint note
by counsel was also submitted. After discussion, it was noted that in an
appeal to the Inner House it would be necessary to establish a positive
case based on the right to treasure in udal law and linking this right to
land tenure. It was decided that Mr Davidson should discuss the matter
with his senior; that Professor T B Smith should be consulted; that the
name of a Norwegian authority on udal law be obtained; that Professor
MacRitchie consult Professor Daube (Professor of Jurisprudence and a
noted expert on Roman law); and that, as soon as possible, a decision
should be made whether there should be an appeal.

Following the process of consultation, it appears that an executive
decision was made to appeal, but this was not recorded in a University
Court minute.

Decision on reclaiming motion

The Inner House upheld the decision of the Lord Ordinary. The
opinions of Lord Patrick and Lord Mackintosh (concurred in by

Lords Strachan and Guthrie) accepted that it was correct to see Bell's statement as accurate in reflecting the essential controlling position that all previously owned things which come to light and appear to be ownerless are Crown property. Albeit academic in so far as *bona vacantia* encompassed treasure, Lord Hunter's sole dubiety on the issue of hidden was brushed aside, with Lord Mackintosh holding that the epithet "hidden" meant no more than "concealed" – with reference to "the state or condition" in which the items were found without implication for the owner's intention.[32]

Lord Mackintosh's opinion spoke to the defenders' case coming from the Lord Ordinary to the Inner House

> "radically changed by a lengthy amendment of the record which had in the interval been made by the defenders to the effect that the disposal of the said objects fell to be regulated in terms of a legal code attributed to the Norwegian King Magnus ... which the defenders in their amendment aver 'still forms part of the law of the islands of Shetland'".[33]

T B Smith's diligent efforts were the basis of the positive case presented to the Inner House which was far removed from the essentially negative argument before the Lord Ordinary. It was now submitted that the matter was governed by the late 13th-century code of Magnus which had not been repealed or superseded. Under this law, it was contended, any interest in a find of treasure fell to be divided equally between landowner, finder and the Crown. Concerning this, the defenders now sought a proof – ie a trial – to establish the matters of fact contended for. Lord Patrick summarised the issues concerned as follows:

> "They asked for a proof of their averments that prior to the pledge of the islands to the Kings of Scotland in 1468 the law of the islands was Norse; that a legal code which is attributed to the Norwegian King Magnus, the Lawgiver, which came into force about 1274, would have governed the disposal of the objects if they had been discovered prior to 1468; and that that code would have given the objects into the joint ownership of the King, the finder and the owner of the Udal land on which the discovery was made."[34]

These averments of fact, Lord Patrick observed, are followed by a statement of law that the code of King Magnus "still forms part of the

---

[32] 1963 SC 533 at 559–560.
[33] At 557.
[34] At 555.

law of the law of the islands of Shetland"; the learned judge went on to note the critical nature of this issue of law in that "unless the code of Magnus is still part of the law of the Shetlands it would serve no purpose to prove the previous averments of fact".[35]

Lord Patrick did not doubt that "the law of Norway applied in the islands prior to their pledge to the kings of Scotland" but saw it as "another matter" whether the code of Magnus regarding ownerless moveables prevailed.[36] In the absence of any text in Scottish institutional writings, he found it "impossible to hold" that the code contended for was extant as part of Shetland law so as to "today prevail over the competing right of the admitted sovereign".[37]

Lord Mackintosh concurred and concluded that the defenders had "failed to show that the law or rule of the code of Magnus upon which they now found is still part of the law of Scotland in the islands of Shetland".[38] The relevance of the institutional writers in this matter was clear to Lord Mackintosh:

> "Our institutional writers from Stair to Bell inclusive agree that the right to *bona vacantia*, including treasure, pertains to the sovereign and although all of them were well aware that certain specialities in our law applied in the islands of Orkney and Shetland ... there is no trace in their works of any special or exceptional treatment of the subject-matter of *bona vacantia*, including treasure, having been given to these islands."[39]

This, then, was the end of the matter in terms of the legal process. It would be most surprising if an appeal to the House of Lords was not considered. Simply on the basis of the effort made by T B Smith, it might have been felt worthwhile to go to the ultimate court.

It is interesting, however, to note that T B Smith considered, or came to consider, that the decision of the Inner House was flawed in so far as a certain substantive argument, presented by counsel in the reclaiming motion, was not dealt with by the court. In an essay published some 10 years after the litigation, in the definitive work on the treasure, he states that before the Inner House the second defender – landowner James Budge, who was formally represented by Smith, leading Kemp

---

[35] At 555.
[36] *Ibid.*
[37] At 556.
[38] At 563.
[39] *Ibid.*

Davidson – presented a public law argument questioning the legality of an "extension" of the Crown's rights on its acquisition of Shetland.

> "[B]y accepted rules of public international and British constitutional law the prerogative rights of the Crown which are merely concerned with property perquisites do not extend even to conquered or annexed territory unless or until the acquiring state alters the law of such territory."[40]

Smith goes on to observe that, on this point, "the Court expressed no view whatsoever, despite the fact that the Crown had adduced no counter argument".[41] In a footnote to this statement, Smith says that "[i]n the circumstances, the actual decision is not a conclusive precedent even in the Court of Session were similar facts to be litigated again".

The public law point was not raised as a new issue, by amendment of the pleadings for the reclaiming motion, as, of course, the new issue of the King Magnus code was. It accordingly did not have to be dealt with specifically but could be rejected by implication. That the Inner House took the view that the municipal law of Scotland, at any rate by the early 17th century, had replaced Norse law in Shetland in all but a few well-known respects – of which udal tenure was the most significant – might be taken to amount to an implied answering of the point in question. The opinion of Lord Patrick contends for a chronology of Scots law displacing Norse rules.[42] The Crown's position probably was that it did not need to address this issue not specifically pleaded and, in any event, answered by implication in the general argument that Scots law came to be controlling except in the few well-known areas of Norse survival, unless, of course, called upon by the court to respond. Smith's precedent point does not seem to carry weight; but it is not a naive point, as I previously said,[43] and I take this opportunity to correct that.

Appeal to the House of Lords?

A special meeting of the University Court was held on 7 August 1963 to consider the Inner House's rejection of the appeal in the opinions issued on 2 August. It was decided that an appeal to the House of

---

[40] T B Smith in Small *et al* (n 2 above) at p 150.
[41] At p 151.
[42] 1963 SC 533, 556.
[43] "T B Smith's Property" in Reid and Carey Miller (n 1 above) at 194, n 135.

Lords should be marked, that Mr Cramb should consult with counsel
and with Professor Smith and that the Court should consider further
action in the light of what Mr Cramb ascertained.

Following the circulation of papers arising from Mr Cramb's
actions, a second special meeting was held on 18 October 1963. At
this meeting, it emerged that there was no support for an appeal to
the House of Lords. Counsel for the defenders did not recommend an
appeal and this was probably conclusive. A joint note of the Dean of
Faculty W I R Fraser QC and C K Davidson dated 18 September 1963
is instructive as to how they saw the court's reaction to the argument
Smith devised and they presented. They saw a "determination ... to
approach the problem solely from the point of view of Scots law" as
an attitude which "does less than justice to the defenders' positive
argument" which although "highly refined" was "not in sympathy
with the practical attitude of the Courts today".

Smith's position was slightly more positive. He felt "that there
was a possibility that the University might be successful in an appeal
to the House of Lords, but that, nevertheless he would not consider
the prospect favourable". The likelihood that Smith considered the
Second Division approach establishment-minded if not parochial is
supported by comments he made in the anonymous piece, already
referred to, published soon after the litigation. Speculating as to the
circumstances, possibly involving a Viking raid, in which the treasure
was hidden, Smith observes that this was what "Lord Patrick during
argument in the Treasure Case called 'Old unhappy far off things'".[44]

It was decided by the University Court that there should not be an
appeal.

Post-decision developments

Rather remarkably in the circumstances, the treasure remained in
the possession of the University in the Marischal Museum for some
2 years after the decision of the Inner House in favour of the Crown. As
late as 8 June 1965, the University Court considered a letter from the
QLTR indicating that the treasure must be deposited in the NMAS and
suggesting that the writer visit Aberdeen, on a date convenient to the
Principal, to discuss the necessary arrangements. It was decided that
Mr Cramb and Professor O'Dell be invited to attend with Principal
Wright when he met the QLTR.

[44] Note 8 above at 188.

That Principal Wright was pursuing Principal Taylor's policy to, if necessary, acquire the treasure by purchase is absolutely clear. A Court minute of 12 October 1965 intimates that the Principal made a public offer of £8,000 to the NMAS for the treasure. A minute of 9 November 1965 records the response of the Chairman of Trustees to the offer to purchase for "£8000 on condition that the treasure was exhibited permanently in Shetland" but that they were "unanimously of the opinion that having been appointed custodians by the Crown they were not in a position to dispose of the silver".

The University produced a press statement reflecting this offer. The release noted that the treasure had been valued by the Keeper of the NMAS at £6,000; also, although the trustees had advised that they were not in a position to dispose of the treasure, it was observed that the NMAS proposed to lend the hoard to Shetland for the opening of the new Lerwick Museum.

A petition was organised in 1965, calling for the St Ninian's Isle treasure to be deposited in the new Lerwick museum. A well-known figure, Jo Grimond, MP for Orkney and Shetland, lent his support and wrote to Principal Wright on 2 September 1965: "I have written again to the Secretary of State but I wonder if you think, in view of the present situation, that we can muster some new high level support."

The Secretary of State for Scotland responded in a letter of 26 November to the effect that, while this was not an easy decision, the conclusion was that because of the importance of the St Ninian's silver it should be part of an appropriate national collection; however, it could go to the new Lerwick Museum on a 3-month loan.

Taylor and Smith: a chemistry of personalities?

Principal Taylor and Professor T B Smith were the prime movers, in distinct roles, in Aberdeen University's assertion of right over the St Ninian's Isle treasure. In terms of the Shetland interest, possibly as part of a northern Scottish solidarity which this exceptional man from Keith felt, Taylor took the matter to his heart and pursued diplomatic statesmanship backed, as he perceived it, by legal right.

Taylor, educated at Keith Grammar School and Aberdeen University, was a remarkable individual of moral conviction and resolute but endearing personal qualities. He practised as an advocate in the 1920s and 1930s and served as Advocate Depute from 1929 to 1934. Appointed Professor of Scots Law at Aberdeen in 1935, as successor to Alexander Mackenzie Stuart, Sir Thomas became Principal in 1948 and held office until he died unexpectedly on 19 July 1962, about 2 months before Lord Hunter's decision of 10 September 1962 against the University. A University Court meeting of 10 October 1962 recorded a minute of appreciation to the late Principal, a man whose "vision, fairness and determination ... far more than the authority of his office" enabled him to "secure the cooperation of many widely different people"; a "man of strongly held convictions and firm opinions" who "combined, in an unusual degree, the qualities of the stout champion and of the peace-maker".

The University Court minutes and Taylor's statements and speeches surely demonstrate these personal qualities in the controlling role he exercised from the time of the St Ninian's Isle find until his death 4 years later. Indeed, it is apparent that the approach and direction in which he had led the University Court were continued, by the Court, after his death. It seems unlikely that the decision against an appeal to the House of Lords would have been different had Taylor been alive to participate.

The roles of Taylor and Smith were quite different, the former diligently working on a day-to-day basis to achieve the outcome he wanted to see, the latter in the role of advocate preparing and presenting legal submissions. A letter of 12 March 1963 from Smith to Gordon, Falconer and Fairweather WS, the University's solicitors in Edinburgh, shows Smith in this role. The letter was written from Harvard University, where Smith was working. Advising that he would be returning from the US by ship leaving on 15 June, Smith says that he would be on leave from Edinburgh University and "shall be free to make the St Ninian's Isle Treasure case my exclusive concern". The opinion of Professor Knut Robberstad – the basis of the case Smith developed to present, via amended pleadings, before the Inner House, commencing on 25 June 1963 – was dated 8 May 1963.

The St Ninian's Isle treasure find was an event with natural ingredients of drama and fascination; to this, the remarkable Shetland history factor added a perspective which gave scope for a dimension of originality seldom seen in the prosaic world of civil litigation. But, of course, the extent and level of the original, radical, legal presentation of the case before the Inner House had much to do with Professor T B Smith being at the helm.[45]

---

[45] The writer has commented on this in "T B Smith's Property" in Reid and Carey Miller (n 1 above) at 192. On an aspect of this comment, see n 43 above.

The magnitude of Smith's endeavours in the St Ninian's Isle case reflected the vigorous enthusiasm which he typically showed in the many causes he espoused. But, almost certainly, powerful senses of loyalty and duty also played a part. A collegiate bond between Smith and Taylor has already been referred to. About 20 years after the treasure litigation, on St Andrew's Day 1981, Smith gave a lecture at Aberdeen to inaugurate a "Lord President Cooper Prize in Comparative Law". Of this, the writer, having organised the event, can speak first hand. The lecture title "While One Hundred Remain: Scots Law, its Historical and Comparative Dimensions", referring to the Declaration of Arbroath, itself tells something of the man. Referring to a new phase in law teaching at Aberdeen "made possible by the late Principal Sir Thomas Taylor", Smith continued:

> "[o]n his appointment as Principal of the University in 1948 I was selected to be his successor as Professor of Scots Law on a full-time basis, and was given the opportunity to encourage the building up of a full-time Faculty. If I am indebted to Lord Cooper for inspiration I am even more indebted to Principal Taylor for the opportunity to dedicate my life to teaching and research in Scots Law and Comparative Law".[46]

Later Smith says that Principal Taylor "gambled recklessly on me" as someone who "[f]ar from having established a reputation as a jurist" had a background essentially in military service. In Kenneth Reid's 2003 C M S Cameron McKenna lecture in honour of T B Smith, published as the opening contribution in a recent study evaluating Smith's contribution, the author notes that the gamble "turned out to be gloriously successful" and "Smith's energy and enthusiasm were prodigious".[47] It is very much evident that these characteristics were in full flow in the treasure case, at least partly, it is suggested, manifesting Smith's loyalty to Taylor who had appointed an outstandingly well qualified and apparently brilliant but completely untried 33-year-old to an ancient university foundation chair.[48]

Smith's industry was recognised by Lord Hunter – possibly the person in the best position to do so – commenting in a British

---

[46] Sir Thomas Smith, "While One Hundred Remain" 1984 Aberdeen University Review 229 at 230.

[47] "While One Hundred Remain" in Reid and Carey Miller (n 1 above) at 7.

[48] H L MacQueen, "Two Toms and an Ideology for Scots Law" in Reid and Carey Miller (n 1 above) at 44; 44–45 throws further light on Taylor's appointment of the brilliant young Smith.

Academy tribute after Smith's death. Stating that in 1956 Smith became a Queen's Counsel – "evidence that he never divorced himself completely from work in the Courts" – Hunter added that this was later demonstrated

> "by his appearance in the litigation concerning ownership of the St Ninian's Treasure, found in Shetland where some Norse law survives. In this litigation he unearthed, with typical industry, some forgotten enactments in the Legal Code of King Magnus Hakonsson 'The Law-mender', a medieval Scandinavian Monarch".[49]

Smith's departure to a new post in Edinburgh, soon after the St Ninian's Isle treasure find, did not dampen his enthusiasm for the Aberdeen University quest to establish a right to retain it. Lady Smith recently told the writer of the enthusiasm with which her late husband and Principal Taylor pursued the St Ninian's Treasure matter in the interests of the University of Aberdeen.

But an irrepressible spirit possibly met its limit when it came to appearing before the Inner House. Lord Hope of Craighall, as a student, was present at the Second Division hearing in June 1963. In 1992, as Lord President, he wrote the foreword to a collection of essays published as a tribute to Professor Sir Thomas Smith QC:

> "It was uncharacteristically of him in court, clad in wig and gown and seen only from behind. I could not see his face, as I was then a student and was sitting in the public benches. Nor did I hear him speak, as most of the speaking on the side which he was representing was done by the then Dean of Faculty, W I R Fraser, QC. C K Davidson was his junior and the junior on the other side was J P H MacKay – an illustrious gathering indeed. The occasion was the hearing in the Second Division of the reclaiming motion in the St Ninian's Treasure Case, *Lord Advocate v University of Aberdeen and Budge* 1963 SC 533. It seemed to me at the time that it was an act of some courage on his part to venture into court, with the Dean's permission since he was not in active practice at the Bar. The novelty and importance of the issues certainly justified his appearance in that case and his contributions undoubtedly influenced the standard of debate. But I doubt whether the experience, in what was essentially a supporting role, was one which he enjoyed."[50]

---

[49] "Thomas Broun Smith 1915–1988" (1992) 82 Proceedings of the British Academy 455 at 460.

[50] D L Carey Miller and D W Meyers, *Comparative and Historical Essays in Scots Law* (1992), xii.

As Lord Hope suggests, a factor which may have added to the inherent tension of Smith's appearing was that his recently published *Short Commentary on the Law of Scotland* – to some a groundbreaking blueprint for the development of the law – had probably not been well received by the senior judiciary.

Lord Mackay of Clashfern, Lord Chancellor from 1987 to 1997, sole survivor of the "illustrious gathering", recalls that Smith, inexperienced as a pleader, made a very learned presentation but the judges, particularly the precise and penetrating Lord Patrick, gradually became impatient. Lord Mackay also notes that, when the Crown's turn came, it was obvious that the reclaiming motion had failed despite the best efforts of the formidable combination of counsel.[51]

Conclusion

The St Ninian's Isle treasure can be seen today in the National Museum of Scotland where it is one of the collection highlights.[52] The treasure was returned to the Lerwick Museum in 2008 for the 50th anniversary of the find. The website entry shows the outstanding beauty of many of the objects. A cryptic account of the find tells only of the schoolboy immediate finder, almost as if the true facts should be forgotten as security against any re-emergence of a Shetland/Aberdeen claim to custody; a fear that T B Smith's "[t]here may yet be laughter in Valhalla"[53] could somehow come to pass.

Principal Taylor's agenda appears to have been to assert the rights and importance of Aberdeen, Shetland and the North of Scotland generally against the perceived hegemony of the Edinburgh establishment. This highlights the tensions that exist within Scotland as well as between it and its more dominant neighbour. Shetlanders still identify themselves with their Norse ancestry and the coming of the Scottish Parliament has thrown into relief the sometimes strained relationships between distinctive parts of the nation.

What is clear is that the case gave full rein to the creativity which was the hallmark of T B Smith, a man who provided inspiration, whether personally or by reputation, to so many who now influence the development of Scotland's distinctive legal system.

---

[51] I am most grateful to Lord Mackay for his letter in response to my enquiry.

[52] www.nms.ac.uk/our_collections/collection_highlights/st_ninians_isle_treasure. aspx.

[53] T B Smith in Small *et al* (n 2 above) at p 165.

Chapter 8

GIVING UP OR LETTING GO
Law Hospital NHS Trust v *Lord Advocate*

Sheila A M McLean

The assumption that acts that cause or result in death can be easily accommodated within the laws of homicide has in recent times been open to a number of challenges, most specifically when they occur in a clinical context. Behaviour that would result in a criminal charge were it to occur outside of this setting is treated differently when doctors or other health care professionals are involved. There are, of course, good reasons for this. Surgery, after all, would amount to an assault were I to conduct it, but if it is done by a professional surgeon in good faith and to benefit the patient it would surely be objectionable, not to say bizarre, to hold the doctor criminally liable. Thus, even although the State reserves to itself the right to declare certain behaviour criminal, so too it has the authority to recognise that the same activity is lawful within certain contexts.

However, the simple example of surgery disguises the complexity of decisions that may arise in the modern medical setting; decisions that may knowingly result in the death of a patient. End-of-life decisions in the clinical context have long troubled health care professionals, medical associations and society as a whole. Until relatively recently, however, they have only rarely been engaged with by the law and, more specifically, by the courts. That it is now necessary for the law to consider these situations is a direct product of the sophistication of contemporary medicine and science. As Lord Hope said in the case of *Law Hospital NHS Trust* v *Lord Advocate*:

> "Medical science has now advanced to such a degree that many techniques are now possible which only a generation ago would have been unthinkable. The ability to prolong life by artificial means has

reached such a stage that it is possible to nourish the body and preserve
it from disease so that life, in the clinical sense, may be continued
indefinitely."[1]

While the law is relatively clear in the case of some end-of-life decisions,
such as assisted suicide or voluntary euthanasia, there are cases
where the liability and responsibility of clinicians have traditionally
been more opaque. While professional ethics might serve to provide
some guidance to physicians and other health care professionals as
to what is the "right" action in the clinical sense, increasing concern
about possible exposure to criminal charges or civil liability has driven
doctors into the courtroom to seek reassurance that what seems
clinically appropriate is also legally permitted. Nowhere is this more
evident than in situations where patients are diagnosed as being in
what used to be known as a persistent vegetative state, but is now
more commonly referred to as a permanent vegetative state (PVS).

First described by Jennett and Plum in 1972,[2] this is a condition in
which an individual is irreversibly comatose. Although the individual
can breathe unaided, and existence can therefore be maintained for
a considerable period of time with assisted nutrition and hydration
(ANH) and appropriate treatment with antibiotics if needed, the
person will never awaken from their coma – they will never again
interact with others. In effect, their condition can be described as
a "living death".

That the person is alive, however, is not in doubt; consequently, they
remain holders (albeit unconsciously) of fundamental rights, such as
the right to life. The major problem for the law, then, is the extent to
which existence in PVS should be maintained, or, to put it another
way, is it ever permissible to bring such an existence to an end and,
if so, how and in what circumstances? Answering this question is a
matter of considerable importance, as at any given time there may be
hundreds of people in PVS in the United Kingdom alone.

The first opportunity for courts in Scotland to consider this thorny
question arose in 1996 in the case of *Law Hospital NHS Trust* v *Lord
Advocate*, but this was not the first UK case. Three years earlier,
England's highest civil court, the House of Lords, had cause to address

[1] 1996 SC 301 at 307.
[2] B Jennett and F Plum, "Persistent vegetative state after brain damage. A syndrome
in search of a name" (1972) 1 *Lancet* 734.

this subject in the case of *Airedale NHS Trust* v *Bland*.[3] Since this case was referred to at some length in the Scottish decision, and since it also highlights some interesting differences between Scottish and English law, the *Bland* case will be considered briefly first.

Airedale NHS Trust v *Bland*

In this case, a young man, Anthony (Tony) Bland, was catastrophically injured in the Hillsborough football stadium disaster. Having been declared to be in a PVS, his doctors, with the support of his parents, petitioned the court for a declaration that it would not be unlawful to withdraw the nasogastric tube that was providing him with nutrition and hydration. The inevitable, and intended, consequence of this would be Tony's death – effectively by dehydration. The case ultimately reached the House of Lords and it is on this judgment that what follows will focus. If the court were to grant the declaration sought, it had two difficult tasks to contend with. First was the question of what duties doctors owe their patients in these circumstances, particularly since it is well established that they cannot be forced to provide medical treatment against their best judgment. Second, it had to deal with the matter of whether or not a doctor would be criminally liable should he or she deliberately withdraw life-sustaining treatment without the consent of the patient. In other words, there were issues about both civil and criminal liability.

By somewhat circuitous routes, each of the judges in the House of Lords concluded that it was legally permissible to withdraw ANH, but their reasoning was by no means harmonious. For some, the critical question seemed to focus on whether or not the provision of ANH was equivalent to the provision of any other "medical" treatment. If so, then the issue was simplified to the question of whether or not doctors could be obliged to continue treatment that they believed to be futile. While it is possible to argue that the provision of food and water is basic care and not medical treatment,[4] the fact that its provision involves medical skills and that the medical profession regards it as medical treatment was sufficient to persuade some of their Lordships. Others focused more closely on the question of best interests; could it

---

[3] *Airedale NHS Trust* v *Bland* (1993) 12 BMLR 64.
[4] For discussion, see S A M McLean, "From Bland to Burke: The Law and Politics of Assisted Nutrition and Hydration" in S A M McLean (ed), *First Do No Harm: Law, Ethics and Healthcare* (Ashgate, 2006) at pp 431–446.

be in Tony Bland's interests to be maintained in a condition where he was permanently insensate? Finally, some (but by no means all) were content to use the purported distinction between acts and omissions to reach a conclusion. On this argument, given that we are generally responsible for our acts but not for our omissions, failure to continue ANH could be categorised as an omission and therefore would be not be unlawful.

Because of the variety of approaches taken, it is worth briefly taking a closer look at them. Confronting the argument that ANH was "not medical treatment at all, but simply feeding indistinguishable from feeding by normal means",[5] Lord Keith declared himself satisfied that the regime to which Tony Bland was subject (including the provision of ANH) amounted to "medical treatment and care". In any event, he declared that "the administration of nourishment by the means adopted involves the application of a medical technique".[6] Lord Goff agreed, and also addressed the futility question. As he said:

> "I cannot see that medical treatment is appropriate or requisite simply to prolong a patient's life when such treatment has no therapeutic purpose of any kind, as where it is futile because the patient is unconscious and there is no prospect of any improvement in his condition."[7]

While accepting that Tony Bland was undoubtedly alive for all legal purposes, the fact that the decision-making took place within a clinical setting and used clinical expertise rendered it "medical" and therefore subject to the tests normally applied in clinical negligence cases; essentially what a responsible body of medical practitioners agree to be the appropriate course of action. The doctor is not liable when acting on sound diagnosis and in good faith either for not offering treatment in certain cases or for withdrawing it in others. For Lord Goff, "[i]n each case, the doctor is simply allowing his patient to die in the sense that he is desisting from taking a step which might, in certain circumstances, prevent his patient from dying as a result of his pre-existing condition".[8]

Lord Browne-Wilkinson also situated the debate within the context of doctors' duties. Applying the test that was then widely used in medical negligence cases, he declared that

[5] At 106.
[6] *Ibid.*
[7] At 116.
[8] At 113.

"if there comes a stage where the responsible doctor comes to the reasonable conclusion (which accords with the views of a responsible body of medical opinion) that further continuance of an intrusive life support system is not in the best interests of the patient, he can no longer lawfully continue that life support system: to do so would constitute the crime of battery and the tort of trespass to the person. Therefore he cannot be in breach of any duty to maintain the patient's life. Therefore he is not guilty of murder by omission".[9]

Despite his reliance on this test, he nonetheless recognised the unease that such a decision might generate, not least because it permitted the slow, lingering death of the patient while the law, then and now, would prohibit a doctor from ending the patient's life quickly.[10] While this may appear bizarre, it rests fundamentally on the distinction drawn in law between acts and omissions. Lord Mustill was unwilling to ignore the problems associated with the use of such a distinction, noting that the true issue at stake in this case was that "the authority of the state, through the medium of the court, is being invoked to permit one group of its citizens to terminate the life of another".[11] Thus, whether or not an event could be described as an act or an omission, his sense was that "however much the terminologies may differ, the ethical status of the two courses of action is for all relevant purposes indistinguishable".[12] Indeed, he described the judgment as emphasising "the distortions of a legal structure which is already both morally and intellectually misshapen".[13] Finally, albeit almost as an aside, he discounted the applicability of the test of accepted medical practice in cases of this sort, saying that "the decision is ethical, not medical, and that there is no reason in logic why on such a decision the opinion of doctors should be decisive".[14]

Despite some apparent disagreement as to the principles upon which the case should be decided, the House of Lords unanimously agreed that the ANH could be discontinued and Tony Bland died some days later. At the same time, the House of Lords declared that all similar cases should be subject to the scrutiny of the courts, presumably in part on the basis that a more disinterested decision could be taken

[9] At 129.
[10] At 131.
[11] *Ibid.*
[12] At 132.
[13] *Ibid.*
[14] At 143.

there, but also because in effect the decisions taken affect both civil and criminal liability in such circumstances.

Scots law often prides itself on being independent of that elsewhere in the United Kingdom and, despite the fact that the House of Lords (now the Supreme Court) is the highest civil court in the United Kingdom, it has no authority in Scotland when it comes to matters that are potentially criminal. So, how would the Court of Session respond to this difficult challenge when Law Hospital sought its authority to remove ANH from Mrs Janet Johnstone?

The facts of the case

Mrs Johnstone had apparently attempted suicide in January 1992, and was subsequently diagnosed as being in a PVS. Some 3 years after she was diagnosed, Law Hospital NHS Trust, ultimately with the support of Mrs Johnstone's family, sought an assurance from the Court of Session that should doctors withdraw ANH they would not be liable in either the civil or the criminal law. The case came first before the Lord Ordinary, Lord Cameron, who referred it to five judges in the Court of Session, given its complexity and importance. The Lord Advocate was involved in the public interest and a curator *ad litem* was appointed to Mrs Johnstone.

The Lord Advocate contended *inter alia* that the Court of Session had no jurisdiction as the declarator sought covered not just civil law matters (in which the Court of Session has jurisdiction) but also matters of criminal liability (in which it does not). Nonetheless, the Court of Session held that it did have jurisdiction, although, as we will see, the Lord Advocate's concerns were taken seriously. What was not in doubt, so far as the Court of Session was concerned, was the validity of the clinical diagnosis and the certainty of its consequences. Lord Hope, the Lord President, described Mrs Johnstone's condition as follows: "She cannot see, hear, feel pain or pleasure, communicate by word or movement or make voluntary movements of any kind."[15] Nor, it was accepted, would she ever recover. Lord Hope noted that this case:

> "belongs to a group of cases which have been recurring with increasing frequency in recent years where the courts are being asked to give their authority to actions to be taken by medical practitioners which raise acute questions of moral or ethical principle".[16]

---

[15] 1996 SC 301 at 305.
[16] At 306.

The ethical dilemma centred on how it was right to treat someone who is legally alive, who could with continued nutrition and hydration survive perhaps for many years, but who had no hope of regaining a life with any quality. The clinical dilemma revolved around a number of factors, one of which almost certainly was whether or not it could ever be appropriate to continue to use scarce resources – in particular the time and expertise of the doctors and nurses who must care for her – in the case of a patient for whom no benefit (in terms of cure or improvement) was possible. Most importantly, of course, was the question of what duties the doctors owed to their patient in this situation. The legal issue was whether or not it could be lawful knowingly to bring about the death of a patient.

From the ethical point of view, it could be argued that the value attributed to the sanctity of life irrespective of its condition is superior to any other considerations. Simply put, life – in whatever form – is the supreme value and where it can be sustained it should be. However, this rather extreme position is counter-intuitive for those who would hold that mere existence is not the same as life. On this argument, assuming the diagnosis to be correct and its consequences certain, one should look to the *quality* of Mrs Johnstone's existence, perhaps also to that of her loved ones whose suffering as a result of her continued existence in PVS can be imagined with some degree of certainty, and incorporate this into the decision. Some might even argue that, since Mrs Johnstone had apparently attempted to kill herself, the ethical dilemma is less grave since she clearly did not want to live – a decision that, while not legally binding, should nonetheless be persuasive as evidence as to what she would now want to happen. It should, however, be noted that at least one newspaper report suggested that, on first being admitted to hospital, when she was still conscious, she did accept treatment.[17]

For the clinicians, continued care was either futile or otherwise an inappropriate use of resources. The primary task of clinicians is to save life, or at least to attempt to improve the quality of life for those who are suffering; where this is not possible, their responsibilities to other patients are also relevant. While the focus of the law has generally been on the one-on-one relationship between doctor and patient, doctors are acutely aware that they also have an obligation to ensure

[17] G Murray, "The public dilemma of a loved one's life or death", *The Scotsman*, 3 March 1996.

that resources are wisely used; in other words, they have a professional obligation to *all* of their patients. How these are to be reconciled when conflict arises is one of the more difficult decisions for clinicians (and managers) in modern health care, given the competing interests of patients and particularly those in potentially equal need.

For the law, of course, the dilemma was how to act in a manner that was both principled and appropriate where no parliamentary guidance was available and the courts were confronted with novel and highly complex questions. While this is obviously an extremely sensitive issue with many components, both ethical and clinical, Lord Hope was clear that it was one in which the law must be engaged. As he said, "the question whether it would be lawful to cease to provide or to withhold treatment cannot be left to the doctors. This is a matter for the law, and it must be decided by the courts, so long as there is no declaration on the matter by Parliament".[18] Having accepted that the Inner House of the Court of Session did have jurisdiction to hear this case, it was also made clear that the ultimate decision was for the Lord Ordinary; the Inner House's function was to elucidate the issues and offer guidance but not to make the final decision. As was true in the House of Lords in the *Bland* judgment, the ultimate decision was approached by slightly different routes, although each judge approved the final conclusion.

For Lord Hope, the question rested on what was best for the patient. As he said, "the issue is in the end a single and indivisible one, as to whether it is in the patient's best interests that her life should be prolonged by the continuance of the life sustaining medical treatment which she currently receives".[19] Lord Cullen agreed, saying that:

> "the single unifying principle which underlies both the long-established practice of the appointment of tutors-dative and the authorisation of the carrying out or withdrawal of medical treatment is that the court, when called on to do so, will exercise a jurisdiction to determine what should be authorised as being in the best interests of the person who is unable to give authority or consent for himself or herself".[20]

Lord Mulligan expressed some concern over the use of the best interests test in such cases, but was satisfied that a negative application of the test was appropriate; that is "it is not in the best interests of the patient

[18] At 307.
[19] At 317.
[20] At 325.

to be kept alive by artificial means where the court is satisfied that the diagnosis is so clear and the prognosis so futile that the ward truly has no interest in being kept alive".[21]

Lord Clyde, on the other hand, was less confident that this was indeed the central issue, saying:

> "In the course of the discussion before us it was said that the power should be exercised for the benefit of, or for the welfare of, or in the best interests of the ward. But while in the context of some medical situations such expressions may be of value I find less assistance in such language when the choice is between life of a sort and death. It seems to me that in a case such as the present the question for the court is whether in light of the material put before it it is or is not just and proper to grant the authorisation in the circumstances as viewed from the position of the patient."[22]

In his view, this was a matter that is intimately linked to the clinical evidence and the consequent responsibilities of doctors to their patients. He was satisfied that "no benefit would be achieved by continuing the treatment".[23] That being so, there was no remaining obligation on doctors to continue the treatment and the nature of their continuing duties "would be towards securing her comfort and dignity for the concluding days of her life".[24] Although he conceded that the acts/omissions distinction might in some cases provide a way of answering the question before the court, he neatly side-stepped the potential problems associated with this, instead finding "greater strength in the submission that if there is in the circumstances no longer a duty to continue with a system of life support there would be no crime committed by the discontinuance of that system".[25]

The Court was ultimately satisfied by the medical evidence as to Mrs Johnstone's diagnosis and prognosis and also that this was a matter over which it had jurisdiction. The case was therefore referred back to the Lord Ordinary, subject to the caveat that, while he could issue a declarator in the case, it was not competent to include criminal matters within it. In delivering his judgment, Lord Hope made it clear that "[s]ome other solution must be found as to how the reassurance

[21] At 329.
[22] At 325.
[23] At 321.
[24] *Ibid.*
[25] *Ibid.*

in regard to the criminal consequences of that conduct can be given to the pursuers and the medical practitioner".[26]

The social aftermath

While the Tony Bland case generated seemingly endless media and academic commentary, by and large there was no personal attack on the parents whose love for their son drove them to the agonising decision that his life should not be maintained. Mr Peter Johnstone, on the other hand was less fortunate. In particular, the tabloid press had a great deal to say, much of it negative and highly personal. Indeed, commenting at the time, Gavaghan said that the complex question raised in the *Law Hospital* case "faced the constant danger of being overshadowed by tabloid speculation as to the nature of Janet Johnstone's relationship with her husband, the possible reasons behind her attempted suicide, and Peter Johnstone's much publicized ostracization by many other residents of the small Lanarkshire town".[27] Newspaper coverage included comments such as "Last night her husband Peter Johnston [*sic*] spoke for the first time about his controversial legal bid and vowed 'I WANT TO KILL MY WIFE'".[28] Mr Johnstone's attitude was also reported in the same newspaper in the following terms:

> "Cold-heartedly Johnston admits: 'I've been through hell and back. It's time I got back on my feet. I've got an awful lot to live through before I can get back to normality. It's been one thing after another – a man can only take so much ... As a butcher, I have killed cows, pigs and sheep to put them out of their misery. As far as I am concerned, removing this tube would be no more or less'."[29]

The same article said "Hard-drinking Peter has become a virtual leper in the one-time mining community because of his obsession with his wife's death".[30] Other coverage was somewhat more sympathetic, for example quoting Mr Johnstone as saying "The decision is taking so long. The whole family has been under tremendous strain because

---

[26] At 312.
[27] C Gavaghan, "When the thread finally breaks", available at http://www.euthanasia.cc/jj.html (accessed on 13/8/2009).
[28] "Please kill my wife", *Sunday Mail*, 27 August 1995.
[29] A Gold, *Sunday Mail*, 27 August 1995, pp 8–9.
[30] At p 8.

of it. I feel so helpless. What happens next is out of my hands".[31] Certainly, there can be little doubt that the family of Mrs Johnstone was subject to an intense level of scrutiny which revealed some initial disagreement between them and some external ill-feeling towards them.

Irrespective of the public speculation about the Johnstone family and the motivation behind their legal action, as we have seen, the Inner House of the Court of Session referred the case back to Lord Cameron, who issued a declarator on 24 April 1996.[32] The commentator Ian Bell, rather than engaging with the real or imagined flaws in Mr Johnstone or his family, re-focused the debate on the person at the centre of this entire case – Mrs Janet Johnstone herself. Declaring that Scots law "has begun finally to appear coherent, humane and just", he concluded that "Janet Johnstone, a mind destroyed and a body eerily preserved, could not now tell you what justice is – but at least she is about to get some".[33] Mrs Johnstone died on 31 May 1996.

The legal aftermath

Despite the insistence of the Inner House that decisions in such cases were for the law and not for the doctors, somewhat curiously it did not insist that every case should be heard by the courts. The consequence of this would seem to be that doctors may, and probably have, made equivalent decisions in a number of cases without reference to the courts, based on their interpretation of what the Court of Session said. Whether or not court involvement would make a difference is, of course, moot and will be considered in a little more depth later. Since the Court of Session has no authority in criminal matters, it would in any case be unable to reassure doctors whose concerns about criminal liability which is, after all, likely to be of equal if not greater concern to doctors and hospitals as possible civil consequences where treatment withdrawal is contemplated. The court did, however, indicate that it was for the Lord Advocate to make the decision as to whether or not prosecution would be taken; indeed, in the course of the hearing of the case, he indicated that he would consider the court's judgment once delivered and issue an appropriate statement. This was forthcoming

[31] G Stewart and J Robertson, "Family pleads for death with dignity", *The Scotsman*, 23 March 1996.

[32] *Law Hospital NHS Trust* v *Lord Advocate (No 2)* 1996 SLT 869.

[33] I Bell, "Justice and humanity over the last great taboo", *The Scotsman*, 12 April 1996.

shortly after the judgment, and consolidated in guidance issued in October 2008.[34]

In the guidelines, the preference for seeking court authority was repeated. It was also indicated that:

> "The Lord Advocate will not authorise the prosecution of a qualified medical practitioner (or any person acting upon the instruction of such a practitioner) who, acting in good faith and with the authority of the Court of Session, withdraws, or otherwise causes to be discontinued, life sustaining treatment or other medical treatment from a patient in a persistent, or permanent vegetative state (PVS), with the result that the patient dies."[35]

This immunity will not automatically extend to those who have no prior court authority, but on the other hand "if doctors and those acting on their instructions were acting in accordance with accepted medical practice and had exercised the proper degree of care expected of them, it would be very unlikely that any prosecution in the public interest would be brought against them".[36] Any death in such circumstances, with or without court authority, must, however, be referred to the procurator fiscal. In Scotland, therefore, while the prudent doctor might be wise to seek the authority of the court before withdrawing ANH from a patient in PVS, it is not mandatory to do so even although it will directly affect criminal as well as civil liability. However, to the author's knowledge, only one case has been raised in the Court of Session since Janet Johnstone's case was decided.

In 1996, Lynn Grant was admitted to Raigmore Hospital in Inverness for a normal delivery of her baby. Reportedly, however, the doctors decided on an emergency caesarean section in the course of which Mrs Grant was deprived of oxygen and suffered brain damage. Although her baby was born safely, Mrs Grant was left in a PVS. The hospital paid a sum of damages in compensation to her family, and Mrs Grant continued to survive with the assistance of ANH. In 1999, her husband commenced legal action in the Court of Session, seeking authority for discontinuation of the ANH to allow his wife to die. He

---

[34] DEATH AND THE PROCURATOR FISCAL Information and Guidance for Medical Practitioners. Produced by Crown Office and Procurator Fiscal Service October 2008; available at http://www.copfs.gov.uk/Resource/Doc/13546/0000506.pdf (accessed on 13/08/2009).

[35] Para 17.2.

[36] Para 17.3.

explained that his wife had in the past discussed what should be done if she ever ended up in such a condition, and had made it very clear that she would not want to survive. His action was raised after much soul searching to respect his wife's views and allow her to "die with dignity". In the event, the Court of Session was never fully to hear the case – Mrs Grant died peacefully on 14 July 2000.

These are difficult, sensitive and emotional cases and it is important that the courts handle them with care in the absence of parliamentary guidance. Following the judgments of the House of Lords and the Court of Session, and the fact that this question is not a priority for any political party in the United Kingdom, it seems more than unlikely that any such guidance will be forthcoming in the foreseeable future. This places a highly significant burden on our courts which must satisfy themselves of a number of crucial factors and raises questions about the approach adopted in Scots law.

First, the entire process of decision-making hinges on the accuracy of the clinical diagnosis. While PVS is an accepted condition with clear diagnostic tests, a lingering doubt remains in the minds of some as to the accuracy of diagnosis, at least in some cases. For example, it has been reported that patients diagnosed in PVS have regained consciousness and the ability to communicate for short or longer periods. Most recently, the media reported on the case of Ron Houben.[37] Mr Houben was a 20-year-old student when he was involved in a serious car crash, following which it seems that he was diagnosed as being in a PVS. His family refused to believe that he was not aware of what was happening and at no stage do they appear to have considered requesting that his treatment be discontinued. Mr Houben is now claimed to be able to engage in minimal communication using one finger and a touchscreen attached to his wheelchair. He is said to have indicated that for the 23 years during which he lay in an apparently irrecoverable condition, he was aware of what was going on around him although he was unable to communicate. His true condition was, it is alleged, only identified following a specific type of brain scan that was not available when he was first diagnosed.

What credence should be given to this story, or others, is unclear but it does emphasise the need for clear, accurate and thorough diagnosis. One potential problem with the current approach of Scots

---

[37] For information, see http://news.aol.com/article/ron-houben-says-he-heard-everything-for/780187 (accessed on 06/01/2010).

law is that doctors may reach their conclusions without their evidence being forensically scrutinised since it is not necessary for cases to be adjudicated on by a court of law. On the other hand, of course, courts are reluctant to critique medical evidence especially where – as in the case of PVS – it will likely have been the result of a most careful and corroborated clinical judgement. Indeed, in one English case, although the patient did not fulfil all of the criteria laid down by the Royal College of Physicians' diagnostic criteria for PVS, the court nonetheless authorised removal of ANH.[38] In any case, as Mason and Laurie point out, it would seem that it follows as night does day that once a diagnosis of PVS is made "the conclusion follows automatically that the patient's best interests dictate the termination of assisted feeding and, indeed, there may well be an obligation on the doctor to discontinue treatment".[39] Still other cases have arisen in which removal of ANH has been authorised even although it is accepted that the patients were not fully in a PVS,[40] despite the fact that it might be reasonable to assume that the *Bland* judgment had been intended only for those diagnosed as being in a PVS and not for those who are in "near-PVS".

A second consideration relates to the manner in which both the House of Lords and the Court of Session approached the entire issue. At no point, certainly in the Court of Session, was it canvassed that the case should be decided against the backdrop of human rights, such as the right to life contained in Art 2 of the European Convention on Human Rights which was subsequently incorporated into UK law by the Human Rights Act 1998. Since this legislation was enacted subsequent to the *Bland* and *Johnstone* cases, would its terms have affected the decisions? It seems not. Although the cases which have arisen subsequent to the Human Rights Act becoming law have been English, since the Convention rights apply equally throughout the United Kingdom, it can reasonably be concluded that similar decisions would be reached in the Scottish courts. In the case of *NHS Trust A* v *Mrs M; NHS Trust B* v *Mrs H*,[41] the High Court was satisfied that the removal of ANH from patients in a PVS did not breach their

---

[38] *Re H (adult: incompetent)* (1997) 38 BMLR 11.
[39] J K Mason and G T Laurie, *Mason and McCall Smith's Law and Medical Ethics* (7th edn, 2006), at p 585, para 16.114.
[40] See, eg, *Re G (adult incompetent: withdrawal of treatment)* (2001) 65 BMLR 6.
[41] (2001) 58 BMLR 87.

rights under the Convention, specifically Art 2 (the right to life), Art 3 (prohibition of cruel and inhuman treatment) and Art 8 (the right to respect for private and family life). Indeed, it was even suggested that to continue treatment to which the patient had (obviously) not consented could amount to a breach of Art 8 rights.

Conclusion

There is no way of knowing whether or not the apparent drift from insistence on a clear diagnosis of PVS to other less severe cases is happening in Scotland since no reported cases exist since that of Mrs Johnstone, but it is possible that it is. The problem is that, while most people (but by no means everyone) probably approve of the outcome in these cases, the justifications for permitting it are occasionally opaque and may seem odd especially when coupled with other end-of-life decisions where the death of the patient is strenuously resisted even if it is what the individual competently wants. Is it time for consolidation and reconsideration of all law at the end of life in Scotland? Maybe, but one prognosis can be made with considerable confidence – it won't happen in my lifetime.

Chapter 9

FOLLY, GUILT AND MORE FOLLY
The McCaig Cases

Robert Rennie

It might be supposed that one can dispose of one's property by will or other testamentary writing much as one pleases.[1] However, it has always been clear that certain conditions are ineffectual. Unlawful conditions or conditions against public policy (*contra bonos mores*) are, according to Bell,[2] regarded in law as impossible. McLaren put it in this way:[3]

> "A trust is said to be unlawful as contravening the policy of the law, where the trust purpose is either illegal or immoral *per se*, or is coupled with a condition which the law will not enforce. There is moreover, a class of trust purpose which, although neither immoral in their object nor prohibited by any positive law, are yet discountenanced on ground of public policy."

What is *contra bonos mores* or contrary to public policy changes with the times. Testamentary provisions in favour of mistresses[4] have in the past been attacked as being granted in consideration of cohabitation.[5] A bequest in a testamentary document in favour of a woman on condition that she left her husband has been held (and presumably still would be held) to be unenforceable.[6] Bell notes[7] that a condition

---

[1] Apart from the legal rights which can be claimed by a spouse or children.
[2] Bell, *Prin*, s 1785, one of the landmark writers on Scots law.
[3] McLaren, *Wills and Succession*, i, para 569 at p 291, the leading Scottish authority on succession.
[4] A term which might be difficult to define nowadays.
[5] See *Durham* v *Blackwood* 1622 Mor 9469.
[6] *Wilkinson* v *Wilkinson* (1871) LR 12 Eq 604.
[7] *Prin*, s 1785.

annexed to a provision to a wife or a husband restraining her or him from a second marriage is valid.[8]

Given current views on marriage and cohabitation, it may be assumed that such conditions would be unenforceable now. A bequest may be invalid because it is simply too ambiguous to be interpreted. There is also a trait of authority to the effect that a bequest must identify either individual beneficiaries or discernible public benefit. There is a tension between the unfettered right of a person to dispose of his or her money in accordance with his or her own wishes and the principle that any bequest must not be contrary to public policy and must be directed to individual or public benefit. This conflict is best illustrated by looking at the various cases where a will or other testamentary document directs that a large sum of money be used to erect a memorial of extravagant proportions to the testator or members of his or her family.

The most celebrated cases of course relate to the McCaig family.[9] The cases reported between 1905 and 1907 were brought by Catherine McCaig against the University Court of the University of Glasgow who were the sole trustees under a will by her brother, John Stuart McCaig. The case in 1915 involved Catherine McCaig's trustees. The legal dispute, however, in each case was almost identical. In the first case, Catherine McCaig sought to challenge the provisions of her brother's will on the grounds that these provisions were vague and uncertain and did not convey any beneficial interest to an individual person, a body of persons or the general public. It is one of the oddities of these cases that Catherine McCaig's own testamentary disposition contained very similar provisions which were also challenged on her death on the same grounds. It may be, of course, that Catherine McCaig's conscience troubled her after her victory in the first case and that she resolved to make reparation to her brother's memory by attempting to fulfil his wishes in her own will.

The McCaigs – the cast assembles

John Stuart McCaig, who was also known as John Stuart McCaig of Muckairn and Soroba, was the second son of Malcolm McCaig,

---

[8] Bell cites *Foulis* v *Gilmours* 1672 Mor 2965; 2 Brown Supp 160; and *Kidd* v *Kidd* (1863) 2 M 227.

[9] *McCaig* v *University of Glasgow* (1905) 13 SLT 565 (Outer House); 1907 SC 231; (1906) 14 SLT 600 (Inner House); *McCaig's Trustees* v *Kirk Session of United Free Church of Lismore* 1915 SC 426.

who was a farmer, and Margaret Stewart. He was born at Clachan, Isle of Lismore, Argyll, on 11 July 1823 and he died aged 78 on 29 June 1902 at John Square House, Oban in Argyll. He is described in various documents as being a draper's assistant, inspector of poor, merchant, banker and gas works director.[10] He has also been described as an art critic and a philosophical essayist. What is clear is that he was a wealthy businessman and a banker with the North of Scotland Bank.[11] At one time, he owned the north pier in Oban. He is, however, best remembered for the tower-like structure on Battery Hill overlooking Oban. From the outside it resembles the Colosseum in Rome. John Stuart McCaig paid for the erection of this tower at a cost of £5,000.[12]

There was to be a museum and an art gallery and a central tower. Mr McCaig's main wish was that there be statues of himself, his parents and his brothers and sisters. Only the outer walls have ever been completed and the tower is generally referred to as McCaig's Folly. John Stuart McCaig had eight brothers and sisters. He had an elder brother, Duncan, who was at one time a captain and honorary major in the Argyllshire Volunteer Artillery, but is also described in various census as a draper, merchant or banker. His younger brother, Dugald, is referred to as an Inland Revenue Officer and his brother Donald as a minister at Muckairn, Argyll. Another brother, Peter, died in infancy. His sisters Jane, Peggy (Margaret) and Anne, are described as milliners, possibly working from premises in Sauchiehall Street, Glasgow, and his other sister Catherine (the one who brought the first action against the University of Glasgow) is described simply as an annuitant in the 1871 census. None of the McCaigs had any issue and indeed none appears to have married. John Stuart McCaig died, survived by his sister, Catherine McCaig, and a brother, Duncan McCaig. Duncan McCaig died on 22 July 1902 and, accordingly, Catherine McCaig would then have been John Stuart McCaig's sole next-of-kin and heir-at-law (assuming he had died intestate), as Duncan McCaig himself left no issue. John Stuart McCaig left heritable estate with a yearly rental income of between £2,000 and £3,000 and moveable estate amounting to about £10,000 – substantial assets in those days.

---

[10] I have gleaned much of the personal information on the family from Wikipedia.
[11] The bank was absorbed by Clydesdale Bank Ltd.
[12] Equivalent to over £500,000 in today's (or perhaps yesterday's) money.

Act 1, scene 1: John Stuart McCaig's will and codicil

John Stuart McCaig left a holograph (hand-written) will dated 20 January 1900 and a holograph codicil dated 18 February 1902. In terms of the holograph settlement, he provided:

> "I, ... being resolved to settle my affairs so as to prevent all disputes after my death, in regard to the succession to my moveable means and real estate hereby nominate and appoint the Court of Session or Supreme Court of Scotland as my Trustees and executors, who shall manage and administer the trust by the appointment of a Judicial Factor from time to time as the circumstances of the management and Administration may require from time to time. The purpose of the Trust is that my heritable property be not sold but let to tenants, and the clear Revenue or Income be used for the purpose of erecting monuments and statues for myself, brothers and sisters on the Tower or circular Building called the Stuart McCaig Tower situated on the Battray Hill above Oban the making of these statues to be given to Scotch Sculptors from time to time as the necessary funds may accumulate for that purpose, also that artistic Towers be built on the hillock at the end of Airds Park in the Parish of Muckairn and on other prominent points on the Muckairn estate, and on other prominent places on the various estates : Such in particular on the Meolreor of Balagown lying North-east of Kilachonich Farm house, my wish and desire is to encourage young and rising artists and for that purpose prizes to be given for the best plans of the proposed statues towers &c. before building them. ... I give full power to the Trustees to sell the property of the Gas Works which is not to include Battary hill and Tower that goes with the unsalable Estate or otherwise called the Muckairn, Soraba, Inverlonin and Kilmore properties. My real purpose and intention is that this Trust is to be perpetual for all time comming and that is the reason of appointing the Court of Session as Trustees with the Auditor of the said Court of Session to audit the Accounts yearly at the Legal Fees. And should the Court of Session decline the acceptance of the Trust then and in that case which I hope and trust will not happen I appoint the College of Glasgow to be the Trustees to carry out the foresaid purposes and real written intentions of this will of mine. ..."

There is obviously a certain amount of vanity involved in the trust purposes, but the philanthropic side of John Stuart McCaig in wanting to encourage young artists is also in evidence. In his codicil, John Stuart McCaig sought to more fully describe and explain his real wishes and meaning and in his own words to prevent the possibility of a vagueness in construing the settlement.[13] In the codicil, he provided:

> "I do hereby mean by College of Glasgow the University of Glasgow. … Further in order to avoid the possibility of vagueness of any kind, I have to describe and explain that, I particularly want the Trustees to erect on the top of the Wall of the Tower I built in Oban statues in large Figures of all my five Brothers and of myself namely Duncan John Dugald Donald Peter and of my father Malcolm and of my mother Margaret and of my sisters Jean Catherine Margaret and Anne and that these Statues be modelled after photographs. And where these may not be available that the Statues may have a family like-ness to my own photograph or any other member of my foresaid family and that these statues will cost not less than One thousand pounds Sterling[14] and that money to come out of the accumulated clear Revenue. … Moreover I wish and direct that the Sum of three hundred pounds per year be paid to such of my Brothers & Sisters as may survive me as long as they live."

Wisely, as it turned out, and possibly in anticipation of all that was to follow, the Court of Session declined the office of trustees. Just why the University of Glasgow accepted office as trustee will become apparent when one considers the first court action. Donald McGregor, the solicitor in Oban who had been factor on the estate, was appointed judicial factor *ad interim* on the estate for any right or interest competent to him. At the time of John Stuart McCaig's death, only the outer walls of the tower had been completed.

Act 1, scene 2: *Catherine McCaig* v *Court of the University of Glasgow and another*[15]

On 27 January 1903, Catherine McCaig had signed a deed of corroboration and assignation which contained a homologation and ratification of John Stuart McCaig's original settlement and codicil. She also granted an assignation and conveyance in favour of the University Court of the University of Glasgow for behoof of the University of all her right title and interest present and future original and accrescing in the whole estate of John Stuart McCaig. The deed further bore that,

---

[13] A vain hope.

[14] By an earlier settlement, dated 19 June 1893, in a direction with regard to the erection of family monuments, the testator provided that the sum to be expended was "not to be less than £1000 sterling on each such monument".

[15] (1904) 12 SLT 145.

after the statues and two towers had been erected, the University Court
was to apply the free revenue of the estate in creating, equipping and
endowing a chair to be called the "John Stuart McCaig Chair" in the
University for the teaching of sculpture, painting, music or other fine
art or kindred subjects; and, should any revenue still be available, it
was to be applied in teaching agriculture. The action which is reported
in 1904 was an action of reduction of the assignation. It was averred
by Catherine McCaig that she had been told by Donald McGregor,
the judicial factor, that, with the exception of the annuity, she had
no interest in or claim on the estate. Apparently, she had asked Mr
McGregor to obtain the opinion of counsel, but he had not done
so. It was averred that Donald McGregor had brought an extended
document to Catherine McCaig and asked her to sign it without her
having the benefit of independent advice.

On being advised by an independent law agent that in fact the
testamentary writings of John Stuart McCaig were of doubtful validity,
and indeed did not dispose of his whole estate, she brought the action
of reduction. The action was heard by Lord Low in the Outer House
of the Court of Session. Lord Low approved two issues to go to a jury.
The first was whether the pursuer Catherine McCaig, in granting the
deed, had done so under essential error and, secondly, whether this
error had been induced by Donald McGregor.

The University Court of the University of Glasgow appealed against
the judgment of Lord Low.[16] As it happens, the case never went
before the jury, the pursuer having been advised to take a more direct
course.

Act 1, scene 3: *McCaig v University of Glasgow and others*[17]

In this action, which was heard by Lord Dundas in the Outer House
of the Court of Session, Catherine McCaig sought declarator that the
testamentary settlement and codicil were void from vagueness and
uncertainty as to their meaning and effect and that she, as heir-at-law
and next-of-kin of John Stuart McCaig, was entitled to succeed on
intestacy to his whole estate with certain unimportant exceptions. The
action was not brought on the ground that John Stuart McCaig was of

---

[16] *McCaig v University Court of the University of Glasgow and another* (1904) 6 F 918;
12 SLT 174. In a judgment which is reported in half a page, the Second Division
of the Inner House refused the appeal.

[17] (1905) 13 SLT 565.

unsound mind at the time he executed the testamentary documents, although of course it was accepted that the provisions of these documents were "peculiar and fanciful", as Lord Dundas himself put it:[18]

> "The question is whether these writings in whole or in part, are void from uncertainty, or as being against public policy, or from unworkability, or upon any other ground known to the law."

Lord Dundas dealt with three main issues. In the first place, there was the argument that the testamentary documents did not actually operate as bequests to any identifiable person and so did not create any beneficial trust; accordingly, the estate could not be said to have been diverted away from the heir. In answer to that, Lord Dundas stated:

> "A Truster may, I apprehend, do what he wills with his own provided his testamentary disposition is expressed with sufficient clearness and is not contrary to public policy or morals."

Lord Dundas also gave John Stuart McCaig credit for having philan-thropic motives. He went on to say:

> "I think that when the settlement is read as a whole, it appears that Mr McCaig's object was really two-fold, and embraced both the encour-agement of Scottish arts and artists and the erection upon his estate of family statues and artistic towers. Each of these aims was intended to be a means toward the achievement of the other."

In relation to the statues, Lord Dundas was of the view that the directions were neither vague nor uncertain nor unworkable, although he did accept that the scheme might be characterised as eccentric or of doubtful wisdom. He did, however, have some difficulty with the towers and accepted that the directions in the testamentary documents were open to more serious attack in respect of vagueness and uncertainty both in conception and expression. Nevertheless, he came to the conclusion, not without hesitation and reluctance, that the wishes and desires of the truster had been expressed with sufficient clarity to enable practical trustees to carry them out. He was further of the view that the directions were not in respect of an illegal object nor an object which was entirely unbeneficial. He concluded:[19]

---

[18] (1905) 13 SLT 565 at 566.
[19] *Ibid* at 567.

"The scheme may be fantastic, and may result in what most people
will consider waste of money. But the money was Mr McCaig's and the
project is neither, so far as I can see, contrary to public policy or morals,
nor more vague and indefinite in scope than some of the schemes which
have been held to be within the recognition of the law."

The second issue which was considered by Lord Dundas was whether
or not at some time in the future the scheme set out in the testamentary
documents might prove to be unworkable. If that happened, Lord
Dundas's view was that Catherine McCaig or those who held her right
could come back to the court under altered circumstances and then
succeed in obtaining the judgment sought. Alternatively, he was of
the view that, if the trust were to be construed as a public trust, the
trustees themselves could come back to the court and ask the court to
approve a *cy près* scheme.

The third issue was whether or not, construing the testamentary
documents as a whole, they did actually dispose of the whole estate
or whether there was in law a partial intestacy. Lord Dundas had no
difficulty in holding that the words used by John Stuart McCaig in the
documents were clearly indicative of an intention to dispose of his
whole estate. Catherine McCaig then lodged an appeal and the case
went to the Inner House.

Act 1, scene 4: *McCaig v University of Glasgow*[20]

When the case called before the Inner House, two additional pleas for
the pursuer, Catherine McCaig, were added by amendment. The first
plea was to the effect that, since the testamentary documents made no
beneficial disposal of the estate except in relation to the direction for
payment of annuities, they were ineffectual to exclude the rights of the
pursuer as sole heir in heritage and movables. The second plea was to
the effect that the provisions of the testamentary documents relative
to the erection and building of monuments, statues and towers were
not valid or effectual to exclude her rights as sole heir in heritage and
movables. Accordingly, she was entitled to decree. In terms of the first
conclusion of the summons, the University of Glasgow, who by now
must have rued the day it ever accepted office as trustee, plead that
John Stuart McCaig, having conveyed his whole means and estate to
it as trustee, it was entitled to *absolvitor* and also that the testamentary

---

[20] 1907 SC 231.

documents were not void or ineffectual from vagueness or uncertainty or otherwise. For good measure, the defenders (technically the University Court) having plead that all parties were not called, Catherine McCaig brought a supplementary action against, among other people, the University of Glasgow and the Senatus of the University of Glasgow.[21] The actions were then conjoined.

Essentially the same arguments were made before the Inner House. In the first place, it was argued that there was no beneficial bequest of heritable and movable estate as only the income was to be used for the trust purposes and, in any event, it was not clear who could actually enforce the provisions as there was no public interest which would have given the Crown or a member of the public in an *actio populais* (an action on behalf of the public) a title to sue. Accordingly, it was argued there was a resulting trust in favour of the heir-at-law. Secondly, it was argued that the trust purposes were too vague and indefinite and, accordingly, it would be impossible to say what would actually amount to a breach of trust. It was argued that this was not a charitable or educational bequest and, accordingly, the court would not be able to assist the trustees by approving a *cy près* scheme. It was argued that the class of "young and rising artists" was not sufficiently definite. Thirdly, it was argued that the trust purposes were void and ineffectual as being contrary to public policy.

It was argued for the trustee that any conveyance to trustees for purposes which were sufficiently definite was enough to divest the heir. It was accepted in this argument that in the future there might come a point in time when the trust's purposes were entirely fulfilled and there could be then a resulting trust to the heir-at-law, but that was not sufficient ground for declaring the trust purposes ineffectual from the outset. Moreover, it was argued for the defenders that there was no need for any identified person or public interest to be benefited; all that was necessary was that the purposes be definite and intelligible and not *contra bonos mores* (contrary to public policy). Where there was some purpose which did not benefit an individual, the Crown had a title to enforce the trust in an *actio popularis*. In a telling phrase, it was argued that, however, whimsical and eccentric the testator's post-death purposes were, if they were intelligible and definite they must be carried out. There was nothing impracticable or inexplicable about

---

[21] One can only imagine the consternation in the Senate Office on receipt of the summons.

the trust at the present time and it did not matter that the trust might appear to be for the glorification of the testator's memory.

In the Outer House, Lord Dundas had taken the view that a testator could more or less do as he wished with his own money provided the trust's purposes were intelligible and not contrary to public policy. When one reads the judgments of the judges in the Inner House in the 1907 report of the 1906 appeal it is quite plain that their view of Mr McCaig and his right to do what he liked with his own money was radically different from the view of Lord Dundas. At the end of the day, the judges also based their decision on the point that the estate had not in fact been beneficially disposed of. However, an analysis of what was actually said in the judgments indicates that at least three of their lordships had formed a very definite view as to whether or not a court should allow extravagant trust purposes of this nature. The views of the Lord Justice-Clerk were plain from the outset. He said:[22]

> "Now what was it that Mr McCaig expressed in the Deed? What was his desire and intention? He seems to have been possessed of an inordinate vanity as regards himself and his relatives, so extreme as to amount almost to a moral disease, though quite consistent with sanity."

His Lordship went on to point out that there was no bequest to anyone in the testamentary documentation and accordingly there was no beneficiary for whom John Stuart McCaig has disinherited his heir. His Lordship went on to hold that it could not be suggested that any young or rising artists would have any title to come forward as beneficiaries because there was no educational trust. The Lord Justice-Clerk's judgment is short, sharp and very much to the point. Lord Kyllachy was more circumspect. He relied more heavily on the lack of disposal of beneficial ownership of the estate. He did not express his final opinion on the contention that the purposes of the trust were void from uncertainty; neither did he give an opinion on whether or not the trust purposes were contrary to public policy. He did, however state:[23]

> "For I consider that if it is not unlawful, it ought to be unlawful, to dedicate by testamentary disposition, for all time, or for a length of time the whole income of a large estate – real and personal – to objects of no utility, private or public, objects which benefit nobody, and which have

[22] 1907 SC 231 at 239.
[23] *Ibid* at 242.

no other purpose or use than that of perpetuating at great cost, and in an absurd manner, the idiosyncrasies of an eccentric testator. I doubt much whether a bequest of that character is a lawful exercise of the *testamenti factio*."

Having indicated that he did not need to give an opinion on this point, Lord Kyllachy went on in the same vein:

"Indeed I suppose it would be hardly contended to be so if the purposes, say of the trust, were to be slightly varied, and the trustees were, for instance, directed to lay the truster's estate waste, and keep it so; or to turn the income of the estate into money, and throw the money yearly into the sea; or to expend the income in annual or monthly funeral services in the testator's memory; or to expend it in discharging from prominent points upon the estate, salvoes of artillery upon the birthdays of the testator, and his brothers and sisters."

Towards the end of his opinion, however, Lord Kyllachy stated that he preferred to rest his judgment on the doctrine already expressed, namely that there could be no divestiture of a man's heirs or next-of-kin except by means of beneficial rights validly constituted in favour of third parties. He also held for good measure that there was no charitable or educational purpose. He did, however, hint[24] that he was having some difficulty in treating the trust purposes which involved a competition among Scottish artists seriously.

Lord Stormonth-Darling indicated that he agreed with much of Lord Dundas's opinion. In particular he supported the view that testamentary documents expressed with sufficient clarity should be given effect to providing they were not contrary to public policy or morals. He did, however, feel that Lord Dundas had erred in rejecting the broad and bold argument taken up by the pursuers that a proprietor of Scottish heritage could not deprive his heir by mere words of disinheritance.

Lord Low was even more circumspect in his judgment: he simply held that, to disinherit the heir-of-law or defeat the rights of an executor, it was necessary that the estate should actually be given to some other person. He took the view that the capital was not dealt with at all in the testamentary documents. He also took the view that there was no-one who could actually enforce the trust purposes, rejecting the notion that there was an educational or charitable trust.

[24] 1907 SC 231 at 243.

The decision of the Second Division has sometimes been cited as authority for the proposition that, if a trust confers no substantial human benefit, then it may be contrary to public policy.[25] What the court actually held was that, on a proper construction of the testamentary documents, there was no beneficiary (private or public) and, accordingly, the heir was not divested. As a subsidiary issue, the Court decided that the purposes were not specific enough for a public trust for educational or charitable purposes.

Act 2, scene 1: Catherine McCaig's will and codicil

One might suppose that Catherine McCaig, having battled her way through the courts and scored a notable victory in setting aside her brother's will, would have left sensible provisions in her own will The bulk of her estate was after all inherited from her brother, John Stuart McCaig. She left a trust disposition and settlement dated 18 April 1908 and a codicil dated 20 June 1910. In the trust disposition and settlement, she directed that a statue of her late brother Major Duncan McCaig be erected in an open space in front of property in Breadalbane Street, Oban. She also directed that a sum necessary to provide for the cost of the statue and for laying out the open space was to be a first charge on the free capital of her estate. The trustees were directed never to dispose of the open space. Duncan McCaig appears to have had some standing in the community in Oban. He was a captain and honorary major in the Argyllshire Volunteer Artillery and was awarded the Volunteer Officers' Decoration in 1892. The trustees were to hold the remaining capital and apply the income to the cost of repair to Miss McCaig's heritable properties and in disencumbering them of bonds. Any surplus income was to be divided in the following manner: (a) a supplement to the annual stipend of the minister of the United Free Church on the Island of Lismore to the extent of twenty pounds; (b) payment to the Town Council of Oban of twenty pounds per annum for the deserving poor; (c) an annuity of thirty pounds and two annuities of twenty pounds to three individuals. Any further remaining income was to be divided into three equal parts to be applied in the assistance of the education and maintenance of Gaelic speaking students at Scottish schools, universities or church colleges, providing lectures to further the knowledge and study of

[25] G L Gretton and A J M Steven, *Property, Trusts and Succession* (Tottel Publishing, 2009), 23.11.

the Gaelic language and literature and for the purpose of erecting and equipping a building on certain subjects in Oban to be called the "McCaig Memorial Institute".

It was, however, not the provisions of the trust's disposition and settlement which were to cause the difficulty but the provisions of the added codicil. The remarkable thing is that the terms of the codicil mirror to a great extent the provisions of Catherine McCaig's late brother's codicil which she was apparently so keen to attack. The codicil was in the following terms:

"I do hereby further provide and declare that my Trustees shall duly carry out purposes first and second of my foregoing trust-disposition and settlement, but that before proceeding to administer my trust-estate as further directed by my said trust-disposition and settlement, they shall in so far as may not have been done at the time of my death – (1) convert the McCaig Tower on the Battery Hill, Oban into a private enclosure by putting suitable railings in the apertures near the ground levels and erecting a suitable tower and gate; (2) clear all the ground within the tower, level the same, and lay it out in such manner as may be found most protective and suitable; (3) erect statues made of bronze within the tower and on the inside of and around the wall thereof of my father and mother and all my brothers and sisters and also of myself; declaring that said statues shall be erected either upon a ledge or upon balustrades as my trustees shall determine, the said statues to be place in the following order, in which order they shall also be erected from time to time as funds permit, viz:– the statues of my father and mother in the centre facing the doorway, and those of my brothers and sisters on each side of them in the following order, on my father's right hand the statues of John, myself Catherine, Donald and Anne, and on my mother's left hand Duncan, Jane, Dugald and Margaret, and opposite to the statues of my father and mother a statue of Peter my brother who died in infancy; and I declare it to be my instructions that all the statues are to cost not less than one thousand pounds each and to bear suitable inscriptions, and in the event of there being difficulty in getting a suitable likeness of my father, I direct that his statue shall be made to bear a family likeness to my brother the late John Stuart McCaig; and I further provide and declare that the cost of the above works at the McCaig Tower and of the various statues shall be made a charge upon the free revenue only, and shall not be made charges against capital, and that when these works have been completed and all the statues hereinbefore provided for erected, the upkeep of the said tower and statues shall become a first charge upon the revenue of my trust-estate; my trustees being bound to properly upkeep the McCaig Tower and

statues in all time coming out of the revenue of my trust-estate; and I
provide and declare that my trustees shall be bound to retain in all time
coming and not to sell or dispose of the McCaig Tower and statues; and
I provide and declare that upon completion, but not upon completion
of the above works and statues, the other purposes detailed in my trust-
disposition and settlement, commencing with purpose third shall come
into force and effect subject to the proper upkeep of the said McCaig
Tower and statues out of revenue."

The net effect of this codicil of course was to postpone payment of the
supplement to the annual stipend of the minister and the payment to
the Town Council for the deserving poor, as well as the annuities and
the provision for the support of Gaelic-speaking studies.

Catherine McCaig died, in her 85th year, on 1 July 1913, leaving free
estate estimated at £30,000 and yielding a free income of approximately
£2,000.

Act 2, scene 2: *McCaig's Trs v Kirk-Session of United Free Church of Lismore; sub nom McCaig's Trs v Magistrates of Oban*[26]

Presumably, the terms of the codicil did not go down well in the
manse at Lismore, nor in the Council Chambers in Oban. Neither
would it have pleased Bella McCaig, Maggie McNaughton and
Jessie McNaughton, the three ladies who were entitled to annuities.
Moreover, it would not have escaped anyone's notice, including the
trustees of Catherine McCaig, that the provisions of the codicil bore
a remarkable similarity to the provisions of John Stuart McCaig's
codicil which were so vigorously attacked by Catherine McCaig
herself. It was decided to bring a special case to the Inner House of
the Court of Session, at which the trustees and the other parties were
all represented. Two questions of law were put to the Court. The first
was whether the Church, the Town Council and the annuitants were
bound to submit to the trustees postponing the payments to them
until all the statues and other works had been erected and completed
as well as until the third purpose of the original trust disposition and
settlement had been fulfilled.[27] The second question was whether
or not these parties were entitled to payment of the provisions in
their favour out of the free revenue of the trust estate subject only to

[26] 1915 SC 426; (1915) 1 SLT 152.
[27] Income to be applied to repairing heritable properties and disencumbering them of bonds.

implement of the first, second and third purposes of the original trust disposition and settlement.[28]

The case was heard before the Second Division on 20 and 21 January 1915; Lord Dundas did not sit.[29] The Division comprised the Lord Justice-Clerk (Lord MacDonald[30]), Lord Salvesen and Lord Guthrie. Since the Lord Justice-Clerk had joined in the decision in the former case, his judgment was restricted to agreeing with the views of the other two judges. The rubric in the report of the case[31] is to the effect that the Court held that in respect of their unreasonable, extravagant and useless character the directions were invalid and could not receive effect. The rubric also indicates that opinions were given to the effect that the directions in the codicil were contrary to public policy. It is also indicated in the rubric that the earlier case of *McCaig* v *University of Glasgow*[32] was followed. The terms of the rubric are in marked contrast to those of the rubric in the earlier case. While the judgments in the case involving John Stuart McCaig's will and codicil indicated strong views on the part of the judges in relation to the extravagance of the provisions, the actual ground of decision was that, there being no party beneficially interested in or capable of enforcing the provisions, the heir-at-law was not disinherited. The decision in the second case involving Catherine McCaig's will and codicil is based on different grounds. The views of the judges are given in even more trenchant terms.

No objection was taken to the provisions in the trust disposition and settlement relative to the erection of the statue to Major Duncan McCaig. In the previous case, the McCaig Tower was referred to as a colosseum-like structure. In the second case involving Catherine McCaig's will and codicil, it is likened to the outer wall of a Spanish bullring, perhaps a less classical allusion.

Lord Salvesen made reference to the judgment of Lord Kyllachy in the previous case. In particular, he agreed that there was nothing against the validity of a will directed to the provision on a customary

[28] That is, ignoring the provisions of the codicil.
[29] It will be remembered he was involved as the Outer House judge in the case involving John Stuart McCaig's will and codicil.
[30] Lord MacDonald had presided over the Second Division when it heard the case concerning John Stuart McCaig's will and codicil. He resigned as Lord Justice-Clerk on 30 June 1915.
[31] 1915 SC 426.
[32] 1907 SC 231.

and rational scale of a burial place for a testator or a suitable monument to his memory. Lord Salvesen made reference to memorial statues to historical personages to which the public had access and to memorials to local celebrities unknown outside the district. On this basis, it was possible to support the provisions in the original trust disposition and settlement for the erection of the statue to Major McCaig; but in relation to the provisions of the codicil, Lord Salvesen stated:[33]

> "The expenditure of this large sum on statues which was directed apparently from motives of personal and family vanity will serve no purpose, all the less seeing that the family has virtually become extinct. It can be of no benefit to the public, because the enclosure to which the statues are to be erected is one to which they will have no right of access."

While Lord Salvesen indicated that he could find no distinction in law between the case before him and the previous McCaig case, he also held that the bequest was contrary to public policy on more than one ground. In the first place, he was of the view that the provisions of the codicil were "a sheer waste of money". Secondly, he was of the view that the Court could not support a bequest which could only gratify the vanity of testators who had no claim to be immortalised. He criticised both John Stuart McCaig and Catherine McCaig, pointing out of course that either of them could, while alive, have used their own money to erect the statues. He said:[34]

> "For many years they had apparently contemplated the erection of similar statues but they could not bring themselves to part with the money during their own lifetimes. Such considerations do not restrain extravagance or eccentricity in testamentary dispositions, on which there is no check except by the Courts of law. ... The prospect of Scotland being dotted with monuments to obscure persons who happened to have amassed a sufficiency of means, and cumbered with trusts for the purpose of maintaining these monuments in all time coming, appears to me to be little less than appalling."

Lord Guthrie felt that there were certain features of the case which distinguished it from the earlier case involving John Stuart McCaig's will and codicil. In the first place, in Catherine McCaig's case, there was no identifiable heir. In the second place, he felt that in John Stuart

[33] 1915 SC 427 at 433.
[34] *Ibid* at 434.

McCaig's case the bequests were more contrary to good sense, more unnatural and more referable to a morbid desire for self glorification. Lord Guthrie came to the conclusion that, while a desire to record the virtues and perpetuate the memory of parents and brothers and sisters was natural, customary and reasonable, the method of carrying out that desire in this case was the precise opposite. He came to this conclusion for no fewer than seven reasons: (i) because the memorials already erected were sufficient to perpetuate the memory of the family members; (ii) because the sites for the statues were inappropriate in relation to the people to be commemorated; (iii) because of the method of commemoration by bronze statues of such people; (iv) because in relation to two of the people (Miss McCaig's father and her infant brother Peter) there were no materials for making any accurate representation; (v) because the cost of the recumbent statue of the infant Peter was to be no less than £1,000; (vi) because there was no limit of price; and (vii) because two statues were proposed for Major Duncan McCaig.

Lord Guthrie stated that whether a testamentary provision was sufficiently contrary to public policy to warrant the court's interference would in all cases be a matter of degree. However, he was clear that in this case the provisions were contrary to public policy. He said:[35]

> "If anybody went to see the statues, supposing they represented faithfully the persons to be commemorated, it would not be to admire them but to laugh at them, and perhaps to philosophise on the length to which morbid family pride may drive an otherwise sensible person. These statues would not in fact achieve Miss McCaig's object of perpetuating an honourable memory. They would turn a respectable and creditable family into a laughing stock to succeeding generations."

There seems little doubt that, in the second case, their Lordships were less well disposed to the notion that testators can do as they wish with their own estate. Of course, their Lordships may simply have been understandably annoyed that virtually the same issue should come before them on two separate occasions and that somehow Miss Catherine McCaig had not learnt anything from her previous victory. One must also bear in mind that, at the time this case was being heard, the First World War was raging and many young men would not be immortalised in statues. To have to come to a view yet again in relation

---

[35] 1915 SC 427 at 438.

to what many would have regarded as wasteful provisions at such a time may also have resulted in stronger language being used. What is clear is that the Court moved away from simply deciding that there had to be some identifiable beneficiary to the point where they were quite happy to criticise the provisions as contrary to public policy.

Other follies

In the judgments in the *McCaig* cases, reference was made to other, more reasonable, testamentary provisions which direct trustees to erect monuments. Whether such provisions cross the "McCaig line" is a matter of fact and circumstance in each case. The test is whether or not the provisions are an abuse of the *testamenti factio* (the right to make a will). It was put rather colloquially by Lord President Clyde in this way:[36]

> "There are of course unwise and even eccentric people who leave behind them unwise and eccentric wills. These are entitled to respect just as much as the wills of wise and sober-minded people. But the principle seems (if I may state it in a popular way) to be that, just as a mad person cannot make any will, so a sane person cannot make a mad will."

In *MacKintosh's Judicial Factor* v *Lord Advocate*, the testatrix provided that her whole estate should be expended on the erection of a vault on ground to be purchased. She directed that the remains of her uncle and aunt should be exhumed from the grave in which they had been buried for many years and buried along with her own remains in the vault. However, the testatrix was of illegitimate birth. Accordingly, as the law stood in 1935, she was not legally related to the so-called uncle and aunt. The court held that her estate had fallen into intestacy and therefore fell to the Crown in respect that she could not direct an application for the exhumation and re-interment of persons to whom she was not related. What is interesting about the case is the differing views of the judges in relation to the nature of the bequest itself. The Lord President was of the view that the direction was perfectly valid. He was of the view that the *McCaig* cases were not easy to understand and that there was considerable conflict of opinion amongst the members of the courts who delivered the judgments. In a sympathetic passage, he said:[37]

---

[36] *MacKintosh's Judicial Factor* v *Lord Advocate* 1935 SC 406 at 411.
[37] *Ibid* at 411.

"One tries to place oneself in her position. She had not been married and had no children; and, owing to a defect of status under which she suffered by no fault of her own she was without a living relative in the world. … As it appears to me, she, not unnaturally sought such consolation as might be derived from the assurance that her remains were to rest alongside the remains of the only two people in the world with whom she had any relation. It is no doubt impossible to look at her plan for the realisation of such a project without a smile; and it is impossible not to be impressed by the grossly disproportionate character of the project. But I do not, for myself, see my way to say that it constitutes an abuse of testamentary power."

The Lord President summed up his feelings in a sentence of almost child-like delicacy when he said:

"The result is that I am not prepared to condemn the testator's direction to erect this little mausoleum for three – for herself and her only known relatives – as coming within the class of extravagant direction which on the authority of the McCaig cases, ought to be refused effect."

Lord Blackburn was less sympathetic than the Lord President. He said:[38]

"I should have been prepared to hold that it was such a preposterous and extravagant scheme, and such a complete waste of money, as to entitle us to refuse to allow the estate of the testatrix to be thrown away in attempting to carry out that part of her scheme."

Another example of the application of *McCaig* cases is *Aitken's Trs* v *Aitken*.[39] In that case, the testator was the last of a family which had been connected with a particular burgh for centuries. In his will, the testator expressed a desire that a monument should be erected in memory of his family and himself. This however was no ordinary monument. It was to be a massive equestrian bronze statue, of artistic merit, of himself as champion riding the marches on a site in one of the main streets of the burgh, then occupied by shops and dwelling houses of which he was proprietor. This would have involved the demolition of these buildings which were on the High Street. The judges in the Inner House held that the directions were invalid, but interestingly enough all for different reasons. Lord Sands took the view that, although the object of the bequest was in itself not unreasonable, the method for carrying it out was irrational and destructive of that object. According

---

[38] *MacKintosh's Judicial Factor* v *Lord Advocate* 1935 SC 406 at 413.
[39] 1927 SC 374.

to Lord Blackburn, the directions were invalid because they were contrary to public policy. Lord Ashmore held that the directions were invalid because they conferred no benefit on anyone. Of more interest, perhaps, were the observations of Lord Sands and Lord Ashmore to the effect that it was possible to disinherit an heir-at-law, not only by a specific bequest of heritage to another person, but also by its dedication to any valid purpose. It will be remembered that, in the first *McCaig* v *University of Glasgow* case,[40] the basic ground of the decision was there was no identified beneficiary who might enforce the directions in the testamentary document.

The matter was considered again more recently in *Sutherland's Tr* v *Verschoyle*.[41] In that case, a testatrix by holograph will directed her trustees to devote the trust estate to house, arrange and preserve for perpetuity her "valuable art collection". The trustees were directed to transfer the collection to St Andrews and to obtain a house there with a resident caretaker. The total value of the works of art in her possession was almost £12,000. However, only one or two were valuable, and the collection as a whole was described as a "heterogeneous conglomeration with no group of material sufficient to illustrate an historical or educational theme". A special case was presented, and reference was made to *MacKintosh's Judicial Factor* v *Lord Advocate*, the *McCaig* cases and *Aitken* v *Aitken's Tr*. The Lord Justice-Clerk admitted that *prima facie* the bequest appeared to confer a substantially greater public benefit than in the other cases, but he took the view that one had to look at the collection as a whole and its viability to be publicly exhibited in perpetuity. The court ruled that, in the circumstances, the direction was so wasteful as to be contrary to public policy. The Lord Justice-Clerk accepted that it was only in the most exceptional circumstances that courts would interfere with the express wishes of a testator, but in this case any public benefit which would arise from implementing the bequest would be so minimal that implementation would be grossly extravagant and so completely wasteful as to be contrary to public policy. The other three judges simply concurred.

Epilogue

It is I think fair to say that there is no general rule or principle which can be stated with any degree of certainty. It is obvious that there

---

[40] *McCaig* v *University of Glasgow* 1906 SC 231.
[41] 1968 SLT 43.

are two opposing principles or at least one principle and a number of opposing principles. The main principle of course is that a man or woman can do as they wish with their estate in a will or other testamentary writing. Against this principle, there seem to be a number of qualifications:

(a) the direction or purpose may be void by reason of uncertainty;[42]
(b) a direction or purpose may be void if it is to be regarded as contrary to public policy or *contra bonos mores*;
(c) a direction or purpose may be void if it appears to confer no substantial human benefit;[43]
(d) a direction or purpose may be void if, although conceived as fulfilling some sort of public or quasi-public function does not actually confer an appropriate and reasonable benefit upon the public.[44]

The case reports contain many derogatory remarks concerning the directions of various testators. Examples would be "vanity," "extravagance", "sheer waste of money", "no claim to be immortalised", "appalling", "morbid desire for self glorification", "injurious to public amenity", "unnatural and unreasonable", "useless waste", "laughing stock", "crazy directions" and "mad will".

It is, of course, extremely difficult to say what would today be regarded as contrary to public policy or indeed *contra bonos mores*. There may be those who would argue that there is no distinction between the two in any event. In 1939, Miss Elizabeth Lindsay (otherwise Campbell) who was a Roman Catholic directed her executor to have a fixed sum invested, the income of which was to be handed over half-yearly to a named church to provide bi-weekly masses for her late mother and herself. In a further direction, she provided that another sum should be invested and the income applied to provide a weekly supply of fresh flowers to be placed on the grave of her mother and herself. To modern eyes, both of these directions might seem reasonable and indeed "sane" and hardly *contra bonus mores* or against public policy. Moreover, they are neither ambiguous nor vague and there appears to be a definite, if private, purpose. Nevertheless, the Second Division of

---

[42] *Lee Hardie* v *Morison* (1899) 7 SLT 42.
[43] *McCaig* v *University of Glasgow* 1907 SC 231.
[44] *Aitken's Trs* v *Aitken* 1927 SC 274.

the Inner House of the Court of Session held that, although provision of funds to provide masses was valid because it was in substance an endowment of a particular church for an act of public worship, the direction to provide funds for a weekly supply of fresh flowers was invalid in respect that it conferred no benefit on any person or class of persons and was intended merely to perpetuate an act begun by the testatrix and so was too indefinite and unreasonable to receive effect. The petition by the executor was heard by four judges[45] (Lord Justice-Clerk Aitchison with Lords Mackay, Wark and Jamieson). The Lord Justice-Clerk had no doubt that the bequest of £1,000 to apply the income and perpetuity for putting flowers on a grave was invalid. It was the amount that was the problem for him. However, he based his judgment on the "cardinal principle" that, by the law of Scotland, there could be no divestiture of a man's heirs or next-of-kin except by means of beneficial rights validly constituted in favour of third parties. This is rather odd in as much as earlier in his judgment he said that it would be quite in order for a sum to be set aside to maintain a grave.

As an epilogue to this epilogue, it should be noted that Ann McCaig, sister to John Stuart and Catherine, also set up a trust of her own, but this trust did not find its way to the Court of Session. In her trust disposition and settlement dated 27 June 1901 and registered in the Books of Council and Session on 22 April 1902, she is designed as being of 303 Sauchiehall Street, Glasgow and of Corran Mhor Villa, Oban. She directed her trustees to hold the residue of her estate for the United Free Church of Scotland and to accumulate income until £30,000 had been gathered. This sum was to be used to pay for the erection and completion of a church at a site which she had already acquired in Oban. As might befit any bequest by a McCaig, the church was to be in the style of a cathedral and to be known as "Christ's Church". It took some time to accumulate the necessary funds, by which time the United Free Church had reunited with the Church of Scotland, but the church was built and the dedication and opening services took place on 20 and 23 June 1957. However, controversy arose in 1983 when there was a proposed union between a number of churches in Oban, resulting in the united congregation having four places of worship including Christ's Church, Dunollie. A proposal of the kirk session to return the church to Ann McCaig's trustees was vetoed by the presbytery on 3 March 1987. Eventually, after appeals

[45] *Lindsay's Exr* v *Forsyth* 1940 SC 568.

to the Synod and the General Assembly, the Presbytery of Lorne and Mull passed a deliverance on 7 December 1988, stating that the Corrin Esplanade Church (Christ's Church) should be retained. This decision was appealed to the Synod but that appeal was dismissed. Title to the church is now vested in the Church of Scotland General Trustees, but they hold title for the Ann McCaig's trust which is still running.

Chapter 10

SPARE THE ROD
Campbell and Cosans v United Kingdom

Kathleen Marshall

Two stories

When 15-year-old Jeffrey Cosans decided to take a short cut home from school through a cemetery, he could hardly have imagined that this would be the start of a 6-year legal battle that would become known across the world and that would affect the lives of millions of children.

Jeffrey was a pupil at Beath Senior High School in the Fife town of Cowdenbeath. On 23 September 1976, the Assistant Headmaster noticed him walking in the school grounds near the cemetery, which was out of bounds for pupils. When questioned, Jeffrey admitted that he had intended entering the cemetery and the Assistant Headmaster ordered him to report the following morning for corporal punishment for disobeying school rules. This traditionally took the form of one or more strokes of the "tawse" – a leather belt designed for that purpose. Jeffrey discussed the matter with his father and, on his advice, Jeffrey reported to the Assistant Headmaster as required but refused to accept corporal punishment. The school's response was to suspend him from attendance until he agreed to submit to the punishment. This was later modified to an offer by the school that he could return if his parents agreed that Jeffrey would obey the school's rules, including its disciplinary arrangements. They refused to agree to this condition, insisting that their son should never be subjected to corporal punishment. Jeffrey never returned to school and his parents were threatened with prosecution for failing to secure his attendance. On 1 October, Jeffrey's mother, Jane Cosans, submitted a complaint to the European Commission for Human Rights, alleging breaches of her own human rights as a parent and those of her son.

The Commission already had before it a complaint submitted the previous March by Grace Campbell, a medical secretary from Glasgow. She was concerned about the possibility of her 6-year-old son, Gordon, being physically punished at his State school – St Matthew's Roman Catholic Primary School in Bishopbriggs, near Glasgow. While no such punishment had been administered or threatened, it was standard practice at the school. Mrs Campbell had sought, but failed to obtain, an assurance that her son would not be punished in this way.

The Commission declared both applications admissible and, after written submissions and oral hearings, decided in 1979 that the applications should be considered together.

Scots law before Campbell and Cosans

The common law of Scotland recognised the rights of parents, teachers and others with care of a child to administer reasonable physical chastisement to the child.

In 1828, the law was described by John Erskine in his influential *Institute of the Law of Scotland*. He observed that parents had a power to exercise over their children:

> "that degree of discipline and moderate chastisement upon them, which their perverseness of temperament or inattention calls for".[1]

The power to chastise was also recognised as belonging to other carers and to schoolteachers. Thus, in 1848, the judge in the case of *Muckarsie* v *Dickson*, finding a teacher guilty of a severe beating of a pupil at Auchtermuchty involving about 14 lashes with the tawse attached to a stick, said:

> "It is clear that a teacher of a public school, being bound to see that the pupils behave correctly, is entitled to administer chastisement when the pupils deserve it; but it must be moderate, and without any cruel or vindictive feeling or passion."[2]

In 1964, the case of *Gray* v *Hawthorn* involved the repeated assault of an 11-year-old with a leather strap for a succession of very minor misdemeanours. He received eight strokes within a period of 2 hours for things such as having dirty hands and knees, having an untidy

---

[1] A B Wilkinson and K McK Norrie, *The Law Relating to Parent and Child in Scotland* (1993), p 177, quoting Erskine, *Institute of the Law of Scotland*, I, vi, 53.
[2] *Muckarsie* v *Dickson* (1848) 11 D 4, per LP Boyle at 5.

bag, and misspellings. The court of appeal upheld the finding of guilt
by the lower court. There appeared to be no deliberate defiance or
breach of discipline on the boy's part and the teacher's assaults on him
amounted to persecution. Lord Guthrie pronounced:

> "There is no doubt that a school teacher is vested with disciplinary
> powers to enable him to do his educational work and to maintain proper
> order in class and in school, and it is therefore largely a matter within
> his discretion whether, and to what extent, the circumstances call for the
> exercise of these powers by the infliction of chastisement. … It is only if
> there has been an excess of punishment … that it can be held to be an
> assault. In other words … whether there has been … evil intent …"[3]

There had been debate about whether carers other than parents
were able to exercise their power independently or whether this was
delegated from the parent.[4] This had implications for the *Campbell and
Cosans* case. If the teacher's power was exercised by delegation, the
parent could withdraw the delegation and thereby prohibit the use
of corporal punishment. If the teacher's power was independent, the
parent had no such authority to prohibit corporal punishment by a
teacher.

In effect, the power of discipline was generally viewed as an
integral aspect of the relationship between teacher and pupil rather
than a delegation from a parent.[5] In 1981, after Jeffrey Cosans' refusal
to accept corporal punishment, but before the matter had been
pronounced upon by the European Court of Human Rights, the law
of Scotland was explained by Lord Justice-Clerk Wheatley in *Stewart
v Thain*.[6] In this case, the headmaster of a school in Dunoon had
called at the home of a difficult 15-year-old pupil after his adopted
father had written expressing the opinion that "it is about time he
was taught a lesson by some authority other than mine". The home
situation was tense and it was agreed that the headmaster would
take the boy away for punishment. He took the boy to his own home,
sought to calm him through "relaxing therapy", then told him to
drop his trousers to receive punishment. The boy was made to bend

---

[3] *Gray* v *Hawthorn* 1964 JC 69 per Lord Guthrie at 75.
[4] Wilkinson and Norrie (n 1 above), p 177.
[5] Wilkinson and Norrie use slightly less forceful words at p 178 and cite two cases:
McShane v *Paton* 1922 JC 26, per Lord Salvesen at 31, and *Brown* v *Hilsom* 1924
JC 1, per Lord Cullen at 5.
[6] *Stewart* v *Thain* 1981 JC 13, per LJ-C Wheatley at 18.

over a piece of furniture. The headmaster lifted the waist-band of his underpants and smacked him on the upper part of his buttocks about four times, with increasing severity. When the form of the punishment later came to light, the father reported the matter to the police and the headmaster was charged with indecent assault. He was acquitted and the procurator fiscal appealed against the acquittal. In refusing the appeal, Lord Justice-Clerk Wheatley accepted the law set out in earlier cases such as *Gray* v *Hawthorn* concerning the independent disciplinary power of a school teacher. In the circumstances of *Stewart* v *Thain*, he accepted the view that the headmaster was also acting in a sense *in loco parentis*. Therefore, in the circumstances of this case and for *this* boy, the punishment was neither unnatural nor excessive.

Although rooted in the common law, the powers of reasonable chastisement were recognised by statute. In 1889, the Prevention of Cruelty to, and Protection of, Children Act was the first statute aiming to prevent cruelty to children. Section 14 said:

> "Nothing in this act contained shall be construed to take away or affect the right of any parent, teacher, or other person having the lawful control or charge of a child to administer punishment to such child."

During the parliamentary debates on the Bill,[7] concern had been expressed that this anti-cruelty legislation would be exploited by the newly-formed Society for the Prevention of Cruelty to Children in order to prevent corporal punishment. Mr Kelly MP insisted that the Society was out to "persecute" teachers by inviting people to send them information about instances of cruelty to children, which the Society would investigate at no cost to the informer. What is more, the informer's identity would be kept secret. Mr Kelly commented:

> "All over the country the Society are trying to get up these hole-and-corner inquiries and to induce people, under the promise that the names of informers will be kept private, to bring all sorts of charges against a most deserving class of persons – the masters and teachers in our schools."

The Government Minister hastened to reassure Mr Kelly that:

> "Not one single summons has been taken out by the Society against a teacher, and in only one instance was a scholar's expenses paid by the Society."

[7] *Hansard*, HC, 3 July 1889, cols 1381–1386.

He was:

> "anxious to give the teachers an assurance that all reasonable moderate punishment they may have to administer as discipline would not subject them to any liability under the Act".

The Children and Young Persons (Scotland) Act 1937 was the successor to the 1889 Act. Section 12 set out to prohibit cruelty towards children under the age of 16, but, like its predecessor, it was careful to safeguard the common law rights of reasonable chastisement. Section 12(7) said:

> "Nothing in this section shall be construed as affecting the right of any parent, teacher or other persons having the lawful control or charge of a child or young person to administer punishment to him."

Even if the law remained relatively static, practice did not. The following paragraphs will show how the category of what might be regarded as "reasonable" or "moderate" has changed significantly over the years.

The practice of school corporal punishment

Corporal punishment in schools is an ancient tradition, but not a consistent or unchallenged one. In *The History of Corporal Punishment*, George Ryley Scott traces its roots from the biblical sayings attributed to Solomon, through ancient Greece, the European Middle Ages and up to modern times, across all classes of society. Yet it was rejected by significant figures such as Confucius and Quintilian, and the lasting damage caused by beatings was noted by Erasmus and other historical figures.[8]

The severity of some school discipline is evidenced by a Scottish case of 1699, in which a schoolmaster, Robert Carmichael, was found guilty of beating one of his pupils to death. It was reported that:

> "It was found by the jury that the prisoner did three times successively make the deceased be held up, and severely lashed him on the back, 'and in rage and fury, did drag him from his desk, and beat him with his hand upon the head and back with heavy and severe strokes, and after he was out of his hands he immediately died'. That after the boy's death, the side of his head was swelled, and there were livid marks on it,

---

[8] G Ryley Scott, *The History of Corporal Punishment* (1996), Ch VIII.

and the marks of many stripes on the back and thighs. Although these circumstances, as well as a rattling noise in his breast upon the third beating, and a good quantity of blood being found under his body after death which had issued from the stripes on his back, afford Complete conviction (the body was not opened) that he died of the beating; yet the lenity of the court in this instance seemed to increase with the barbarity of the criminal, and they only sentenced him to receive seven stripes, and to be banished Scotland for life."[9]

The same issues were being discussed and addressed in England. A few years before the *Carmichael* case, Hale's *Pleas of the Crown* (1674) had noted:

"[If] by struggling the child or scholar or servant dies, this is only *per infortunium*. ... If done with a cudgel or other thing not likely to kill, it will be manslaughter: if done with a dangerous weapon likely to kill ... or maim ... murder. ... Yet though the correction exceeds the bounds of moderation, the court will pay a tender regard to the nature of the provocation."[10]

The fact that the *Carmichael* case was prosecuted indicates that it was, thankfully, an extreme, but more general practice in Scotland is highlighted by an extract from *The Edinburgh Review* of 1830:

"For all offences, except the most trivial, whether for insubordination in or out of school, for inability to construe a lesson, or to say it by heart, for being discovered out of bounds, for absence from chapel or school – in short, for any breach of the regulations of the school – every boy, below the 6th form, whatever be his age, is punished by flogging. This operation is performed on the naked back, by the head master himself, who is always a gentleman of great abilities and acquirements, and sometimes of high dignity in the church."[11]

Evidence from school "punishment books" shows a recurring pattern of beatings for very minor transgressions. Analysing such an English resource covering the years 1930 to 1956, one commentator noted that pupils aged 8 to 11 were given between one to four

---

[9] Percy, Reuben and Sholto, *The Percy Anecdotes* (originally published from 1820 to 1823: facsimile on line at www.mspong.org/percy; originally sourced from George Ryley Scott, *The History of Corporal Punishment*, 82–83).

[10] Hale, *Pleas of the Crown*, vol 1, 31, 261. Quoted by P Newell in *Children Are People Too: The case against physical punishment* (1989) at p 99.

[11] Quoted by Ryley Scott (n 8 above) at pp 83–84.

strokes of the cane for offences such as "inattention, bad work and 'inbred tiredness'". Other crimes included "inertia", "not trying", "idiotic behaviour" and "stealing and lying". "Talking", "laughing" and "disobedience" also brought physical retribution.[12] He concluded:

> "The number of canings over the years is clearly related to the character and style of the headmaster in office …"[13]

Attitudes began to mellow in the 1960s. In February 1968, a Code of Practice for state schools was agreed between the Scottish Education Department and the teachers' unions and distributed to all local authorities. It was identified as a step towards a desired elimination of corporal punishment which, in the meantime, was to be administered only as a last resort and after clear warnings. "The tawse" was the only permissible instrument of punishment. It was to be used only on the hand and was not to be used to punish poor work, truancy or lateness, unless it could be established that it was the child's fault.[14] While the Code had no statutory force and was not incorporated into teachers' contracts, it was something that might be referred to in civil or criminal proceedings or disciplinary cases.

Despite that, a study in Edinburgh in 1974 showed that over two terms there were 10,000 uses of the belt on only 70,000 pupils.[15] A 1977 survey by the Educational Institute of Scotland showed that 36 per cent of 12- to 15-year-old boys were belted at least once in 10 school days, and that 21 per cent of them were strapped three or more times during that period.[16] In 1980, Edinburgh University's Centre for Educational Sociology surveyed 40,000 school leavers and found that

[12] S Merry, "The good old days, eh?" in *Independent*, London, 3 October 1996.
[13] *Ibid.*
[14] Liaison Committee on Educational Matters (Scottish Education Department, Association of Directors of Education and Teachers' Associations), "Elimination of Corporal Punishment in Schools: Statement of Principles and Code of Practice" (1968). Quoted in the judgment of the European Court of Human Rights in *Campbell and Cosans*, para 16. See also Heatherbank Factsheet 12, *The Belt*, available at http://www.gcal.ac.uk/heatherbank/pdfs/fs12belt.pdf; and D Henderson, *TES*, 8 January 1999. On a personal note, as a teenager in upper secondary school in 1968, I can remember some rumours about changes in the rules on physical punishment – which was freely administered at my school – but no-one of course dared to let the pupils into the secret!
[15] Newell (n 10 above), p 134.
[16] www.corpun.com/scotland.htm.

only 1 in 20 boys had gone through secondary school without getting the belt.[17]

In the light of this history, we may be tempted to consider corporal punishment in schools as a long-standing tradition that has gone unchallenged until recent decades. But that would be wrong. The grievances children have felt about their brutal treatment are likely often to be have been nursed silently. Occasionally, however, they have emerged into public discourse.

In 1669, a "Children's Petition" was presented to Parliament by a "lively boy". It was described as:

"A modest remonstrance of that intolerable grievance our youth lie under, in the accustomed severities of the school-discipline of this nation."[18]

It suggested that:

"[Any] person, who by sweetness and gentleness, or by the gravity of their deportment and countenance, or else by prudence and contrivance, is not able to awe and keep a company of youth in obedience without violence ... is not fit for that function."[19]

In 1698, the petition was reformulated into a pamphlet in an attempt to persuade MPs to promote a Bill to control the use of corporal punishment in schools.[20]

Protests continued to appear sporadically across the UK. In 1792, a pupil at Westminster School condemned the use of corporal punishment in a school magazine and was expelled for his efforts. His name was Robert Southey and he went on to become Poet Laureate. In 1889, schoolboys demonstrated on London's Albert Embankment under banners demanding "No Cane".[21] In 1969, school pupil organisations held protests in London with the banning of caning as one of their demands.[22]

---

[17] www.corpun.com/scotland.htm quoting "Children under shadow of the belt," *Daily Record*, 26 November 1980.
[18] C B Freeman, "The Children's Petition and Its Sequel", *British Journal of Educational Studies*, vol 14, no 2 (May 1966), 216 – 223, quoted in Newell (n 10 above), 112.
[19] Quoted in Teachers TV: *The Behaviour Timeline,* accessed at www.teachers.tv/behaviour/timeline.
[20] Newell (n 10 above), Appendix 1, 131.
[21] These two examples are drawn from Heatherbank Factsheet 12, *The Belt*.
[22] Newell (n 10 above), Appendix 1, 134.

Peter Newell's 1989 book *Children are People Too: The case against physical punishment* lists a whole succession of attempts to ban school corporal punishment both locally and nationally from 1905 on. One of the major difficulties was the resistance of teachers to any change. Thankfully, this was not universal. 1968 saw the formation of STOPP (Society of Teachers Opposed to Physical Punishment) and the period following that witnessed increasing attempts by education authorities to ban the practice, some of which were successful.[23] The book also lists countries that had already banned school corporal punishment, starting with Poland in 1783.[24]

In Scotland, the Pack Committee (appointed by the Secretary of State for Scotland) recommended in 1977 that corporal punishment be eliminated by a gradual process encouraging consensus rather than by legislation. Interestingly, it reported that pupils too preferred corporal punishment to other methods of discipline.[25] But there are other views on this too.[26]

Debates about corporal punishment tended to speak about the rights of parents, teachers and carers. "Rights talk" gained an increasingly higher profile after the passing of the European Convention on Human Rights in 1950 – but it was still largely about the rights of adults.

The European Convention on Human Rights

The European Convention for the Protection of Human Rights and Fundamental Freedoms (ECHR) was adopted by the Council of Europe in 1950. It built on the 1948 Universal Declaration of Human Rights, which had been passed by the United Nations General Assembly as a response to the horrors perpetrated by totalitarian regimes during the Second World War. The stated aim of the Convention was "securing the universal and effective recognition and observance" of the rights set out in that Declaration.[27] The Council saw fundamental human

---

[23] Newell (n 10 above), Appendix 1 and Chapter 5.
[24] Others include: Netherlands (1820s); Belgium (1867); Austria (1870); Finland (1872); France (1881); Soviet Union (1917); Turkey (1923); Rumania (1948); Portugal (1950); Sweden (1958); Cyprus, Denmark and Spain (1967); and West Germany and some cantons of Switzerland (1969).
[25] These aspects of the report are referred to in the *Campbell and Cosans* judgment by the European Court of Human Rights at para 18.
[26] See, eg, the website of the Children Are Unbeatable Alliance, which has a section devoted to children's views: http://www.childrenareunbeatable.org.uk/pages/views.html.
[27] ECHR, Preamble.

rights as a common agenda among the States that were beginning
to form a European identity, and the collective enforcement of those
rights was something that could bind European States together. Until
1998, the enforcement mechanisms underpinning the Convention
included both a Commission and a Court of Human Rights. Cases
directed at the Court were filtered first by the Commission which
considered the application and made a decision about whether it
was admissible. The Commission was also charged with fact finding,
attempting conciliation between the parties with a view to reaching
a "friendly settlement" and giving a preliminary opinion on the merits
of the case.[28]

Over the years, the Convention was amended and augmented by
a series of "protocols", one of which is relevant to the *Campbell and
Cosans* case.

The arguments before the Commission

While the earlier protests against corporal punishment referred to
above arose from children, the case of *Campbell and Cosans* v *United
Kingdom* was taken to the European Commission by the childrens'
mothers. They claimed that:

1. The use of corporal punishment in schools breached Art 3 of
   the ECHR – the absolute prohibition of torture or inhuman
   or degrading treatment or punishment, which applied also to
   children; and
2. The use, or threatened use, of corporal punishment against their
   children breached the applicants' rights as parents to ensure
   that their children's education was in conformity with their (the
   parents') philosophical convictions (Art 2 of Protocol 1 to the
   ECHR).
3. Mrs Cosans also complained that Jeffrey's suspension from
   school was a denial of his right to education set out in Art 2 of
   Protocol 1.

The debates conducted between the parties both by written submissions and in the oral hearing focused on a number of questions:

[28] R Reed and J L Murdoch, *A Guide to Human Rights in Scotland* (2001), pp 67–68.
The Commission was abolished in 1998 in an attempt to speed up the progress
of cases.

- Did corporal punishment fall within the ambit of Art 3? And, if it did, were the pupils "victim" as required by the then Art 25(1), given that neither of them had actually been beaten?
- Could the method of discipline be regarded as part of "education and teaching" in terms of Art 2 of Protocol 1, or was it something separate that was not covered by the Convention?
- Could the parents' views on corporal punishment rightly be regarded as a "philosophical conviction"?
- Had Jeffrey Cosans been denied the right to education by virtue of his suspension? He had been suspended for nearly a whole school year, from 24 September 1976 until he reached school leaving age on 31 May 1977.

The mothers argued that the corporal punishment threatened was both degrading and inhuman and therefore breached Art 3 which was designed to prevent serious interference with human dignity. The children were "victims" because, even though no corporal punishment had actually been inflicted on them, there was a serious risk of that happening, and also because the very possibility of corporal punishment contaminated the ethos of the school. The parents viewed themselves as indirect victims because of the moral damage to them resulting from the situation. They pointed out that a number of the member States of the Council of Europe had banned corporal punishment in schools. This was relevant because the ECHR was seen as an evolving instrument, with the Court able to adapt its interpretation to common standards emerging amongst member states.[29]

The UK Government argued that moderate punishment on the hand with the "tawse" could not be considered to be torture or inhuman or degrading treatment or punishment. Scotland's domestic law and the 1968 Code of Practice on the administration of corporal punishment provided adequate safeguards against excess. Furthermore, methods of discipline did not form part of the functions of "education and teaching" addressed by Art 2 of Protocol 1, but rather formed part of the "arrangements under which these functions were carried out".[30] The Government therefore believed that the form of discipline chosen

---

[29] This approach was exemplified in the case of *Tyrer* v *United Kingdom* (1980) 2 EHRR 1, in which judicial birching of a 15-year-old on the Isle of Man was held to constitute degrading punishment in breach of Art 3.

[30] European Commission Report, para 52, p 18.

was not a matter addressed by that provision. Even if that argument failed and the Court felt that it *did* form part of "education and teaching," the Government argued that the parents' views on the matter could not be regarded as a "philosophical conviction". Article 2 of Protocol 1 linked "philosophical convictions" with religious convictions. In the Government's view, this showed that, to fall within the scope of the article, the conviction concerned had to be part of some sort of "creed". It had been inserted into the text to make allowance for agnostic convictions and had not been intended to open the door to any sort of moral belief or preference. The Government did not think preferences about disciplinary punishment met that test. The discussions that had led to the article's inclusion in the protocol showed that:

> "the object of this Article was to protect the prior rights of parents to choose the education to be given to their children and to set up a guarantee against totalitarian regimes, which subordinated the child to the benefit of the State and sought systematically to expose it to ideological propaganda".[31]

On a more practical note, the Government insisted that corporal punishment was used only to the minimum degree necessary to keep order and this use was supported by significant proportion of Scottish parents and teachers.

Nor, in the Government's view, had Jeffrey Cosans been denied the right to education. All that was required by the article was that there was access to education and Jeffrey had that access provided he obeyed the school's reasonable disciplinary rules.

The Commission's opinion

The Commission's report on the case is dated 16 May 1980. It felt the mothers' case was strongest where it presented their opposition to corporal punishment as a "philosophical conviction". It was not persuaded by the Government's argument that the method of punishment was not part of "education". "Education", the Commission said, "is generally understood as meaning not only theoretical instruction in a strict sense, but also generally the development and moulding of children's character and mental powers" (para 80). Discipline was an integral part of this (para 81).

[31] European Commission Report, para 51, p 17.

The Commission acknowledged the original aim of the reference to "philosophical convictions" that the Government had pointed out, but that did not mean it was to be interpreted so narrowly as to cover only pseudo-religious views. Demanding that standard would mean the article would apply to very few parents, which was clearly *not* the intention. However, it would also be unhelpful to interpret the phrase too widely. The Commission concluded that:

> "as a general idea, the concept of 'philosophical convictions' must be understood to mean those ideas based on human knowledge and reasoning concerning the world, life, society etc., which a person adopts and professes according to the dictates of his or her conscience. These ideas can more briefly be characterised as a person's outlook on life including, in particular, a concept of human behaviour in society" (para 92).

The report concluded:

> "As regards the present two applicants, the Commission is satisfied that their views on the use or threatened use of physical violence as a means of disciplining young children are indeed views of a clear moral order concerning human behaviour in respect of young children at school and in society at large. Furthermore, on the facts as established by the Commission, there is no indication whatever to show that these views are not genuinely held by them" (para 93).

Having decided that opposition to corporal punishment was a "philosophical conviction", the Commission went on to consider whether the parents' rights had actually been breached. It accepted the need for discipline in schools and was careful to point out that it would be reluctant to conclude that other punishments, such as extra homework, also fell within the scope of the article. Extending the category too far would make school life "impracticable". It was irrelevant that most parents supported the use of physical punishment. If it was a matter of "philosophical conviction", numbers did not matter (para 97). The Commission's conclusion was that:

> "The United Kingdom Government has failed to respect the applicants' philosophical convictions contrary to the second sentence of Article 2 of Protocol No 1" (para 101)

> "The Commission therefore concludes by nine votes against five that the failure to respect the applicants' philosophical convictions constitutes a

violation of the second sentence of Article 2 of Protocol No 1 to the Convention" (para 106).

The Commission decided that it did not have to explore Mrs Cosans' argument that Jeffrey had been denied the right to education because of his suspension. The facts were so linked that they felt this claim could be subsumed into the violation of rights that they had already proclaimed (paras 107–111).

They took the same approach with regard to the argument about whether the mothers were "victims". Even if they were not, they were acting as the guardians of their children who, the Commission decided, were potential victims:

> "It cannot be excluded that ... children may be affected by the existence of physical violence around them and by the threat of a potential use on themselves of corporal punishment" (para 116).

The Commission then turned to the major question about whether the corporal punishment threatened breached Art 3 of the Convention – the absolute prohibition of ""torture" or "inhuman or degrading treatment or punishment". They were quick to conclude that it was not torture and could not be regarded as "inhuman". On the circumstances of the cases presented to them, they concluded that the mothers had failed to convince them that the nature of what had been threatened was severe enough to be regarded as "degrading". In order for a punishment to be regarded as "degrading":

> "the humiliation and debasement involved must attain a particular level ... the assessment is, in the nature of things, relative: it depends on all the circumstances of the case and, in particular, on the nature and context of the punishment itself and the manner and method of its execution".[32]

The fact that no corporal punishment had actually been administered in the current cases made the measurement of severity impossible. The Commission was careful to conclude, however, that this did not mean that they thought school corporal punishment could never breach Art 3 (para 124).

In a dissenting opinion, Mr Klecker, a member of the Commission, concluded that there *had* been a breach of Art 3:

---

[32] Para 120, citing the judgment in *Tyrer* (n 29 above), para 30.

"Until the 20th century, physical chastisement was commonplace in all European countries, in the home as well as at school. Frequently inflicted by husbands on their wives and by masters on their apprentices, it sometimes took the form, in barracks and on board ship, of the most inhuman cruelty. The fact is that, having declined everywhere, it can nowadays be legally inflicted only on children. Corporal punishment amounts to a total lack of respect for the human being; it therefore cannot depend on the age of the human being" (paras 7 and 8 of the dissenting opinion attached to the Commission's report).

The European Court of Human Rights

The European Court of Human Rights considered the case on 28 September 1981 (oral hearings) and 29 January 1982 and delivered its judgment on 25 February 1982.[33] It accepted the view that the teacher's right to physically chastise a pupil, according to the law of Scotland, was independent of the parental right, rather than delegated by the parent. Its exercise was left largely to the discretion of the teacher, being subject only to the common law and any conditions contained in the teacher's contract of employment.

The Court said Art 3 could apply even if the boys had not actually been physically punished, because the mere threat of conduct prohibited by Art 3 could itself amount to "inhuman treatment" (para 26). However, the cases under examination did not meet the standard for this. There was no evidence that the threat had caused the boys suffering of a sufficient level to trigger Art 3. Nor could the situation be considered "degrading" because no punishment had taken place.

The Court gave much closer consideration to the claim that there had been a breach of Art 2 of Protocol 1 in respect of lack of respect for the parents' philosophical convictions. It agreed that corporal punishment fell within the scope of "education" for the purposes of that article:

"Education of children is the whole process whereby, in any society, adults endeavour to transmit their beliefs, culture and other values to the young, whereas teaching or instruction refers in particular to the transmission of knowledge and to intellectual development" (para 33).

Corporal punishment was:

[33] The case is reported as *Campbell and Cosans* v *United Kingdom* (1982) 4 EHRR 293.

"when used, an integral part of the process whereby a school seeks to achieve the object for which it was established, including the development and moulding of the character and mental powers of its pupils" (para 33).

It also supported the Commission's view that parental objections to corporal punishment could fall into the category of "philosophical convictions":

"such convictions as are worthy of respect in a 'democratic society' … and are not 'incompatible with human dignity' and which do not conflict with the fundamental right of the child to education'" (para 36).

In the Court's view:

"The applicants' views relate to a weighty and substantial aspect of human life and behaviour, namely the integrity of the person, the propriety or otherwise of the infliction of corporal punishment and the exclusion of the distress which the risk of such punishment entails. They are views which satisfy each of the various criteria listed above; it is this that distinguishes them from opinions that might be held on other methods of discipline or on discipline in general" (para 36).

It was not enough for the Government to argue that it was moving towards a consensual abolition of corporal punishment. This did not constitute "respect" for the applicants' philosophical convictions. The Court therefore agreed with the Commission's conclusion that the mothers' rights to respect for their philosophical convictions had been breached (para 38).

While the Commission had felt it unnecessary to examine the issue of Jeffrey's suspension from school and whether this was in breach of his right to education, the Court felt it must look at the matter. It noted that there was a substantial difference between the two breaches alleged in relation to Art 2 of Protocol 1. The issue about philosophical convictions was about the right of the parent. The argument about the right to education was about the right of the child (para 40). It could not therefore be subsumed into the first issue as the Commission had argued. Jeffrey's return to school was conditional upon his parents agreeing to something that went against their philosophic convictions and was in breach of their rights:

"A condition of access to an educational establishment that conflicts in this way with another right enshrined in Protocol No. 1 cannot be described as reasonable … There has accordingly also been, as regards Jeffrey Cosans, breach of the first sentence of that Article" (para 41).

The Court therefore at least acknowledged the concept of the rights of the child, but it is ironic that the decision in such a critical child rights issue turned mainly on the rights of parents to direct whether their children should be beaten or not.

Contemplating the prospect of parents being allowed to forbid schools to beat their children, the *Guardian* newspaper reported:

> "The ruling, legally binding on the Government, received a mixed reaction. Teachers' unions expressed concern, corporal punishment abolitionists are calling for a total ban and the Department of Education side-stepped any hasty commitment."[34]

The impact of the decision

Campbell and Cosans has been described as "undoubtedly the crucial event in the campaign against school beating".[35] It became clear to everyone – not least the UK Government – that the European Court was taking the matter seriously. The fact that there were others cases waiting to emerge onto the European stage showed that this was an issue that was not going to go away. One case in particular forced the Government's hand.

While the *Campbell and Cosans* case was proceeding through the European Court, an English school corporal punishment case was under consideration by the European Commission. *Mrs X v United Kingdom* centred on a 14-year-old who had received "a few strokes of the cane" from her headmistress. According to the Commission's report, dated 17 December 1981, "A doctor found that this caning had produced weals on the buttocks (one over a foot long) and hand. The child was in discomfort for several days and traces of the caning remained for a considerably longer period".[36] As in *Campbell and Cosans*, the child's mother claimed a breach of her child's rights under Art 3 in respect of degrading treatment or punishment, and a breach of her own rights as a parent under Art 2 of Protocol 1 to have her

---

[34] G Parry, *Guardian*, 26 February 1982.

[35] Newell (n 10 above), p 114.

[36] European Commission of Human Rights, *Mrs X v United Kingdom*. Report of the Commission adopted on 17 December 1981, para 5.

child educated in accordance with her own philosophical convictions. The Commission declared the case admissible and then followed its usual practice of trying to mediate a "friendly settlement" between the parties. The Government clearly realised that it was not in its interest to pursue the case and agreed to pay the applicant £1,200 plus costs. More interesting from our point of view was the requirement for "The dispatch of a circular letter by the central Government to the local education authorities stating that the use of corporal punishment might in certain circumstances amount to treatment contrary to Art. 3 of the Convention".[37] This was an interim measure forced on the Government by the *Mrs X v UK* case.

However, it was clear that something more substantive was required to implement the *Campbell and Cosans* judgment. In 1983, the Department of Education issued a consultative document, *Corporal Punishment in Schools*. It proposed a scheme allowing parents to opt their children out of the corporal punishment regime. This suggestion formed the substance of the Education (Corporal Punishment) Bill which was introduced in the House of Commons in 1985 and was widely ridiculed as being unworkable, unprincipled, unfair, "dotty" and "one of the silliest pieces of legislation that has ever come before the House".[38]

This last comment was uttered by Lord Stewart of Fulham who criticised the idea of a register showing which children were allowed to be beaten:

> When all this is done – when the register is prepared, the parents have made up their mind once and possibly changed it again, and the father and mother, if they disagree, have somehow reached an agreement on what is to be done – we are still left with the situation ... in which two children in the same class who have committed the same offence can be punished in quite a different manner. ... [T]he Bill ... puts the teacher in a position where two pupils have behaved in a very similar manner, in a manner that deserves rebuke or punishment, and one of them can receive corporal punishment while the other cannot. ... Well, all I can say is, let her try persuading the boy who has received the corporal punishment in those circumstances that that was fair, and she will not get very far with it. This was clear enough to a member

---

[37] European Commission of Human Rights, *Mrs X v United Kingdom*. Report of the Commission adopted on 17 December 1981, para 8.

[38] See *Hansard*, HL, vol 463, cols 479–518 (3 May 1985) and HL, vol 465, cols 1314–1333 (4 July 1985).

of the Government, the noble Baroness's colleague, the Lord Advocate, when he pleaded the British case before the Court of Human Rights. I shall quote what he said on that occasion: Lord Mackay, Lord Advocate, speaking for the Government during the hearing of Campbell and Cosans case before the European Court [said]: 'It would not be feasible to have a system in which children in the same class were differently treated in this respect according to the view of their parents because it must be a fairly fundamental practice of any reasonable system of discipline in a school that it should be seen to be fair'. Exactly the same view, though in different words, was expressed by Sir Vincent Evans, the British judge on the Commission, who dissented from the majority view of the Commission."

A further complication was that, in order to achieve consistency with the status of 16-year-olds in Scottish educational legislation, it had been felt necessary to make a special provision for Scotland so that, where a pupil was 16 or over, it was the pupil, not the parent, who could opt in to or out of the corporal punishment regime. Lord Mulley commented:

"[W]hat seems to me an extraordinary concept in the Bill is that a 16-year-old can go to the school authorities and say, 'Please put me down on the list so that I may be caned.' I should have thought that that was an almost impossible expectation. If you must have this nonsense of registers, I should think the most simple method would be to make the age of 16 an age above which corporal punishment cannot be employed against children, either in Scotland or in any other part of the United Kingdom."

On 4 July 1985, Baroness David moved an amendment to turn the Bill into an abolitionist measure. It was carried by 108 votes to 104. The Government took fright and hastily withdrew the Bill.

Still, something had to be done to implement the *Campbell and Cosans* judgment, but the Education Bill introduced the following year in the House of Lords was silent on the matter. On 17 April, 1986, during the Committee stage, peers voted, by 94 votes to 92, to insert an abolitionist measure. When it moved into the House of Commons, the Education Secretary, Kenneth Baker, announced that there would be a free vote on the issue. This kicked off an energetic campaign to persuade members to vote for abolition. On the day of the vote, 22 July, early editions of the *Evening Standard* carried a photograph of the bruised buttocks of a 13-year-old boy who had, 5 days previously, received five strokes of the cane for not doing well enough in an exam. Campaigners circulated the story to members thought to be wavering.[39] The abolitionist amendment was carried by only one vote – 231 votes to 230 – after a three and a half hour debate – to become S 47 (for England and Wales) and s 48 (for Scotland) of the Education (No 2) Act 1986. The ban took effect on 15 August 1987. However, it applied only to pupils in state schools or whose education was funded or supported by the state. Privately funded children at independent schools were not protected.

Teachers' views

The opposition of teachers to a ban had long been cited as a strong reason for retaining corporal punishment. When papers from the late 1960s were released under the 30-year rule, they showed that this opposition had persuaded ministers against a ban. Instead, they had set up a Liaison Committee on Educational Matters to consider the matter. Members included an umbrella group of unions, headteachers, employers and civil servants. They worked for two years to produce the 1968 Code, referred to in *Campbell and Cosans*, which was seen as a step in phasing out corporal punishment. In 1967, the Scottish Secondary Teachers Association had advised Ministers that teachers would not be prepared to give up the belt "until a proved alternative is forthcoming". Other teachers associations thought the Code merely reflected emerging practice.[40] So, there was disunity amongst the professional ranks. However, Newell identifies a "sudden conversion of the teachers' unions" following the decision in *Campbell and Cosans* so that, by the time the 1986 Bill was under consideration, most had already adopted abolitionist policies.[41] And indeed, by the time the 1986 Act was passed, practice in Scotland had already changed. Baroness Cox, moving the Second Reading of the 1985 Bill had noted:

> "The Secretary of State for Scotland has encouraged gradual elimination of corporal punishment and that process has been largely completed. That is a rather different policy from that in England and Wales, where many parents and teachers see a place for the moderate and reasonable use of that sanction in schools."[42]

---

[39] Newell (n 10 above), p 122.
[40] D Henderson, "Soft on teachers, soft on the belt" in *Times Educational Supplement*, 8 January 1999.
[41] Newell (n 10 above), p 117.
[42] *Hansard*, HL, vol 463, col 482 (3 May 1985).

Nevertheless, the prospect of a ban had the potential to cause consternation among some members of the profession. A Scottish headmaster, reflecting on that time, commented on staff anxiety about implementing a decision to ban the belt on an experimental basis:

> "Panic swept through the meeting. Teachers feared anarchy might ensue from telling students of our decision."

Their fears proved groundless:

> "Far from their being mayhem, the students reacted well and most parents accepted the decision although, sadly, over the years, a number requested that their child be belted."[43]

Despite periodic attempts by individuals and small groups to reintroduce corporal punishment in schools, the mainstream professional associations have strongly opposed it.[44]

As noted above, the ban was not complete. It applied only to publicly funded schools or publicly funded places in independent schools. The saga of opposition to a ban continued in independent schools and, particularly, in a small number of independent, Christian schools.

Independent schools

The catalyst for the move to ban corporal punishment in independent schools was yet another European Court case, *Costello-Roberts* v *United Kingdom*.[45] This was about a 7-year-old boy attending an independent boarding school who had received a "slippering" for talking in the corridor and other minor misdemeanours. The Court judgment relates that he was given "three 'whacks' on the bottom through his shorts with a rubber-soled gym shoe". His mother had placed him in the school knowing that it took discipline seriously but without any specific knowledge of its use of corporal punishment.

The Court said that Art 3 had not been breached as the punishment had not reached the minimum severity test that would allow the Court to conclude that it had been "degrading". However the fact that this case had failed merely on that test led the Government to introduce a

---

[43] Hugh Mackenzie, author of *Craigroyston Days*, quoted in *For whom the Belt Told*, an article by Rosie Free in *The Scotsman*, 14 May 2003.

[44] For example, BBC News Online, "EIS rejects belt classroom call", 7 June 2006.

[45] *Costello-Roberts* v *United Kingdom* (1993) 19 EHRR 1112.

measure to set thresholds for the administration of corporal punishment
in independent schools. The Education Act 1993, ss 293 and 294, made
it illegal for teachers in *any* school to administer corporal punishment
that was inhuman or degrading. A test was identified for this:

> "In determining whether punishment is inhuman or degrading regard
> shall be had to all the circumstances of the case, including the reason for
> giving it, how soon after the event it is given, its nature, the manner and
> circumstances in which it is given, the persons involved and its mental
> and physical effects."[46]

So now the situation was that corporal punishment was banned in
all state schools. In independent schools, it could not be used on any
pupils whose places were publicly funded. It could be used on pupils
whose places were privately funded, but had to be administered in a
way that was not "inhuman or degrading".

The media made some sport out of this. On 1 May 1994, the
Independent on Sunday published an article, "Where to send your
child to school if you want them beaten".[47] The author had been able
to find only four independent schools that admitted using corporal
punishment. The Independent Schools Information Service was
reported as being against corporal punishment and as advising that
this view was shared by most schools. It is open to debate whether
this development was spurred by a philosophical conversion or
mere pragmatism. The *Daily Telegraph* reported an interview with a
headmaster who opined that:

> "[M]ost headmasters in independent schools, faced with two categories
> of pupils, did away with corporal punishment."[48]

His own small school was different. It had no publicly funded pupils
and could therefore continue beating without the unhappy taint of
discrimination.

Corporal punishment in independent schools was finally pro-
hibited for England and Wales by s 131 of the School Standards and
Framework Act 1998 and for Scotland by s 16 of the Standards in
Scotland's Schools etc Act 2000.

---

[46] Education Act 1993, s 293(2) (England and Wales) and 294(2) (Scotland).
[47] P Victor, "Where to send your child to school if you want them beaten"
Independent on Sunday, 1 May 1994.
[48] T King, "Love must come first but caning works, says head", *Daily Telegraph*, 30
October 1996.

Most independent schools accepted this as reflecting what had become common practice. However, opposition remained from a small number of independent Christian schools who regarded physical punishment as a biblical requirement.[49] In the wake of the 1998 English legislation, they took their case to the English courts which were now required, by the Human Rights Act 1998, to take account of the ECHR. In a strange inversion of *Campbell and Cosans*, they argued that the ban on corporal punishment meant there was no longer any opportunity for them to ensure that their children were educated – and beaten – in accordance with their parents' philosophical convictions. The only options open to them were either to defy the ban, or to ask parents to come into the school to administer the punishment themselves when the need arose. The headmaster who led the case, Phil Williamson, is reported as saying:

"The Government is dismantling a tried and tested method. They are erring on the side of children's rights instead of parents' rights."[50]

When the case came to the House of Lords, the schools' approach to corporal punishment was summed up as follows:

"The claimants' beliefs regarding the use of corporal punishment by both parents and teachers are based on their interpretation of certain passages in the Bible. For instance, 'He who spares the rod hates his son, but he who loves him is diligent to discipline him': Proverbs 13:24. They say the use of 'loving corporal correction' in the upbringing of children is an essential of their faith. They believe these biblical sources justify, and require, their practices. Religious liberty, they say, requires that parents should be able to delegate to schools the ability to train children according to biblical principles. In practice the corporal punishment of boys takes the form of administering a thin, broad flat 'paddle' to both

---

[49] It should be noted that other Christian opinion is against corporal punishment. See eg, Churches' Network for Non-Violence, http://www.churchesfornon-violence.org/ which explains its stance as follows: "The Churches' Network for Non-violence (CNNV) has developed out of concern that physical punishment of children has been largely unchallenged by Christian and other religious communities. CNNV rejects all forms of violence against children including corporal punishment in all its forms. We believe positive, non-violent discipline best models the example set by Jesus. All the recorded encounters between Jesus and children were gentle, respectful and compassionate."

[50] A Benson, "Come to school and beat your own children", in *Daily Post*, Liverpool, 22 February 1999.

buttocks simultaneously in a firm controlled manner. Girls may be strapped upon the hand. The child is then comforted by a member of the staff and encouraged to pray. The child is given time to compose himself before returning to class ..."[51]

The House of Lords considered a number of dimensions of the case. Using the concepts developed by the European Court, it concluded that the right claimed by the applicants to manifest their beliefs under Art 9 of the Convention was not absolute. In this case, the Court concluded, government interference was "necessary" to protect the rights of vulnerable children. This was a legitimate aim and the interference was proportionate. There had therefore been no breach of Art 9.

Neither had Art 2 of Protocol 1 been breached. This right to respect for beliefs and philosophical convictions belonged to parents, not teachers. Lord Nicholls of Birkenhead concluded:

"The present case cannot be regarded as comparable to *Campbell and Cosans v United Kingdom* 4 EHRR 293. In the present case, unlike in the *Campbell* case, the claimants' beliefs involve inflicting physical violence on children in an institutional setting. Parliament was bound to respect the claimants' beliefs in this regard, but was entitled to decide that manifestation of these beliefs in practice was not in the best interests of children."[52]

Baroness Hale of Richmond took a strong children's rights approach:

"This is, and has always been, a case about children, their rights and the rights of their parents and teachers. Yet there has been no-one here or in the courts below to speak on behalf of the children. No litigation friend has been appointed to consider the rights of the pupils involved separately from those of the adults. No non-governmental organisation, such as the Children's Rights Alliance, has intervened to argue a case on behalf of children as a whole. The battle has been fought on ground selected by the adults. This has clouded and over-complicated what should have been a simple issue."[53]

She concluded:

[51] *R* v *Secretary of State for Education and Employment and others (Respondents), ex parte Williamson (Appellant)* [2005] HL 15, para 10.
[52] *Ibid* at para 52.
[53] *Ibid* at para 71.

"How could it be justified in terms of the rights and protection of the child to allow some schools to inflict corporal punishment while prohibiting the rest from doing so? If a child has a right to be brought up without institutional violence, as he does, that right should be respected whether or not his parents and teachers believe otherwise."[54]

Wider implications: the "safe parental smack"

The fact that corporal punishment has eventually been banned in all schools, despite opposition from many quarters, has given heart to those who still struggle to end all legitimised violence against children. Despite recent modifications of the law to restrict the scope of legitimate parental violence, the Scottish and UK Governments have shrunk from banning all parental violence against children.[55] The same arguments have been rehearsed as in the school debate about biblical duties and the perceived necessity of this last resort punishment. The same panic has been generated that a ban would lead to the end of civilisation as we know it, with parents jailed and children taken into care as a consequence of what some identify as "a safe parental smack".[56]

When the Scottish Law Commission published its *Report on Family Law* in 1992, it set out the results of its consultation about banning physical punishment in the home. It noted, but dismissed, the proposition that the school ban had led to a decline in school discipline:

"A few of those who were in favour of retaining the parental right of corporal punishment claimed that the abolition of corporal punishment in state schools had led to widespread indiscipline and disruption. Such research evidence as we have been able to assess does not bear this out. Discipline problems were present before corporal punishment was abolished. Indeed 'behaviour tended to be worse in schools with a high level of corporal punishment (which might mean more punishment leads to more rebellion, or more rebellion leads to more punishment). Certainly, it seems that schools with strict punitive strategies [did] not

---

[54] *R* v *Secretary of State for Education and Employment and others (Respondents), ex parte Williamson (Appellant)* [2005] HL 15, para 86.
[55] Scottish law is now set out in s 51 of the Criminal Justice (Scotland) Act 2003, and English and Welsh law in s 58 of the Children Act 2004.
[56] Scottish Law Commission, *Report on Family Law* (Scot Law Com No 135, 1992), paras 2.92–2.102.

avert delinquency'.[57] Since corporal punishment in state schools was
abolished, schools have developed a variety of strategies and sanctions
to cope with discipline problems. Research done in Scotland, at a time
when some schools had voluntarily abolished corporal punishment and
others had not, found that 'irrespective of whether a school employed
corporal punishment, there was a distinct gap between the best and the
worst classroom climates. In the schools which had given up corporal
punishment wholly or substantially, teaching and learning went on as
elsewhere. Standards of behaviour were not generally giving more cause
for concern to teachers, parents or pupils than in other schools. Nor did
the teacher-observers find the behaviour of pupils in the class rooms
detectably different from elsewhere'.[58] None of the schools which had
abandoned, or moved towards abandoning, corporal punishment had
considered re-introducing it. The majority opinion among staff and
pupils was that standards of behaviour were no worse since abolition or
reduction of corporal punishment."[59]

Nevertheless, the Commission rejected the idea of a total ban on
corporal punishment in the home and opted instead for a restriction in
the scope of allowable parental chastisement to take account of some
of the standards set by the European Court.

Since 1992, other European cases have fuelled the move for reform,
in particular *A v UK*. This case, decided in 1998, was about a 9-year-
old boy who had been severely caned by his stepfather on a number
of occasions. On examination, a paediatrician considered that the
bruising on the boy was consistent with the use of a garden cane
applied with considerable force on more than one occasion.

The stepfather had been found not guilty of a charge of assault
causing actual bodily harm. In summing up, the judge advised the jury
as follows:

"What is it the prosecution must prove? If a man deliberately and unjustifiably hits another and causes some bodily injury, bruising or swelling
will do, he is guilty of actual bodily harm. What does 'unjustifiably' mean
in the context of this case? It is a perfectly good defence that the alleged

---

[57] The Scottish Law Commission report cites M Johnstone and P Munn, *Discipline
in School: A Review of "Causes" and "Cures"* (Scottish Council for Research in
Education, 1987), 39 (footnotes omitted).

[58] The Scottish Law Commission report cites C E Cumming, T Lowe, J Tulips and
C Wakeling, *Making the Change: a study of the process of the abolition of corporal
punishment* (Scottish Council for Research in Education, 1981), 3.

[59] Scottish Law Commission, *Report on Family Law*, para 2.91.

assault was merely the correcting of a child by its parent, in this case the stepfather, provided that the correction be moderate in the manner, the instrument and the quantity of it. Or, put another way, reasonable. It is not for the defendant to prove it was lawful correction. It is for the prosecution to prove it was not.

This case is not about whether you should punish a very difficult boy. It is about whether what was done here was reasonable or not and you must judge that …"[60]

The European Court took a different view and ruled that the level of severity involved constituted a violation of the boy's Art 3 rights (protection from inhuman and degrading treatment). The UK Government was in breach of the Convention by failing to provide adequate protection. While the Court did not go so far as to condemn all physical punishment by parents, the case sent out a clear message about the dangers of infringing the rights of children.

Support for a ban on parental physical punishment has also come from other international quarters. The UN Committee on the Rights of the Child, which monitors compliance with the UN Convention on the Rights of the Child of 1989, has persistently and loudly condemned the UK's retention of the defence of "reasonable chastisement".[61] The Council of Europe has also insisted that UK law be changed to protect children. In 2001, the European Committee of Social Rights "General Observation" on corporal punishment advised:

> "Article 17 [of the European Social Charter] requires a prohibition in legislation against any form of violence against children, whether at school, in other institutions, in their home or elsewhere."

In defiance of all this pressure, Scottish law, now set out in s 51 of the Criminal Justice (Scotland) Act 2003, identifies a parental right of "justifiable assault" of their child, but disallows blows to the head, shaking or the use of an implement. English and Welsh law, now set out in s 58 of the Children Act 2004 allows "common assault" on a

---

[60] *A* v *United Kingdom* (1999) 27 EHRR 611.

[61] The Committee considers any legitimised violence as a breach of Art 19 of the UN Convention on the Rights f the Child. It has condemned this breach on each of the three occasions on which it has scrutinised UK compliance, including the most recent report in 2008: United Nations Committee on the Rights of the Child, *Concluding Observations, United Kingdom of Great Britain and Northern Ireland:* CRC/C/GBR/CO/4, 2008, available at http://www.crin.org/docs/CRC.C.GBR. CO.4[1].pdf.

child to be classified as "reasonable punishment" but draws the line at "battery".

Clearly, there is some distance to go to secure for children the legal protection from assault that adults assume as their right. The message from the long road to ban the belt in schools is: don't give in and don't give up.

Conclusion

When Neil Armstrong stepped onto the surface of the moon in 1969, he uttered his famous, well rehearsed and sometimes disputed statement: "That's one small step for man, one giant leap for mankind." It is unlikely that 15-year-old Jeffrey Cosans had similarly rehearsed a historic declaration as he made his way towards the cemetery in Cowdenbeath in 1976. However, it can scarcely be doubted that this event and its consequences, and the energy and determination of two Scottish mothers, precipitated one giant leap for children in Scotland and throughout the United Kingdom. And the story is not finished yet.

Chapter 11

NOT OUR FINEST HOUR
The Lockerbie Trial

John P Grant

The "story" of the Lockerbie trial should, in truth, be about the victims of the destruction of Pan Am Flight 103 in December 1988. It should be about the 259 passengers and crew on the Jumbo jet who lost their lives and the 11 residents of Lockerbie who were killed on the ground. It should, in the words of the Lord Advocate, Colin Boyd QC, on the opening day of the trial, be about "four hundred parents who lost a child, 46 parents [who] lost their only child, 65 women [who] were widowed and 11 men [who] lost their wives; 140 [who] lost a parent; and seven [who] lost both parents". Or it should be about Flora Swire, a talented and vivacious medical student at Nottingham University who, one day before her 24th birthday, boarded Pan Am 103 to visit her American boyfriend for the Christmas holidays, only to have her life ended just after 7 pm on 21 December 1988. Or it should be about Rick Monetti, a handsome 20-year-old student of journalism returning to the United States along with 34 other Syracuse University students after a semester at a British university. Or it should be about Flora and Rick's family and friends.

Sadly, nearly two decade after the Lockerbie disaster and nearly a decade after the trial of those accused of being its cause, the story of the Lockerbie trial has become the story of one man, the only person convicted of causing the disaster, indeed the person convicted of 270 murders, Abdelbaset Ali Mohmed Al Megrahi – and for the wrong reason. Current interest – nay obsession – among politicos and the chattering classes is not, as it certainly should be, about the legitimacy of Megrahi's conviction, but rather the legitimacy and the circumstances surrounding his release from prison in Scotland, on compassionate grounds, to return to his home in Libya: that has become the story of

Lockerbie trial. Both the UK and Scottish Parliaments have held inquiries into Megrahi's release, Westminster investigating the so-called "deal in the desert" between Tony Blair and Libya and Whitehall's role in Megrahi's return to Libya, Holyrood looking into the Scottish Justice Minister's conduct in deciding on compassionate release, ultimately condemning Kenny MacAskill for visiting Megrahi in prison and not having proper regard to the victims' views before taking his decision.

Yet, despite this diverting trivia, there remains an enduring interest in the original trial. Recently, one experienced lawyer added a further casualty to the Lockerbie death-list, the death of justice, resulting from miscarriage of justice at the trial.[1] Books have been written, some by the victims' family members,[2] some by those involved in the investigation,[3] some by commentators placing the trial in a political or legal context,[4] and some by those offering a theory as to why Libya and Megrahi could not possibly be responsible.[5] There are Web sites and blogs galore, many questioning the Megrahi verdict, including one by Megrahi on which has been posted some material that would have been used in his abandoned appeal.[6]

Whatever is the true Lockerbie story, it cannot be the decision of Scottish Justice Minister MacAskill to release Megrahi from Greenock Prison in August 2009 so that he could return to his family in Libya to die. If, as MacAskill admitted when announcing the decision, this compassionate release was nonetheless based on the acknowledgement that Megrahi was a convicted terrorist and mass-murderer, then the American President Barack Obama, Secretary of State Hilary Clinton, Director of the FBI Robert Mueller and the families

---

[1] G Pierce, "The Framing of Megrahi", *London Review of Books*, 24 September 2009. In similar vein, see M Ruthven, "Deception over Lockerbie?", 56 *New York Review of Books*, 8 October 2009.

[2] S and D Cohen, *Pan Am, 103: The Bombing, the Betrayal, and a Bereaved Family's Search for Justice* (2000); K Dornstein, *The Boy who Fell from the Sky: A True Story* (2007).

[3] R A Marquise, *Scotborn: Evidence and the Lockerbie Investigation* (2006); J Crawford, *The Lockerbie Incident: A Detective's Tale* (2006).

[4] J P Grant, *The Lockerbie Trial: A Documentary History* (2004); K I Matar and R W Thabit, *Lockerbie and Libya* (2004).

[5] S Emerson and B Duffy, *The Fall of Pan Am 103* (1991); S Al-Bawab, *Why Libya? The Lockerbie Crisis* (1991); W H Chasey, *Pan Am 103: The Lockerbie Cover-Up* (1995); C Flores, *Shadows of Lockerbie* (1997); R Wallis, *Lockerbie: The Story and the Lessons* (2001).

[6] See particularly http://lockerbiecase.blogspot.com/; www.i-p-o.org/lockerbie_observer_mission.htm; www.megrahimystery.net/.

of the American victims are surely right in condemning MacAskill's decision. On what basis should someone convicted of callously killing 270 innocent people be released from a term of imprisonment that in any case equated ten lives with every year of his jail time? Where in Scottish society and Scots law did MacAskill find this kind of all-forgiving and all-embracing compassion? Certainly not in the High Court of Justiciary which, in hearing Megahi's application for release on bail pending his second appeal 10 months before MacAskill's decision, was not inclined towards any compassion, balancing the severity of the crimes of which he had been convicted with his then-existing medical condition.[7]

If, however, there were bigger fish to fry, commercial fish, then the decision becomes intelligible, if woefully misguided in the message it sends to terrorists everywhere and crassly insensitive to the victims' families. If, and here's the rub, there were serious doubts about Megrahi's conviction – doubts that had already been articulated by the Scottish Criminal Cases Review Commission and that were likely to be confirmed if his second appeal had proceeded – then the avoidance of embarrassment to Scotland and the Scottish legal system (and possibly also compassion from a not uncompassionate man), makes complete sense of MacAskill's decision. After all, who would want a man ultimately found not to be criminally responsible for the Lockerbie atrocity to die in a Scottish prison?

The atrocity

On Wednesday, 21 December 1988, at 6.04 pm, Pan Am Flight 103 pushed back from stand Kilo 14 at Terminal 3 of London's Heathrow Airport and began taxiing to runway 27R for take-off to JFK Airport, New York. On board the Boeing 747 were 243 passengers and a crew of 16, the majority of whom (189) were American citizens. The flight took off at 6.25 pm. Just under 38 minutes later, at about 7.03 pm, while the aircraft was flying at 31,000 feet over the border between England and Scotland, an improvised explosive device detonated in luggage in a container in one of the cargo holds. The aircraft broke up, debris falling in and around the town of Lockerbie over an area of about 845 square miles. All the passengers and crew on Pan Am 103 were killed, along with 11 residents of Lockerbie, all from the town's Sherwood Crescent.

---

[7] *Megrahi* v *HM Advocate (Bail Application)* [2008] HCJAC 68.

The ensuing investigation, involving law enforcement and intelligence personnel from the UK and abroad, focused initially on the recovery of the debris of and from the aircraft. These materials were examined by the Air Accident Investigations Branch (AAIB), an independent part of the Department for Transport, whose report in mid-1990 left no doubt as to the cause of the Pan Am 103 disintegration: "the detonation of an improvised explosive device located in a baggage container positioned on the left side of the forward cargo hold".[8]

There followed a Fatal Accident Inquiry, which reported in March of 1991 and which, like the AAIB report, had no doubt about the cause of the destruction of Pan Am 103: "the detonation of an improvised explosive device located in luggage container AVE 4041 situated on the left side of the forward hold". In his findings, Sheriff Principal John S Mowat QC, who conducted the inquiry, even reconstructed a sequence of events as to how the device came to destroy Pan Am 103: the explosion was caused by a Semtex-type plastic explosive concealed in a Toshiba radio-cassette player in a Samsonite suitcase, which had been transferred in London to Pan Am 103 from Pan Am 103A from Frankfurt without being identified as an unaccompanied bag and having arrived at Frankfurt on a non-Pan Am flight.[9]

Building upon the findings of the AAIB report and the Fatal Accident Inquiry and on the world-wide police investigations, the Procurator Fiscal for the Lockerbie area petitioned the local Sheriff on 13 November 1991 for warrants for the arrest of Megrahi and Al Amin Khalifa Fhimah, both Libyan nationals, on charges of conspiracy to murder, murder, and offences under the Aviation Security Act 1982.[10] To the sequence of events determined by the Sheriff Principal, the petition added the names of the two accused, alleged to be agents of the Libyan intelligence service, and their insinuation of the Samsonite suitcase containing the IED at Luqa Airport in Malta. The warrants were granted. On the very same day, a Grand Jury in Washington DC handed down an indictment against the same defendants, articulating the same sequence of events and, allowing for differences in legal terminology, the same charges.[11]

[8] Aircraft Accident Report No 2/90 (EW/C1094).
[9] See Grant (n 4 above), p 35.
[10] *Ibid*, p 72.
[11] *Ibid*, p 81.

Getting the accused to trial

The focus then shifted to getting Megrahi and Fhimah to Scotland or the United States for trial. It was clear that Libya could not, having no extradition treaty with either the UK or the US, simply extradite Megrahi and Fhimah for trial. Realising this, Britain and the United States sought the help of the UN Security Council, to which, in quick succession, three documents were submitted setting out the US, UK and French demands upon Libya in respect of the Pan Am 103 incident and the UTA Flight 772 bombing over Niger on 19 September 1989 in which Libya was also alleged to have been involved. In sum, these demands were, in respect of Pan Am 103: to ensure the surrender of Megrahi and Fhimah for trial; to cooperate in the investigation and prosecution; to accept responsibility for the actions of its officials; to pay appropriate compensation; to renounce terrorism; to prove that renunciation by concrete actions; and to cease terrorist activities and support for terrorist groups. When these demands were not immediately met by Libya, the three States, all permanent members of the Security Council, secured the adoption of Resolution 731 (1992) of 21 January 1992, which, being non-binding in nature, merely requested Libyan compliance.

Libya's response was that it had satisfied the requirements of the Montreal Convention on Aircraft Sabotage of 1971,[12] by detaining Megrahi and Fhimah and reporting them to its prosecution authorities; that the Montreal Convention gave it the right to prosecute the alleged offenders or to extradite them (as the Convention indeed did); and that Libyan law prohibited the extradition of its own nationals. The demands remaining unmet, a further resolution of the Security Council, Resolution 748 (1992), was adopted on 31 March 1992, transforming the requests of 2 months earlier into binding obligations coupled with air transport and diplomatic sanctions. Twenty months later, on 11 November 1993, the sanctions regime was extended and strengthened by the Security Council in Resolution 883 (1993).

While there was little formal progress to resolve the dispute between the parties, behind-the-scenes activities, particularly in the United Nations, kept the issue alive. In a private initiative in January 1994 by Professor Robert Black, then Professor of Scots Law at Edinburgh University, and Ibrahim Legwell, then head of the Libyans' defence team, a compromise scheme was proposed, whereby the trial would

---

[12] 974 UNTS 177.

take place in a neutral venue before a panel of international judges, with a Scottish presiding judge, and using the rules of Scots criminal law, evidence and procedure.[13] This proposal was swiftly rejected by the UK and US authorities in vehement terms – odd, considering a very similar proposal was put forward to the Security Council as a British and American "initiative" to resolve the dispute.

By 1997, moves towards some resolution of the impasse gained momentum, with a UN-sponsored report as to whether Megrahi and Fhimah could get a fair trial in Scotland concluding that they could if international observers were in attendance.[14] This report received a favourable response from a group of lawyers representing the interests of the accused.[15] The Permanent Mission of Libya to the UN produced a Position Paper in December 1997 reiterating Libya's basic stance, yet accepting the possibility of a trial in a neutral venue before a panel of Scottish judges.[16]

In a joint UK/US letter of 24 August 1998,[17] described subsequently in the Security Council as an "initiative" (though, in view of the 1994 Black/Legwell proposal, it was certainly not that), the two governments proposed the trial of Megrahi and Fhimah before a court of three Scottish judges, using Scots law, procedure and evidence, but sitting in the Netherlands. These proposals were endorsed by the Security Council three days later in Resolution 1192 (1998), after which an agreement was concluded between the UK and the Netherlands to regulate the sitting of the "Scottish Court in the Netherlands", as it was called;[18] and subordinate legislation was passed in the UK to regulate the proceedings of the Scottish Court, particularly those necessitated by the unique features of the trial.[19]

On the basis of these proposals, as endorsed by the Security Council and as clarified in further discussions on the security of the two accused, Megrahi and Fhimah surrendered (or were surrendered) on 5 April 1999 at Valkenburg Air Base, near Leiden, to await trial at

---

[13] See R Black, "The Lockerbie Proposal", 1997 SLT (News) 304; Grant (n 4 above), pp 119–121.
[14] UN Doc S/1997/991 Annex.
[15] Annexed to UN Doc S/1997/1015.
[16] See Grant (n 4 above), pp 135–143.
[17] UN Doc S/1998/795.
[18] Agreement concerning a Scottish Trial in the Netherlands of 18 September 1998, 2062 UNTS 81.
[19] SI 1998/2251.

the Scottish Court in the Netherlands. Thereupon, the UN Secretary-General reported that surrender and the Security Council President confirmed the suspension, but not the complete lifting, of sanctions on Libya.

Prelude to "the trial of the century"

After their arrival in the Netherlands, the accused were moved to a specially-constructed prison block at the Scottish Court at Camp Zeist (or Kamp van Zeist, in Dutch), a former NATO airbase near Utrecht. Under the terms of the agreement with the Netherlands, Camp Zeist was under the jurisdiction and control of the Scottish Court; its premises were inviolable; and, while Dutch law applied unless expressly excluded, the day-to-day operations in Camp Zeist were under the authority of the Scottish Court. In the event, Dutch police maintained security around the perimeter of the Camp, while Scottish police secured access to the site and maintained order within it.

Eleven months later, and after some preliminary court proceedings, just before the beginning of the trial, Joshua Rozenberg, the distinguished legal affairs correspondent and commentator, described the courtroom in these terms:

"The trial of the two Libyans accused of the Lockerbie bombing begins on 3 May inside a £12m facility constructed for the hearing at Camp Zeist in the Netherlands. It is just over a year since Abdelbaset Ali Mohmet Al Megrahi and Al Amin Khalifa Fhima surrendered for trial in a case unique in legal history. Their trial will be held under Scottish law, but at a former military air base in the woods outside Utrecht. Three judges, sitting without the normal jury of fifteen, will decide whether the two Libyans murdered the 270 people who died in the Lockerbie bombing. But those judges will have to peer over large television monitors to see the two accused and the various witnesses. … The monitors, built into large cream-coloured housings, are the most striking feature of the courtroom: they take up much of the desk-space provided for those in court. They can be used to show documents, video recordings, and television pictures from within the court itself. Witnesses will sit at the far end of the court from the bench, which may make it difficult for judges to see their facial expressions and body language. Another striking feature of the court is that press and public will be separated from everyone else by a bullet-proof glass screen running from floor to ceiling; blinds can be raised so that vulnerable witnesses can give evidence without being seen. In Scottish courtrooms the defence advocates are normally seated on the judges' left; at Camp Zeist, they'll have to sit on the other side of the

courtroom so that the accused can be seated close to the door leading to
the cells. Officials working for the Scottish Court Service acknowledge
there have been criticisms of the way the court has been designed; they
say compromises are inevitable when an ordinary criminal trial has to be
held under such extraordinary circumstances." [20]

Three judges were appointed for the Zeist court. The presiding judge,
Lord Sutherland (Ranald Iain Sutherland), was in his late sixties
and this was his last trial before retirement. He had a grandfatherly
demeanour, but his conduct of the trial was assured and firm, if not
severe. Flanking him on the bench were Lord Coulsfield (John Taylor
Cameron) and Lord MacLean (Ranald Norman Munro MacLean),
both junior to Lord Sutherland in years and ranking on the Scottish
Bench. Coulsfield was owlish and intellectual, MacLean elegant and
serious, masking his renowned sense of humour. Indeed, there was no
humour on the Zeist Bench; the judges were rumoured not to enjoy
the trial and the security and other constraints that surrounded it.
All three had, at one time, served as an advocate depute, a normal
stepping stone for progress to the Scottish Bench at the time. A further
judge, Lord Abernethy (John Alistair Cameron), was appointed as
an "additional judge" to stand in on the death or indisposition of one
the three appointed judges. He cut a lonely figure at the far end of
the Bench; and his services were unneeded. While there was a surfeit
of Ranalds and Johns, the multiplicity of Camerons (and there was
another Cameron on the Scottish Bench) compelled John Taylor
and John Alistair to choose judicial titles (Coulsfield and Abernethy
respectively) different from their family names, a customary practice
to avoid confusion.

The Crown case was opened by Colin Boyd QC (now Baron Boyd
of Duncansby), who had been appointed Lord Advocate less than
3 months earlier. Fortunately, the day-to-day conduct of the trial was
conducted by Alistair Campbell, then in his early fifties, and Alan
Turnbull, in his mid-forties. Campbell had a cold and dispassionate
style, while Turnbull was more animated and aggressive. Campbell was
elevated to the Scottish Bench in 2003 as Lord Bracadale (too many
Campbells); and Turnbull was appointed to the Bench in 2006, Lord
Turnbull being then the youngest Scottish judge at the age of 47.

The lead counsel for the two accused were fascinating contrasts. For
Megrahi, William Taylor QC, a very senior criminal defence practitioner,

[20] Available at http://news.bbc.co.uk/1/hi/uk/718403.stm.

was theatrical and unpredictable, giving a performance that might have appealed to a jury but could hardly win over three judges. He coined some memorable terms. If a fact was clear, it was "plump and plain". If he thought or surmised something, he "jaloused" it. Richard Keen QC, for Fhimah, could not have been more different. He was calculating and clinical in all he did; and his background as an advocate in intellectual property cases made him a master of the plethora of scientific evidence that was led. Unsurprisingly, Keen is now a hugely successful Dean of the Faculty of Advocates.

For the opening of the trial and pretty consistently thereafter, a large number of victim's family members were in the courtroom. Under arrangements made with the American Office for Victims of Crime, financial support was available to allow all family members – and not only those of American victims – to attend the trial, and many took advantage of that generosity. Very few members of the general public attended any part of the trial. Certainly, Camp Zeist was in a pretty desolate location, as befits an airbase though not, one would have thought, a court hearing a case involving the largest terrorist atrocity at the time.

The high-tech media centre, converted from the airbase gymnasium, had accommodation for a huge number of media outlets and a huge number applied for accreditation. For most of the trial, the media centre was virtually empty, such was the dry and technical nature of much of the evidence. Even BBC Scotland, *The Herald* and *The Scotsman*, who were the most stalwart media attendees, could not support personnel in attendance for the whole trial. There were some predictable peaks, when the media centre buzzed with the activity of media outlets worldwide: the first day of the trial and the verdict, plus the perceived highlights, which included the evidence of the confused and confusing Edwin Bollier, a partner in MEBO, and the bizarre and pathetic Libya "defector" Abdul Majid Giaka.

The Lockerbie trial

The trial began on 3 May 2000 with the expectation that it would run for a considerable time. Indeed, one the reasons given for the replacement of a normal jury with a bench of judges as fact-finders was that no Scottish juror could be expected to be away from home and work for a year to 18 months. Initially, the prosecution witness list contained 1,160 names, the defence list 121 names; and there were 621 non-documentary productions and 1,867 documentary productions on the prosecution list. However, the prosecution and defence teams were encouraged to, and did, agree on a number of items of evidence, thereby considerably reducing the length of the proceedings. During the final submissions of the Crown in December 2000, the indictment was revised with the deletion of the charges of conspiracy to murder and conspiracy under the Aviation Security Act 1982 and of the reference to Fhimah's membership in the Libyan intelligence service, leaving only charges of murder (in the amount of 270) against each accused. On 31 January 2001, after 38 weeks in which 230 witnesses and evidence were presented in 84 days, the Scottish court announced its unanimous verdict: guilty in respect of Megrahi and not guilty in respect of Fhimah.

While a jury gives no reasons for its verdict, the Scottish Court, composed as it was of three judges in lieu of a jury, was required by the Order in Council governing the proceedings, in the event of a conviction, "to give a judgment in writing stating the reasons for the conviction". Implementing this requirement started badly, for on the day of the verdict the Court published to those attending the trial its reasoned judgment with a mistake in the very first line of the first paragraph: the date of the Lockerbie tragedy was stated to have been 22 December 1988, and not 21 December. This version was hurriedly withdrawn and replaced with a corrected version; but some at the trial thought this did not augur well for what followed.

In its judgment of 90 paragraphs, the trial court essentially convicted Megrahi on the basis of nine findings of fact.[21] These findings can be grouped under two heads, the Swiss connection and the Maltese connection. Under the Swiss connection, the court found that the timer that detonated the improvised explosive device on Pan Am 103 was made by a Swiss company, MEBO, and had been supplied principally to Libya. The Libyan intelligence service had an office adjacent to that of MEBO in Geneva. Megrahi was a member of the Libyan intelligence service. Under the Maltese connection, the court found that the suitcase with the IED contained items of clothing purchased from a shop in Sliema, Malta, called Mary's House. Megrahi was identified by the proprietor of Mary's House, Tony Gauci, as the purchaser of the clothing. The clothing was purchased on 7 December, when Megrahi

---

[21] 2000 SCCR 701. The trial and appeal opinions are available at http://www.scotcourts.gov.uk/library/lockerbie. See also R Black, "The Lockerbie Verdict" (2001) 5 ELR 221.

was in Malta, and not on 23 November, when he was not. The suitcase with the IED was sent on an Air Malta flight from Luqa Airport in Malta to Frankfurt on the morning of 21 December. Megrahi was in Malta on the night of 20–21 December and left the following day. On this visit to Malta, Megrahi travelled on a "coded" (false) passport that was never subsequently used.

In para 89 of its judgment, the court said:

> "We are aware that in relation to certain aspects of the case there are a number of uncertainties and qualifications. We are also aware that there is a danger that by selecting parts of the evidence which seem to fit together and ignoring parts which might not fit, it is possible to read into a mass of conflicting evidence a pattern or conclusion which is not really justified. However, having considered the whole evidence in the case, including the uncertainties and qualifications, and the submissions of counsel, we are satisfied that the evidence as to the purchase of clothing in Malta, the presence of that clothing in the primary suitcase, the transmission of an item of baggage from Malta to London, the identification of the first accused (albeit not absolute), his movements under a false name at or around the material time, and the other background circumstances such as his association with Mr. Bollier [a partner in MEBO] and with members of the JSO [Libyan intelligence service] or Libyan military who purchased MST-13 timers, does fit together to form a real and convincing pattern. There is nothing in the evidence which leaves us with any reasonable doubt as to the guilt of the first accused, and accordingly we find him guilty of the remaining charge in the Indictment as amended."

This "real and convincing pattern" leaving the trial court with no reasonable doubt as to the guilt of Megrahi relies entirely on all nine pieces being in place. The removal of any pieces, like, for example, the identification of Megrahi as the purchaser of the clothing, would, on the logic the court itself adopted, distort the pattern and raise reasonable doubt – something that was clearly in the mind of the Scottish Criminal Cases Review Commission when it reviewed the conviction in 2007.

Some commentators have doubted that these findings in themselves justify a conviction of Megrahi beyond reasonable doubt. One of the UN observers of the trial, Dr Hans Koechler, reported that, overall, the trial was unfair.[22] He was particularly concerned that "foreign

---

[22] 2001/P/HK/17032, available at http://i-p-o.org/lockerbie-report.htm.

governments or (secret) governmental agencies may have been allowed, albeit indirectly, to determine, to a considerable extent, which evidence was made available to the Court"; "that virtually all people presented by the prosecution as key witnesses were proven to lack credibility to a very high extent, in certain cases even having openly lied to the Court"; and that the verdict was based upon "a series of highly problematic inferences".

Megrahi received the mandatory sentence for murder under Scots law, life imprisonment, with a recommended minimum of 20 years before being considered for release. On 24 November 2003, that recommended period was replaced with a mandatory 27 years before consideration for release as the "punishment part" of his sentence, as required by human rights legislation.

The appeal

While many, particularly American family members, were happy with the Lockerbie verdict (if not the sentence) as an acknowledgement of Megrahi's guilt and Libya's role in the terrorist murder of 270 people, a substantial number of others, including some British family members and commentators, remained sceptical about the correctness of the verdict and, indeed, Libya's involvement.

Megrahi appealed the verdict on the ground of a miscarriage of justice, that miscarriage being the misdirection of the fact-finders (by themselves), particularly in inferences drawn from accepted testimony, and on the ground of new evidence. He did not base his appeal, and his counsel did not seek to argue on appeal, that the verdict was one "which no reasonable jury, properly instructed, could have returned".[23] This surprising choice of appeal ground caused the presiding judge, Lord Justice-General Cullen, to ask lead counsel for Megrahi on the first day of the appeal hearing to confirm that he was indeed proceeding on the sole ground of misdirection.

The appeal was heard before a Bench of Five Judges sitting at Camp Zeist, consisting of Scotland's senior judge, the Lord Justice-General (Lord Cullen), in the chair, sitting with Lords Kirkwood, Osborne, Macfadyen and Nimmo Smith. Megrahi's legal team argued that the trial court erred in fixing the date of purchase of items of clothing from Mary's House as 7 December 1988 and in its reliance on Tony Gauci's identification evidence; misdirected itself in inferring that an

[23] Criminal Procedure (Scotland) Act 1995, s 106(3)(b).

unaccompanied bag was transferred to Pan Am 103A at Frankfurt; erred
in its incriminating inference from Megrahi's association with Edwin
Bollier, a partner in MEBO; erred in its incriminating inference on
Mehrahi's use of a "coded" passport bearing the name "Abdusamad" ;
and erred in ignoring an alternative explanation for Megrahi's visit to
Malta on 20–21 December 1988.

The appeal court unanimously rejected the appeal on all grounds
on 14 March 2002 in a judgment of 370 paragraphs.[24] It heard new
evidence, relating to the possibility of the ingestion of the IED at
Heathrow, but concluded that it was not of such importance as to
dislodge the trial court's finding that the IED had entered the system
in Malta. It acknowledged that, in a few instances, the trial court had
found a fact on the basis of a misunderstanding of the evidence or in
the absence of evidence, but discounted these errors as unlikely to
have affected the eventual outcome. As to the weight given to evidence
and the inferences drawn from the evidence at the trial, the appeal
court determined that it was for the trial court to give the appropriate
weight to the evidence. At a stroke, it left the question of inferences to
be drawn from the evidence to the trial judges. The appeal court was
clear that it could not substitute its views on the evidence for those of
the trial court. The whole thrust of the appeal, the limited role of an
appeal court in the Scottish criminal justice system, meant that, while
rejecting Megrahi's appeal, the appeal court did not, as many have
claimed, endorse the trial court's findings. It simply found that the
new evidence and the alleged misdirections were insufficient in law to
overturn the verdict.

Dr Koechler felt constrained to report on the appeal proceedings
too, waxing again about power politics in the trial and appeal leading
to the "incomprehensible" decision of the appeal court, but this time
focusing much of his criticism on the inadequacies of Megrahi's legal
representation.[25]

Reviews and release

In December 2002, Megrahi made an application under the European
Convention for the Protection of Human Rights and Fundamental

[24] 2002 SCCR 701. The trial and appeal opinions are available at http://www.
scotcourts.gov.uk/library/lockerbie. See R Black, "The Lockerbie Appeal" (2002)
6 ELR 385.
[25] 2002/P/RE/17553, available at http://i-p-o.org/koechler-lockerbie-appeal_report.
htm.

Freedoms of 1950,[26] alleging a violation of his right to a fair trial, guaranteed in Art 6. The convention has a sifting mechanism whereby an applicant must satisfy a number of admissibility criteria. A committee of the European Court of Human Rights determined on 11 February 2003 that the application was inadmissible, finding that the material submitted in support of the application "did not disclose any appearance of a violation of the rights and freedoms set out in the Convention and its protocols". Somewhat surprisingly, the determination does not make it clear in what respects Megrahi's application failed the admissibility criteria.

Megrahi then sought a remedy through the Scottish Criminal Cases Review Commission. The Commission (or SCCLC) is empowered by statute[27] to consider cases, from which no further appeal is possible, where it is alleged that a miscarriage of justice has occurred and to refer appropriate cases to the High Court, sitting as an appeal court, for reconsideration. Upon such a reference, the High Court may affirm the verdict, set it aside, or set it aside and authorize a new prosecution. Megrahi's application was lodged with the Commission in September 2003; and its decision was announced in June 2007, that decision being to refer the case to the High Court of Justiciary.

The thoroughness of this review has to be contrasted with the brevity of its decision as announcement to the public. The review took nearly 4 years, when the trial and appeal, between them, lasted a year and a half. The review was conducted under the supervision of Sir Gerald Gordon, a former Professor of Criminal and Scots Law at Edinburgh University, a sheriff for 22 years, a temporary High Court judge for 5 years, author of the highly respected *Criminal Law of Scotland*, long-time editor of the classic Renton and Brown's *Criminal Procedure According to the Law of Scotland* and of the *Scottish Criminal Case Reports*. It is difficult to imagine anyone more qualified to review Megrahi's conviction. After that quality work by quality people, resulting in an 800-page statement of reasons, it is sad that the intimation of the decision should take the form of a 14-page press release,[28] much of which was devoted to data about the Commission and its method of operation.

---

[26] ETS No. 5.

[27] Criminal Procedure (Scotland) Act 1995, ss 194A–C.

[28] Available at www.sccrc.org.uk/viewfile.aspx?id=293.

In that press release, the SCCRC stated that it "has no power under statute to make copies of its statements of reasons available to the public", as indeed it does not, at least not without a permissive Order in Council, which to his credit, Justice Minister MacAskill has sought.[29] The SCCRC is presently seeking consent from those who gave evidence to the Commission to the publication of the full report under an extended power of disclosure authorised in an Order in Council,[30] a commendable initiative of the Scottish Government and, in particular, Kenny MacAskill. Of course, not all who gave evidence will consent. It seems clear that whatever eventually appears will be a heavily redacted version of the original and full report.

There is something wrong in a society committed to transparency that a public body, like the SCCRC, paid out of public funds (£1.1 million for the Megrahi review alone) and charged with an important public function should be restrained by statute from disclosing more than the bare bones of its decision. This becomes intolerable when the statement of reasons concerns a matter of immense national and international importance. Even the press release carried an air of reluctant disclosure: three paragraphs are devoted to condemning media speculation over the previous 3 years, concluding with the statement that the Commission hoped that the publication of the summary "will end some of these inaccurate reports". Media speculation over the largest mass murder in Scottish legal history, the worst terrorist atrocity until 9/11 – intolerable!

In all, while rejecting many of the applicant's grounds of review, the SCCRC identified six grounds where it believed a miscarriage of justice may have occurred. Of the six, two were not revealed in the press release, though it is not too difficult to work out what they were. One concerned the non-disclosure by the Crown before or during the trial of a document from a foreign government concerning the timer used to detonate the IED; and the second concerned the content of that document.

The other four grounds all related to the Maltese connection. Given the centrality to his conviction of the identification of Megrahi as the purchaser of the clothes from Mary's House on 7 December 1988 that were found from the suitcase in which the IED was located, it is worth

---

[29] Criminal Procedure (Scotland) Act 1995, ss 194J–L.
[30] SI 2009/448.

quoting from the relevant parts of para 5 of the press release on that evidence:

> "… the Commission formed the view that there is no reasonable basis in the trial court's judgment for its conclusion that the purchase of the items from Mary's House, took place on 7 December 1988. Although it was proved that the applicant was in Malta on several occasions in December 1988, in terms of the evidence 7 December was the only date on which he would have had the opportunity to purchase the items. The finding as to the date of purchase was therefore important to the trial court's conclusion that the applicant was the purchaser. Likewise, the trial court's conclusion that the applicant was the purchaser was important to the verdict against him. Because of these factors the Commission has reached the view that the requirements of the legal test may be satisfied in the applicant's case.[31]
>
> New evidence not heard at the trial concerned the date on which the Christmas lights were illuminated in the area of Sliema in which Mary's House is situated. In the Commission's view, taken together with Mr Gauci's evidence at trial and the contents of his police statements, this additional evidence indicates that the purchase of the items took place prior to 6 December 1988. In other words, it indicates that the purchase took place at a time when there was no evidence at trial that the applicant was in Malta.
>
> Additional evidence, not made available to the defence, which indicates that four days prior to the identification parade at which Mr Gauci picked out the applicant, he saw a photograph of the applicant in a magazine article linking him to the bombing. In the Commission's view evidence of Mr Gauci's exposure to this photograph in such close proximity to the parade undermines the reliability of his identification of the applicant at that time and at the trial itself.
>
> Other evidence, not made available to the defence, which the Commission believes may further undermine Mr. Gauci's identification of the applicant as the purchaser and the trial court's finding as to the date of purchase."

So, in a nutshell, Megrahi could not be proved to have been in Malta on the date on which the clothing was bought and could not credibly be proved to be the purchaser of the clothing. Absent the full statement of reasons from the SCCRC, we do not know what the Commission thought about the Crown claim, accepted by the trial court, that the

---

[31] That is, "a verdict that no reasonable jury, properly instructed, could have returned": s 106(3)(b) of the Criminal Procedure (Scotland) Act 1995.

suitcase with the IED was "ingested" at Luqa Airport, when that airport was known at the time to have excellent security systems. Nor do we know what the Commission made of the sinister inference drawn by the court from Megrahi's presence in Malta on 20/21 December 1988 with a "coded" passport.

Indeed, there is a great deal that we do not know. But what we do know from the SCCRC press release – that Megrahi could not be proved to be the purchaser of the clothing – is enough to raise the most serious doubts about his conviction. As the Crown case, in the words of Richard Keen QC, representing Megrahi's co-accused, in his final submissions to the trial court, was based on "an inference based upon an inference leading to an inference", then surely the demolition of two major planks in the trial court's reasoning fatally undermines the verdict. Put at its most neutral, while Megrahi may or may not have been complicit in the destruction of Pan Am 103, his conviction is unsafe.

A number of people, including the Lord Advocate, Elish Angiolini QC, in a testy statement, make much of the fact that Megrahi had abandoned his second appeal before being returned to Libya, thereby acknowledging his guilt. That is an over-simplification. He had applied for compassionate release and the Libyan Government had applied for prisoner-transfer – and both fell to be decided by Justice Minister MacAskill simultaneously. Under the Treaty between the UK and Libya on the Transfer of Prisoners (the "deal in the desert"),[32] *prisoner transfer* is permissible only when all legal proceedings are concluded. In the event, there were, until after the decision was taken to allow Megrahi's *compassionate release*, extant legal proceedings – an appeal by the Lord Advocate against the sentence imposed on Megrahi. If he abandoned his appeal so that he could be transferred to a Libyan prison, he was misguided or misled, for the Lord Advocate's appeal was enough to block transfer. However, there is no requirement under the *compassionate release* arrangements[33] that there be no extant legal proceedings. The Scottish Justice Minister's consideration of both applications at the same time muddied the waters. Why Megrahi abandoned his appeal when that was not required for compassionate release is difficult to understand. Why, if he still protested his innocence, did he not let the second appeal

---

[32] The treaty was signed in London on 17 November 2008: Cm 7540.
[33] In s 3 of the Prisoners and Criminal Proceedings (Scotland) Act 1993.

proceed, albeit he would be in Libya, and probably dead, by the time a final decision was made? He may have believed or been induced to believe that the abandonment of the appeal was necessary for the success of either of the two applications.

Whatever the explanation, and while the abandonment of the appeal certainly does not help the credibility of his claims of innocence, three things are clear. One, Megrahi has not stopped protesting his innocence – nor have others with an interest in revealing what they see as the true facts of the Pan Am tragedy. Secondly, decisions about compassionate release made by politicians alone are clearly problematic, however well intentioned and well advised the politician may be. There is, as here, always the appearance that political factors played a part in the granting or refusal of an application for compassionate release. Thirdly, as befits politicians, concern about Megrahi's return to Libya has focused exclusively on the politics of the return decision, and not on whether Megrahi's conviction is sound or what actually happened prior to the awful events of 21 December 1988. Apart from some victims' families and some commentators, where are the demands for a full and independent public inquiry into the entire circumstances of the Pan Am 103 bombing and its aftermath or even a more limited inquiry into the investigation of the atrocity and the prosecution of those thought responsible? Where are the demands for the truth for the victims' families – or even, in light of the SCCRC determination, for Megrahi and his family?

Nor, as many claim, does Libya's acknowledgement of responsibility and payment of compensation in the amount of $10 million for each family *prove* Megrahi's and Libya's guilt. In a carefully worded statement in August 2003, Libya stated that it "accepts responsibility for the actions of its officials",[34] vicarious responsibility *qua* employer of one of its convicted intelligence agents (Megrahi), and not direct responsibility for the Lockerbie bombing. The acknowledgement of responsibility was not, and was not intended to be, an admission of Libyan guilt. The statement was made in a plea to the Security Council that Libya had met all the conditions imposed upon it by the resolutions of 1992 and 1993 and that UN sanctions should therefore be lifted, a plea that was successful in Resolution 1506 (2003) of 12 September 2003. The acknowledgement of responsibility and the compensation

---

[34] Letter from the Permanent Mission of Libya to the UN to the Security Council President of 15 August 2003: UN Doc S/2003/818.

package were the (cynical) price that Libya was prepared to pay for the ending of sanctions, nothing more.

A teachable moment?

Can we now, at this particular moment in time, glean any lessons from these events? And, as a story, does it have a happy ending?

Certainly, the victims' families were kept informed of developments throughout the Lockerbie investigation, trial and appeal in a way not characteristic of the Scottish criminal justice system at the time. Thanks to the generous financial support of the Office for Victims of Crime, part of the American Department of Justice, elaborate arrangements were put in place to allow victims' families to attend parts of the trial or to view the trial as it happened on video links with the court in four "remote locations" (Washington DC, New York City, London and Dumfries). Special arrangements were made to enable the appeal to be streamed live on BBC Online. Successive Lords Advocate, and their officials at the Crown Office, went to substantial lengths to keep the families abreast of developments. The treatment of victims throughout the entire lengthy process has been exemplary – and provides a model for how we should treat all victims of crime and their families.

Equally exemplary were the arrangements for the trial, from the refurbishment of the former NATO airbase at Camp Zeist into a high-tech courtroom and modern prison-block to the thorough yet friendly security arrangements for those wishing to view the trial. If the trial had to be adjourned so that a doorway could be widened to allow debris from the aircraft to be brought into court, if there were hiccups in the simultaneous interpretation of testimony into Arabic, if the cafeteria arrangements for those attending the trial were lamentable, these were but blemishes on what was otherwise a marvelous reflection on the efforts of those involved.

The critical issue was always going to be how well the Scottish criminal justice system handled its "trial of the century". Certainly, the Crown was confronted by a daunting task in prosecuting Megrahi and Fhimah, involving no direct eye-witnesses to the core elements of the crime, involving wholly circumstantial evidence, involving highly-technical scientific evidence and involving events that were at least 12 years old by the time the case got to trial. It was, without question, a huge achievement for the Crown to satisfy three judges beyond reasonable doubt as to Megrahi's guilt, and for the Crown to defeat the Megrahi appeal before a further five judges.

But when commentators question the verdict from the outset, when the only UN observer to comment publicly on the trial calls the verdict incomprehensible and the trial unfair, when even some victims' family members doubt Megrahi's guilt, and when the Scottish Criminal Cases Review Commission, as it happens the final quasi-judicial pronouncement in the matter, concludes that there were six miscarriages of justice, one is forced to the inescapable conclusion that the conviction of Megrahi is unsafe. That is not to say that he was not in some way complicit in the Lockerbie bombing; but what it does say is that he was not rightly and rightfully convicted.

Looking at the broader picture, did the Lockerbie trial prove to be a model for other domestic trials of international terrorists? Given that the 13 international conventions dealing with international terrorism, including the Montreal Convention on Aircraft Sabotage, are premised on the prosecution of international terrorists in regular domestic criminal courts (and not in some international criminal tribunal) and on those accused of terrorist offences receiving a fair trial, one is tempted to think that Hans Koechler is right when he said that "disservice has been done to the important cause of international criminal justice".

A happy ending? There has never going to be a happy ending for the victims' families, but there might at least have been closure in knowing that, after a fair and convincing trial, someone had been held legally responsible and punished accordingly. Abdelbaset Ali Mohmed Al Megrahi will go to his grave with the stigma of 270 deaths, a stigma imposed, wrongly it now appears, by the Scottish criminal justice system. Not our finest hour.

INDEX